*Shakespeare and
Classical Comedy*

Shakespeare and Classical Comedy

The Influence of Plautus and Terence

ROBERT S. MIOLA

CLARENDON PRESS · OXFORD

1994

Oxford University Press, Walton Street, Oxford OX2 6DP

Oxford New York
Athens Auckland Bangkok Bombay
Calcutta Cape Town Dar es Salaam Delhi
Florence Hong Kong Istanbul Karachi
Kuala Lumpur Madras Madrid Melbourne
Mexico City Nairobi Paris Singapore
Taipei Tokyo Toronto
and associated companies in
Berlin Ibadan

Oxford is a trade mark of Oxford University Press

Published in the United States
by Oxford University Press Inc., New York

© Robert S. Miola 1994

All rights reserved. No part of this publication may be reproduced,
stored in a retrieval system, or transmitted, in any form or by any means,
without the prior permission in writing of Oxford University Press.
Within the UK, exceptions are allowed in respect of any fair dealing for the
purpose of research or private study, or criticism or review, as permitted
under the Copyright, Designs and Patents Act, 1988, or in the case of
reprographic reproduction in accordance with the terms of the licences
issued by the Copyright Licensing Agency. Enquiries concerning
reproduction outside these terms and in other countries should be
sent to the Rights Department, Oxford University Press,
at the address above

British Library Cataloguing in Publication Data
Data available

Library of Congress Cataloging in Publication Data
Miola, Robert S.
Shakespeare and classical comedy: the influence of Plautus and
Terence / Robert S. Miola.
Includes bibliographical references and index.
1. Shakespeare, William, 1564–1616—Comedies. 2. Shakespeare,
William, 1564–1616—Knowledge—Literature. 3. Latin drama (Comedy)—
Appreciation—England. 4. Classicism—England—History—16th
century. 5. English drama (Comedy)—Roman influences. 6. Plautus,
Titus Maccius—Influence. 7. Terence—Influence. I. Title.
PR2981.M56 1994   822.3'3—dc20   94–22020
ISBN 0–19–818269–4

Set by Hope Services (Abingdon) Ltd.
Printed in Great Britain
on acid-free paper by
Biddles Ltd.
Guildford & King's Lynn

For Rose

Seneca cannot be too heavy, nor Plautus too light
Polonius (*Hamlet* II. ii. 400–1)

Acknowledgements

THIS study, the companion to *Shakespeare and Classical Tragedy: The Influence of Seneca* (Oxford, 1992), has been fortunate in its benefactors. I give thanks to Loyola College for a sabbatical, summer research fellowship, and other support; to the National Endowment for the Humanities for a senior fellowship, 1987–8; to the editors of *Renaissance Quarterly*, *Philological Quarterly*, and *Comparative Drama* (along with the Board of the Medieval Institute) for kind permission to reprint some material; to the Shakespeare Association of America and the Shakespeare Institute, Stratford-upon-Avon, for providing forums; to other individuals and institutions who invited presentation of the work—the Society for the Classical Tradition at Boston University, Richard Hamilton at Bryn Mawr College, Michele Marrapodi at the Universities of Messina and Palermo. I am also grateful to learned colleagues who offered advice and encouragement: Bernard M. W. Knox, Harry Levin, John W. Velz, David Bevington, friends at the Folger Shakespeare Library, the readers for the Press, and Louise George Clubb, whose work inspired pursuit of the Italian connections. I am greatly indebted to the Loyola University of Chicago Rome Center, especially Paolo Giordano and John Felice, for graciously hosting me and my family (1991–2), thus enabling research at the incomparable Biblioteca Vaticana. In the Eternal City many others were generous with their help and friendship: Piero and Joan Boitani, Nino and Anna Ricciardi, Frank and Chris Fuoco, the Amici di Don Orione, the communities of Santa Susanna and Padre Pio X, and the members of Il Club del Fratino, true colleagues of the mind and heart.

The personal debts are beyond reckoning. The late Timothy S. Healy, SJ, *magister et amicus*, first pointed the way. Throughout, my parents and brother gave faithful and loving support; my children, Daniel, Christine, and Rachel, offered many lessons and much fun; as did my youngest, Rose, to whom I dedicate this book with faith, hope, and love.

Contents

Abbreviations

(i) Journals and Series

AJP	*American Journal of Philology*
CD	*Comparative Drama*
CQ	*Classical Quarterly*
CRPT	Carleton Renaissance Plays in Translation
CW	*Classical World*
LCL	The Loeb Classical Library
MSR	Malone Society Reprints
OCT	Oxford Classical Texts
RD	*Renaissance Drama*
Revels	The Revels Plays
RLDE	Renaissance Latin Drama in England
SJ	*Shakespeare-Jahrbuch*
TAPA	*Transactions of the American Philological Society*

(ii) Individual Works

Adel.	*Adelphoe*
Amph.	*Amphitruo*
Aul.	*Aulularia*
AYL	*As You Like It*
Bacc.	*Bacchides*
Cist.	*Cistellaria*
Eun.	*Eunuchus*
HT	*Heauton Timorumenos*
IO	*Institutio Oratoria*
LLL	*Love's Labour's Lost*
Men.	*Menaechmi*
Mer.	*Mercator*
MG	*Miles Gloriosus*
Most.	*Mostellaria*
Poen.	*Poenulus*
Poet.	*De Arte Poetica Liber*

Pseud. *Pseudolus*
Rhet. *Ars Rhetorica*
Rud. *Rudens*

Abbreviations for other periodicals conform to the listing in the annual *Publications of the Modern Language Association* bibliography. Full citation for works identified in the text and notes by author's name (or name and date) can be found in the Bibliography.

I

Light Plautus

There are no voiceless words that belong to no one. Each
word contains voices that are sometimes infinitely distant,
unnamed, almost impersonal (voices of lexical shadings, of
styles, and so forth), almost undetectable, and voices resound-
ing nearby and simultaneously.

Mikhail Bakhtin[1]

BAKHTIN's 'word', Kristeva explains, is 'an *intersection of textual
surfaces* rather than a point'; 'a dialogue among several writings:
that of the writer, the addressee (or the character), and the contemporary or earlier cultural context.'[2] As in words so in texts, as in
language so in literature. The voices of Plautus and Terence, sometimes distant, sometimes near, significantly form and enrich the
dialogues that constitute drama in western civilization. The surviving plays of Plautus (twenty-one including the fragmentary
Vidularia) and Terence (six) are all *fabulae palliatae*, 'comedies in
Greek dress, i.e. comedies which preserve the themes, characters,
costumes, and stage-settings of the Greek originals.'[3] Composed of
diverbia, verse in iambic senarius to represent ordinary speech, and
of diversely metrical *cantica*, verse for recitative and song, Roman
comedy embodies some of the largely vanished works by
Menander, Philemon, Diphilus, and Apollodorus of Carystus,
while incorporating native Italian traditions, also largely vanished—the Fescennine verses, Atellan farce, dramatic *satura*,

---

[1] *Speech Genres and Other Late Essays*, 124.

[2] Kristeva, *Desire in Language*, 65.

[3] Duckworth, *The Nature of Roman Comedy*, 18. How slender a thread the
future hangs by is evident from the loss of most Greek and Roman New Comedy.
Surviving titles and fragments have been collected by Kassel and Austin, *Poetae
Comici Graeci*, and Ribbeck, *Comicorum Romanorum Fragmenta*. Menander alone
wrote over 100 plays; in the second century Aulus Gellius (*Attic Nights* III. iii.
11–12) noted that 130 plays were circulating under Plautus' name; Suetonius (*Vita
Terenti* 5) records the story that Terence died at sea while carrying back from
Greece 108 plays adapted from Menander.

Graeco-Roman mime.[4] As such they constitute a rhetorical and symbolic vocabulary, a treasury of signifying capacities, a dense and expressive dramatic code that played variously in later generations. Employing the biological metaphor, we can say that the plays of Plautus and Terence, themselves descendants of barely visible forebears, engendered countless progeny, including works by Hrosvit, Ariosto, Berrardo, Trissino, Cecchi, Dolce, Della Porta, Machiavelli, Turnèbe, Garnier, Grévin, Jodelle, Belleau, Larivey, Rotrou, Baïf, La Taille, Molière, Rueda, Molina, Vega, Calderón, Heywood, Shakespeare, Jonson, Middleton, Congreve, Farquhar, Wycherley, Sheridan, Wilde, and Shaw. Mixing freely with the bloodlines of other traditions, appearing in various productions, translations, and refigurations, Plautus and Terence bequeathed to posterity the essential genetic make-up of their genre, dramatic comedy.

The first descendants appear early—*Querolus*, a fifth-century adaptation of *Aulularia*, Hrosvit of Gandersheim's tenth-century versions of Terence *moralisé*, Latin comedies by twelfth-century French writers like Vitalis of Blois, William of Blois, Arnulf of Orléans, Matthew of Vendôme, and by later Italians like Petrarch, Vergerio, Aretino, Alberti, Ugolino, and Piccolomini.[5] The twelve new Plautine plays which Nicolaus Cusanus brought to Rome in 1429 energized the production and reproduction of Roman comedy in Renaissance Europe. Plautus and Terence found new life on stage, in the productions of Pomponius Laetus in Rome and of Ercole I in Ferrara, and also on page, in the *editiones principes* of Terence in 1470 and of Plautus in 1472. There soon arose a considerable critical tradition, beginning with the fourth-century commentaries of Donatus and Evanthius and culminating in the great

---

[4] On the origins of Roman comedy see Duckworth, 3 ff.; Tanner, 'The Origins of Plautine Comedy,' in Marshall (1980), 58–83; Hunter, *The New Comedy of Greece and Rome*, 8–23.

[5] On the French comedies see Lawton, *Térence en France*, 23 ff., the introductions to Crawford, *Secular Latin Comedies*, and Elliott, *Seven Medieval Latin Comedies*; Bate, 'Twelfth-Century Latin Comedies'. On the Italians, Duckworth, 397–8. For the history of Plautus and Terence in later literature see Reinhardtstoettner, *Plautus*; Lumley, *The Influence of Plautus on the Comedies of Ben Jonson*, 1–49; *The Birthe of Hercules*, ed. Wallace, 20–96; Ballentine, 'The Influence of Terence'; Bond, ed., *Early Plays from the Italian*, xv ff.; Norwood, *Plautus and Terence*, 181–92; Bolgar, *The Classical Heritage*, 532–3, 536–7; Duckworth, 396–433. Also helpful are the bibliographies by Hughes, 101–4, and Cupaiuolo, 466–85.

variorum editions of Terence which shaped the understanding and experience of comedy for Renaissance playwrights and audiences.[6]

As well as for readers, especially students. Editions of Plautus and Terence attained great prominence in European school curricula, the latter exercising influence even in the Middle Ages. Italian Renaissance theorists like Navagero praised the playwrights' Latin and rhetoric, usually preferring Terence as 'cultior' and 'limatior', for excelling in 'elegantia'.[7] These qualities earned the praise of Jacques Peletier du Mans, who also observed in 1555 that Terence's plays were 'entre les mains de chacun'. Consequently, teachers like Barzizza, Guarino, and Ascham strongly encouraged study of Terence as a supreme Latin stylist.[8] Administering his purge, Jonson's Virgil advises the poetaster Crispinus to shun Plautus but to 'taste a piece of Terence' every day; 'sucke his phrase / In stead of lycorice' (*Poetaster* v. iii. 540–1). Plautus had his partisans also. Circulating widely was Aelius Stilo's saying that if the Muses wished to speak Latin, they would use only Plautine language: in Angelo Poliziano's formulation, 'Latine vellent etiam si Musae loqui, / Nullis usuras nisi plautinis vocibus'. Jonson repeated the sentence, adding that Plautus was superior in the 'Oeconomy, and disposition of *Poems*'. Petrarch preferred Plautus as did Nashe's Wittenberg doctors, who wanted to see him first in the conjuration of ancients; the humanist Volcatius Sedigitus ranked Plautus second and Terence sixth among Roman comedy writers.[9]

In England as elsewhere, Terence (often accompanied by

[6] On these early editions and commentaries see Dibdin, *An Introduction to the Knowledge of Rare and Valuable Editions*; Sandys, *A History of Classical Scholarship*; Baldwin, *Five-Act Structure*; Herrick, *Comic Theory*; Robbins, *Dramatic Characterization in Printed Commentaries on Terence*; Pfeiffer, *History of Classical Scholarship*; Altman, *The Tudor Play of Mind*; and Smith, *Ancient Scripts and Modern Experience*.

[7] On Terence in the Middle Ages see Theiner, 'The Medieval Terence', *The Learned and the Lewed*, ed. Benson, 231–47; at the reception of Ambrose's sister as a nun, Liberius, Bishop of Rome (352–66), quoted a line of Terence in St Peter's (Sandys, i. 630–1). On the Italians see Weinberg, *A History of Literary Criticism in the Italian Renaissance*, i. 91–2.

[8] For Peletier see Lawton (ed.), *Handbook of French Renaissance Dramatic Theory*, 50; on Barzizza and Guarino, Grendler, *Schooling in Renaissance Italy*, 250; for Ascham see Smith (ed.), *Elizabethan Critical Essays*, i. 27–9.

[9] Poliziano, *Prose volgari inedite e poesie Latine e Greche*, ed. Lungo, 283; Jonson, ed. Herford and Simpson, vii. 641, 618–19; (cf. Quintilian, *IO*, x. i. 99; for Ricci, see Weinberg (ed.), *Trattati di poetica e retorica del Cinquecento*, i. 436); Petrarch, ed. Rossi, *Le familiari*, ii. 34–5. For the references to Nashe and Volcatius see Riehle, *Shakespeare, Plautus and the Humanist Tradition*, 1, 16.

Plautus) became central to the grammar school curriculum. 'I learn'd *Terence*, i' the third forme at *Westminster*' (Induction 46–7) says the boy in Jonson's *The Magnetic Lady*; and Censure in *The Staple of News* complains of student irresponsibility with unintentional irony: 'We send them to learn their grammar and their Terence, and they learn their play-books' (3. Intermean 48–9). The academic appropriation of Roman comedy in the Renaissance was largely a linguistic, rhetorical, and didactic enterprise: commentators provided lexical and metrical information, expository paraphrase, grammatical analysis, explanatory notes, classical cross-references, and the identification of rhetorical figures. Willichius, who prepared an edition used in English schools, considered each scene in Terence an oration and analysed scenes according to the conventional rhetorical scheme—*exordium, narratio, confirmatio, refutatio*, and *peroratio*.[10] This kind of pedagogy, standard in Renaissance editions, attracted satirical notice: Montaigne ridicules the pedant, 'meagre-looking, with eyes-trilling, flegmatike, squalid, and spauling', who 'wil either die in his pursuit, or teach posteritie the measure of *Plautus* verses, and the true Orthography of a Latine word' (tr. Florio, i. 255). Similarly, Marston's Dondolo gibes at the critic who 'has lost his flesh with fishing at the measure of Plautus' verses' (*The Fawn* IV. 208–9).

Of course, the rediscovery of pagan Plautus and Terence, who display so zestfully lust, avarice, and deceit, posed certain problems. The texts of New Comedy become in the Renaissance well marked sites of ideological struggle and exchange. Advocates emphasize the moral utility of the plays. Introducing his French translation of *Andria* (1542), Charles Estienne, for example, declares that New Comedy features 'reformations de moeurs corrompues et lascives'. In prologues to performances of Terence at Westminster school around 1545, Alexander Nowell argues that comedy can be morally edifying, as does the teacher in Gascoigne's *The Glasse of Governement*: 'out of *Terence* may also be gathered many morall enstructions.'[11] Others were not so confident. Speaking of Terence, Augustine warns about the 'vinum erroris'

---

[10] Herrick, *Comic Theory*, 6–7.

[11] For Estienne see Weinberg (ed.), *Critical Prefaces of the French Renaissance*, 92; on Nowell, Smith, *Ancient Scripts*, 141–3; Gascoigne, ed. Cunliffe, ii. 17. See also McPherson, 'Roman Comedy in Renaissance Education'.

served to students by drunken teachers, 'ab ebriis doctoribus' (*Confessions* i. 16). More graphically, Benedetto Grasso condemns Terence for carrying 'a poisonous plague, by which the minds of tender youths, bewitched, become infected and poisoned in the sewer of the vices'. John Rainoldes advises the young either not to read Terence or not to read him all. Not far from these voices is that of Dryden's extremist, Eugenius, who argues that the ancient playwrights fail to provide profit or delight.[12]

On the other side, Giraldi articulates the standard defence that comedy teaches what to imitate and what to avoid, or as Donatus put it, 'quid sit in uita utile, quid contra euitandum'. For presenting the 'rewarde of the good' and the 'scowrge of the lewde', Whetstone argues in the 'Epistle Dedicatorie' to *Promos and Cassandra* (1578): '*Menander, Plautus,* and *Terence,* them selves many yeares since intombed, (by their Commedies) in honour live at this daye.' Citing Quintilian, Guarino affirms that a knowledge of evil is necessary for moral life. Declaring likewise that 'the filthines of euil wanteth a great foile to perceiue the beauty of vertue', Sidney specifically justifies the portrayal of flawed characters like niggardly Demea, crafty Davos, flattering Gnatho, and vainglorious Thraso. Asserting that drama properly presents vices in general not in particular persons, Jonson's Mr Probee clinches his argument with reference to familiar examples: 'Would you aske of *Plautus,* and *Terence,* (if they both liv'd now) who were *Davus,* or *Pseudolus* in the Scene? who *Pyrgopolinices,* or *Thraso?* who *Euclio* or *Menedemus?*' (*The Magnetic Lady* II. Chorus. 14–17). The great schoolmaster of the age, Erasmus, who knew all of Terence by heart and who ranked him first for the learning of Latin style, advised that objectionable parts should confer some benefit, 'si modo sit ingenii dextri praeceptor' ('if only the teacher possess a ready wit').[13]

What specific form this 'dextrum ingenium' might take is well illustrated by the editions themselves, which feature elaborate strategies of reformulation and containment. Commentators typically preface each scene by explaining its 'theses', or moral lessons.

---

[12] Grasso, as quoted by Weinberg, *Literary Criticism,* i. 287; Rainoldes, *Th'over-throw of Stage-Playes,* 123; Dryden, *An Essay of Dramatick Poesie,* 21 ff.

[13] On Giraldi, see Weinberg, *Literary Criticism,* i. 288 f.; Donatus, ed. Wessner, i. 22; Whetstone, ed. Bullough, ii. 443; on Guarino, Grendler, 251–2; for Sidney see Smith (ed.), *Elizabethan Critical Essays,* i. 177; Erasmus, *De Ratione Studii, Opera Omnia,* I–2, 139.

Witness, for example, the commentaries on *Hecyra*, a particularly problematic Terentian play important to *All's Well That Ends Well*. In this play Pamphilus adopts a pretext to reject his wife because he thinks her pregnant by another; when he discovers that he himself is the father, having previously raped the unwed girl in the dark, he magnanimously reaccepts her.[14] The commentaries in the Lyon edition (1560) analyse the action morally and microscopically, in terms of individual actions and general precepts. Originally reluctant to leave his *meretrix* for a wife, Pamphilus nevertheless agrees to the marriage but leaves it unconsummated; thus he illustrates 'quam grauiter adolescentes ferant vxores sibi dari praesertim in ea aetate, qua amoribus liberaliter indulgere possunt, docet haec scena' (628, 'how seriously young men should take wives who are given to them, especially at the age when they are able to indulge freely in lovers, this scene teaches'); his emotional outburst at the discovery of his wife's pregnancy illustrates the power of fortune, 'quae in rebus humanis dominatur, tanquam tyrannus quispiam' (664, 'which rules in all human affairs like some tyrant'). Pamphilus' pretence of filial piety teaches filial piety, 'Quantum debeant parentibus liberi, quantumque pietatis illis exhibere' (674, 'how much children owe their parents, and how much filial respect they ought to show them'); the final questioning of Parmeno about the true facts of the story shows a praiseworthy caution against the enjoyment of false pleasure, 'Prudentis est circumspicere, ne falso gaudio fruatur' (722). Such commentary, perhaps reaching full expression in Stephanus Riccius' collection of Wittenberg commentaries by Melanchthon and other German reformers (1566–8), aggressively fits the text to the sermon instead of the other way around. For the less dextrous there were translations like that of Pandolfo Collenuccio, who adapted *Amphitruo* to praise a contemporary Hercules, his patron Ercole I of Ferrara; anthologies of selected passages like Aldo Manuzio the Younger's *Locutioni di Terentio* and Nicholas Udall's ubiquitous *Floures of Terence*; and, of course, the expurgated editions adopted, among other places, in some Jesuit schools.[15]

---

[14] This plot is entirely conventional, with analogues in Menander's *Epitrepontes* and *Plokion* and Caecilius Statius' *Plocium* (Warmington (tr.), *Remains of Old Latin*, i. 516 ff.). See also Anderson, 'Love Plots in Menander and his Roman Adapters'; Wiles, 'Marriage and Prostitution', in Redmond (1989), 31–48.

[15] On Riccius and this collection see Robbins, 22 ff.; on Collenuccio, Pittaluga, 'Pandolfo Collenuccio e la sua traduzione'; on Manuzio and Jesuit school editions,

The 'ingenium dextrum' that marks the presentation of New Comedy on page also marks its presentation on stage, though the concerns here are theatrical as well as moral. Early performances of classical comedy featured spectacular allegorical intermezzi and pageantry, related to the action either loosely or not at all. The 1487 production of *Amphitruo* at Ferrara, for example, ended with an elaborate procession of Hercules and his Labours; the 1502 version of *Menaechmi* before Pope Alessandro VI featured representations of Fortune and Virtue, 'et facta contentione fra epse quale fosse soperiore'. Wolsey's 1526–7 production of *Menaechmi* at Hampton Court framed the play with a *pastourelle* and a Petrarchan 'triumph of love', thus transposing the errors into courtly romance.[16] In general, as Bruce C. Smith has shown, Renaissance productions of Plautus and Terence imposed didactic messages on the text while magnifying the spectacle and heightening the love interest. Such productions were fairly frequent in England and elsewhere, especially at the universities. In 1510–11 King's Hall staged a comedy of Terence, the first classical production by any college in Cambridge or Oxford. Later statutes encouraged the periodic production of classical comedy at both universities. At the University of Salamanca a 1538 regulation decreed that a comedy by Plautus or Terence or a tragicomedy be presented regularly.[17] To judge by the references in Elizabethan plays, popular audiences were also familiar with productions of Plautus and Terence. In Chapman's *The Gentleman Usher* (I. i. 193 ff.), for example, Sarpego remembers acting the title role in *Curculio*, dons a 'parasite's dress', and quotes several lines of the Latin text.

Familiar from the schoolroom or the theatre, validated by

Grendler, 251–2; on Udall, Baldwin, *Small Latine*, i. 744–7 and *Five-Act Structure*, 375–7. In the fifth century Stobaeus compiled an anthology, which included quotations from Menander and other Greek comic playwrights, for his son's moral edification. One medieval Plautus florilegium survives; see Thomson, 'A Thirteenth-century Plautus Florilegium'.

[16] See Bonino, ed., *Il teatro italiano*, i. 406; ii. 408–9; Smith, *Ancient Scripts*, 134–8.

[17] Nelson, *Records of Early English Drama: Cambridge*, ii. 711; Boas, *University Drama in the Tudor Age*, 16–18; Hosley, 'The Formal Influence of Plautus and Terence', 131; McKendrick, *Theatre in Spain*, 50–1. The university continues to be a congenial home for classical comedy. The University of Warwick recently produced Plautus in translation on a replicated Roman stage; see Beacham, *The Roman Theatre and its Audience*, 86–116.

polemical modes of presentation, Plautus and Terence set the standards for achievement in comic drama. In England Michael
Drayton praises Ben Jonson as rival to the best classical dramatists
in tragedy and comedy, 'Strong *Seneca* or *Plautus*'. Francis Meres
compliments Shakespeare in similar terms: 'As Plautus and Seneca
are accounted the best for Comedy and Tragedy among the
Latines: so Shakespeare among the English is the most excellent in
both kinds for the stage.' John Davies salutes Shakespeare as 'our
English Terence'; the epistle prefacing the 1609 quarto of *Troilus
and Cressida* compares the play to the '*best Commedy in* Terence
or Plautus'. Fitzgeoffrey's epigram, in which he charges Jonson
with stealing from Plautus but then concludes that Plautus now
steals from Jonson in heaven, humorously inverts the standard
rhetoric of praise.[18]

Such estimation naturally incited imitation. Plautus and Terence
found new life in many direct and oblique descendants, which
appeared in various venues—academic, courtly, popular—and in
various forms, including the Spanish *paso* or *entremés* (interlude),
and the Italian scenarios of the *commedia dell'arte*. Renaissance
adoption of Plautus and Terence as dramatic models exhausts the
full range of possibilities—from passing reference, through direct
imitation, to wholesale recreation. Beginning with the lighter end
of the scale we find everywhere casual allusion, direct quotation,
echo, and parody. More substantial are the Latin academic imita-
tions, commencing with Petrarch's lost *Philologia* and Vergerio's
Paulus (*c.* 1390), which transfer the language, rhetoric, situation,
and character of the original texts into entirely new contexts.
Largely forgotten today, such plays significantly accommodated
classical texts to contemporary moral concerns. Writers like
Wimpheling, Reuchlin, and Chilianus in Germany, Gnapheus,
Macropedius, and Crocus in Holland, Grimald, Radcliff, Udall,
and Foxe in England formed a large and influential corpus of New
Comedy *moralisé*.[19] Next there are the vernacular plays that imitate specific plots in Plautus or Terence. In England, for example,

---

[18] For Drayton, see Spingarn (ed.), *Critical Essays of the Seventeenth Century*, i.
138; Meres, ed. Smith, *Elizabethan Critical Essays*, ii. 317–18; Davies, 'The Scourge
of Folly', ed. Grosart, *Complete Works*, ii. 26; *Shakespeare's Plays in Quarto*, 706;
Fitzgeoffrey in Jonson, ed. Herford and Simpson, xi. 370.

[19] On this Latin drama see Herford, *Studies in the Literary Relations of England
and Germany*, 70–164; *The Birthe of Hercules*, ed. Wallace, 45–59; Herrick,
Tragicomedy, 16–62; Bradner, 'Latin Drama'.

we think of the anonymous *The Birthe of Hercules* (*Amph.*); Shakespeare's *The Comedy of Errors* (*Men.* and *Amph.*); Jonson's *The Case is Altered* (*Captivi* and *Aul.*); Heywood's *The Captives* (*Rud.*) and *The English Traveller* (*Most.*); Chapman's *All Fools* (*HT* and *Adel.*). Finally, there are recreations like Bibbiena's *La calandria*, Shakespeare's *Twelfth Night*, and Jonson's *The Alchemist*, plays that take energy and vitality from New Comedic traditions and conventions as well as from specific texts.

Seen overall, the prevailing poetics of creative *imitatio* produced a dazzling variety of results that testifies to the flexibility of the original elements, to their capacity for refigurations endless and surprising. Renaissance adaptations of New Comedy range from the pedestrian transference of *Jack Juggler* to the surprising transformations of Della Porta and Shakespeare, from Heywood's formal experiments to the free-wheeling improvisations of the *commedia dell'arte*, from the mythological comedy of John Lyly to the satirical city plays of Jonson, Middleton, and Marston, from the moral revisionism of Hrosvit, Macropedius, and Foxe to Grévin's anti-romantic *Les Esbahis*, Jodelle's amoral *L'Eugene*, and Machiavelli's brilliantly cynical *La mandragola*. Throughout the entire range of adaptations the humanist project of domestication shows fissures and contradictions; the ancient voices cannot be silenced or ventriloquized but continually sound and resound in unsettling discourses that create, complicate, and subvert comedic actions.

This polyphony, this interplay of voice, everywhere characterizes Renaissance neo-classicism. Deriving partly from the multivocal nature of language itself, partly from the polemical presentation, it gains special intensity from the prevailing practice of *contaminatio*, the combining of several source plays. Montaigne observes the working method of contemporary playwrights:

It hath often come unto my minde, how such as in our dayes give themselves to composing of comedies (as the Italians who are very happy in them) employ three or foure arguments of *Terence* and *Plautus* to make up one of theirs. In one onely comedy they will huddle up five or six of *Bocaces* tales.   (tr. Florio, ii. 97)

As Montaigne might well have gone on to note, Renaissance playwrights frequently combine Plautus and Terence with each other, with Boccaccio or other Italian prose writers, with other classical authors including Seneca and Ovid, medieval literature, folklore, and romance, with the whole assortment of texts and traditions that stretches from antiquity into their own times. Showing Erasmus' 'ingenium dextrum', they turned to the Bible to create fascinating hybrids that were to be both 'dulce et utile'. The new comedic *adulescens* thus becomes a version of the Prodigal Son, for example, in one central and well-attested variation;[20] other neo-classicists—reworked the stories of Joseph, Susanna and the Elders, Judith and Holofernes, Abraham and Isaac, the Crucifixion and the Resurrection. The work of these writers comes to fruition in Cornelius Schonaeus' *Terentius Christianus* (1592), a series of plays that present biblical stories in New Comedic form.

Classical constituents in Renaissance drama, however, are not always so easy to distinguish and assess as they are in these plays. Sometimes they appear blended into subtle, complex, even subversive, new creations. As commentators have long noted, for example, the New Comedic agelast enriches Shakespeare's portrayal of Shylock; there is even a suggested *locus classicus*, Euclio of *Aulularia*, who futilely attempts to lock up Phaedria and who suffers comic distress over the loss of ducats and daughter.[21] But the hard lines of the Plautine configuration blur and deliquesce in the Venetian mist, where the *senex avarus* laments the theft of Leah's ring, turquoise reminder of himself as a young lover, where the Christians mock and spit at the Jew. Agelast, *senex*, pantaloon, usurer, miser, Barabas, Jew, Shylock grows beyond the fixed confines of the Plautine original into a character capable of endless refiguration, into one who assumes radically different identities in different productions.[22]

---

[20] Prodigal Son plays include Gnapheus' *Acolastus* (1529), Macropedius' *Asotus* (1510) and *Rebelles* (1535), Stymmelius' *Studentes* (1549), Ingelend's *The Disobedient Child* (1560), *Nice Wanton* (1560), *Misogonus* (1571), and Gascoigne's *The Glasse of Governement* (1575). On such hybrids see the references above (n. 19), Beck, 'Terence Improved,' and Young, *The English Prodigal Son Plays*.

[21] See, e.g., Lumley, 43–4. Focusing on the confusion between the girl and the gold, MacCary (review of Konstan, 450–1) extends the Euclio–Shylock affiliation back to Menander's Smikrines and up through Molière's Harpagon and Eliot's Silas Marner. (Cf. Jaques in Jonson's *The Case is Altered* and Suckdry in Wilson's *The Projectors*.) *Merchant* also exhibits New Comedic structure. Lloyd-Jones ('Structure', 314) notes that Menander's fifth acts often occur 'as an appendix to the action proper', in an atmosphere relaxed and removed from everyday reality. The ring action in Belmont, long a critical problem, is Shakespeare's version of this traditional New Comedic *komos* or revelry.

[22] On stage history see Lelyveld, *Shylock on the Stage*; Overton, *The Merchant of*

Given so complicated a history, the influence of New Comedy on Elizabethan drama, especially on Shakespeare, has long challenged critical assessment. In effect, early critics denied rather than discerned the influence of New Comedy on Shakespeare. Instead of initiating broader investigation, for example, Shakespeare's obvious indebtedness to *Menaechmi* in *The Comedy of Errors* became a focal point in the 'Small Latine' debate of the eighteenth century. Langbaine's assertion that Shakespeare used Warner's translation instead of the original Latin echoed in the judgements of Rowe, Gildon, Dennis, Pope, and Lennox.[23] Dennis, in fact, asserted that he could 'never believe' Shakespeare capable of reading Plautus 'without Pain and Difficulty' and speculated about the assistance of a 'Stranger' or 'some learned Friend'. Richard Farmer, influential debunker of Shakespeare's classical attainments, jeered at two other putative instances of direct influence, both alleged by George Colman (1765). Farmer observed that the disguise plot of *The Taming of the Shrew* derives from Gascoigne's *Supposes*, not Plautus' *Trinummus*, and that Shakespeare's altered quotation of a line from Terence derives from Lily's grammar rather than the source in *Eunuchus*.

T. W. Baldwin's monumental labours, of course, have long since settled many major points in the debate about Shakespeare's classical learning.[24] Yet the problems which hindered the first attempts to discuss Shakespeare's indebtedness to New Comedy still persist today, albeit in new forms: 1) the failure to recognize the range and variety of New Comedy; 2) a narrow critical approach that privileges verbal echo as evidence of influence; 3) an inadequate understanding of sources, texts, and their relations.

Misperceptions about Plautus and Terence and their role in Renaissance drama still flourish because modern critics remain

Venice, 43–74; Mahood's New Cambridge edn. (1987), 42–53; Bulman, *Shakespeare in Performance*: '*The Merchant of Venice*'.

[23] Vickers (ed.), v. 77; below, Dennis (ii. 291, 292); Farmer (v. 275–6). Riehle (279–83) argues that Shakespeare used the Latin and Warner's translation. But Warner's 1595 translation appeared after Shakespeare's play and the evidence linking the two is not entirely convincing; see Dorsch's New Cambridge edn. (1988), 8–9.

[24] Baldwin (*Small Latine, Five-Act Structure*) demonstrated the centrality of Latin and of Terence (often with Plautus) to the grammar school curriculum, suggested Shakespeare's familiarity with specific New Comedies, and showed that Terentian commentaries probably inspired Elizabethan five-act structure. On the last point, Riehle (89–97) argues vigorously against Terence in favour of Plautus; but in this matter both were probably influential.

generally inattentive to Latin and to the range of Plautus' and Terence's plays. Inherited generalizations obscure the music, richness, and variety of New Comedy and pre-empt investigation into contemporary understanding. One recent essayist, for example, well reflecting on Shakespeare and the traditions of comedy, nevertheless perpetuates without qualification the old distinction between the classical 'urban comedy of manners' and the native romantic comedies of Lyly, Peele, and others. What of the considerable romantic elements in plays like *Miles Gloriosus*, *Rudens*, and *Andria*? And what of New Comedy's demonstrable influence on writers like Lyly, Peele, and others? Another writer provides this representative summary of critical assumptions in a prizewinning study:

Had Shakespeare been willing to accept the donnés and plot formulas of Plautine comedy, there would be no critical debates over his comic denouements. For all to end well in Plautus no character need be chastened or enlightened because no moral issues are raised, and no regret or sorrow is possible in characters who are fixed forever in their stereotypical natures: the parasite must be greedy, the wife shrewish, the servants cunning, the courtesan unscrupulous. In this farcical universe whatever is, is right and most of the difficulties are merely illusory—the result of some 'error' or 'suppose', a misunderstanding about the identity of a hero or heroine.[25]

'Plautine' or New Comedy here does not seem to include the brilliant and sophisticated experiments of Terence, not to mention those of later tradition. And the critic reduces the varied, exuberant, and innovative work of Plautus himself to the errors formula, set in a farcical universe devoid of moral issues, inhabited only by stock characters. *Stichus*, of course, has no errors, and the errors formula does not begin to describe the action of a satire like *Truculentus*, an intrigue play like *Pseudolus*, a mythological travesty like *Amphitruo*, or a maritime romance like *Rudens*. The assertion that New Comedy raises no moral issues, as we have seen, runs directly counter to centuries of humanistic teaching and commentary. And, of course, characters in Plautus and Terence (and also Menander) continually play against their masks, out of

[25] The first writer is Daniell, *Cambridge Companion*, ed. Wells, 101; the second, Ornstein, *Shakespeare's Comedies*, 21. Uncritical reliance on inherited generalizations concerning New Comedy entirely invalidates Rowe's *Thomas Middleton and the New Comedy Tradition*.

their expected roles: Phormio is a parasite who is also a clever servant; Alcumena (*Amph.*) and Sostrata (*Hecyra*) are wronged and
noble wives; Grumio (*Most.*) is a dull-witted, frightened servant;
Bacchis (*Hecyra*), a most scrupulous courtesan, to take only some
obvious counter-examples. With creativity and theatrical verve,
Menander, Plautus, and Terence ceaselessly vary verse and formula, constantly experiment with structure and character, intentionally defy expectation. Later critics might well have heeded
Jonson's Cordatus, who perceived in New Comedy precisely this
independence from tradition as well as the free play of liberty and
invention; Cordatus recalls,

Menander, Philemon, Cecilivs, Plavtvs, and the rest: who have vtterly
excluded the *Chorus*, altered the property of the persons, their names, and
natures, and augmented it with all liberty, according to the elegancie and
disposition of those times, wherein they wrote[.] I see not then, but we
should enioy the same licence, or free power, to illustrate and heighten our
inuention as they did.

(*Every Man out of his Humour*, Induction 261–8)[26]

The second old problem, a narrow critical approach that privileges verbal echo as evidence, also persists today. To be sure, critics have discerned the influence of New Comedy in the
morphology of Renaissance drama—five-act-structure, the double
plot—and in stock characters like the *servus currens*; but claims
for the influence of individual plays still rest largely on the perception of echo.[27] Evidence normally appears in the delusive form of

---

[26] Interestingly, Shakespeare's company performed this play in 1599. Cordatus'
view accords with most informed criticism beginning with Plutarch (*Moralia* 712C),
who noted different kinds of *hetairai* in Menander. On Menander's inventiveness see
also Handley's and Sandbach's essays in *Ménandre, Fondation Hardt Entretiens*
(1–26; 113–36); Webster, *An Introduction to Menander*, 13–24; Arnott, 'Time, Plot
and Character in Menander', 353 ff., as well as his introduction to the Loeb edition,
xxxii–xxxviii; Goldberg, *The Making of Menander's Comedy*; Brown, 'Plots and
Prostitutes in Greek New Comedy'; on the conventionality and originality of Roman
comedy see the seminal work of Fraenkel, *Plautinisches im Plautus*; Duckworth,
384–95; Williams, *Tradition and Originality in Roman Poetry*, 285–95; Wright,
Dancing in Chains; Zagagi, *Tradition and Originality in Plautus*; Hunter, *New
Comedy*, 59–82; Slater, *Plautus in Performance*; Goldberg, *Understanding Terence*.

[27] On five-act structure see above, n. 24; on the double plot see Levin, *Multiple
Plot in English Renaissance Drama*, 225–45; Weimann, *Shakespeare and the Popular
Tradition*, 151–60, 237–46; Levin and Weimann wisely recognize both classical and
native influences. For verbal echoes see Tschernjajew, 'Shakespeare und Terenz';
Simpson, *Studies in Elizabethan Drama*, 13–23, 48. On the limitations of this
approach to literary history see Riffaterre, *Text Production*, 90 ff.

parallel-passages, those inevitably disappointing jumbles of nuga-
tory resemblance, commonplace idea, and faint rhyme. The realities of Renaissance imitation must broaden our conception of
influence to include various manifestations, verbal and also non-
verbal—'transformed convention, rhetorical or structural format,
scenic rhythm, ideational or imagistic concatenation, thematic
articulation'.[28] These realities must also attune criticism to the fact
of mediated or collateral influence. Like other Renaissance playwrights, Shakespeare encountered Plautus and Terence directly and
indirectly—in the drama of his predecessors and contemporaries.
And in non-dramatic works as well. New Comedy influenced
Propertius, Ovid, and Lucian, whose dialogues in turn supply character and situation to Erasmus and others. Boccaccio copied all of
Terence by hand, remembering him significantly in the *Decameron*;
Sidney's *Arcadia* (old version) orders its action according to the
'renaissance Terentian five-act structure', with *protasis*, *epitasis*,
and *catastrophe*, and features a Terentian double plot. Plautus and
Terence shape tales in Bandello, either directly or through an intermediary like *Gl'ingannati*; they also contribute to the ancient
novel, those enormously influential prose romances of writers like
Chariton, Heliodorus, Longus, Xenophon of Ephesus, and
Apuleius.[29] The formative presence of New Comedy in these
works, so important to Shakespeare, argues for wider investigation,
for critical recognition of intertextual presence; in the age of imitation one text always leads into and out towards many others. We
think of Charles Grivel's famous dictum: 'Il n'est de texte que
d'intertexte.'[30]

Grivel and other recent theorists of intertextuality have greatly
expanded our understanding of sources, texts, and their relations.
Current theory has distinguished between two opposite intertextual
perspectives, synchronic and diachronic. Dismissing all notion of

---

[28] See my *Shakespeare and Classical Tragedy*, 6–8 (8).

[29] See Yardley, 'Propertius 4.5, Ovid *Amores* 1.6 and Roman Comedy'; on
Lucian, LeGrand, *The New Greek Comedy*, 17–18; Riehle, 185–97; on Boccaccio's
copying, Sandys, ii. 12; on Sidney, *Poems*, ed. Ringler, jun., xxxviii. See also
Lindheim, *The Structures of Sidney's Arcadia*, 30–1; Parker, 'Terentian Structure and
Sidney's Original *Arcadia*'; Chalifour, 'Sir Philip Sidney's *Old Arcadia* as Terentian
Comedy'; on Bandello, Caliumi, *Il Bandello*, 81 ff.; on romance writers see below,
141 n. The list could easily be extended in other directions: Fernando de Rojas, e.g.,
employs New Comedic character and situation throughout *Celestina*, his seminal
work; see Grismer, *The Influence of Plautus in Spain before Lope de Vega*.

[30] As quoted by Plett, ed., *Intertextuality*, 17.

temporality and hence of sources, the synchronic perspective views all texts as existing simultaneously with each other. 'An endless *ars combinatoria* takes place in what has been variously termed "musée imaginaire" (Malraux), "chambre d'échos" (Barthes), or "Bibliothèque générale" (Grivel).' On the contrary, the diachronic perspective recognizes temporality and thus constructs well-ordered 'archives' (Foucault) of intertextuality that meticulously chronicle 'every code and register its continuities and discontinuities'.[31] The latter perspective opposes the former's potentially endless deferral and dispersion, that kind of detheologized hermeticism in which all signifiers ultimately signify everything or nothing. It enables, rather than precludes, criticism by affording more spacious perspectives in which to work and a set of more subtle instruments for measure.[32]

The need for such and other changes is wittily recognized in Stephen Greenblatt's *pronunciamento*: 'Source study is, as we all know, the elephants' graveyard of literary history.'[33] In his study of Harsnett and *Lear*, Greenblatt dismantles the old dichotomy between sources as background or raw material and the text as free-standing, disinterested work of art, arguing for the permeability of the boundaries between them, situating both in a larger cultural poetics. The primary disadvantage of the new approach—the facile tendency to substitute literary tropes of metaphor and synechdoche for historical analysis and evidence—has become only too clear in recent years, as has the primary advantage, a redefinition of terms that encourages exploration of institutional strategies and cultural dispositions. The study of ancient texts in the Renaissance, no less than contemporary ones, benefits from this redefinition. For they, surcharged with humanistic commentary in editions, adapted in Renaissance productions, translations, and

[31] Plett, ed., *Intertextuality*, 25–6.

[32] The diachronic perspective is discussed and deployed variously by Greene, *The Light in Troy* and *The Vulnerable Text*; Schoeck, *Intertextuality and Renaissance Texts*; the essayists in *Literary Theory / Renaissance Texts*, ed. Parker and Quint. Recent advances, of course, do not negate the important work of earlier scholars: Coulter, 'The Plautine Tradition in Shakespeare'; Duckworth; Doran, *Endeavors of Art*, esp. 152, 171 ff.; Frye, 'The Argument of Comedy', 'Characterization in Shakespearian Comedy', *Anatomy of Criticism*, 163–86; *A Natural Perspective*; Hosley, 'Formal Influence'; Salingar, *Shakespeare and the Traditions of Comedy*; Altman; Nevo, *Comic Transformations*; Paster, *The Idea of the City*; Newman, *Shakespeare's Rhetoric of Comic Character*; Riehle.

[33] 'Shakespeare and the Exorcists', in Parker and Hartman (1985), 163. For a devastating critique of New Historicism and 'Current Literary Theory', as he contemptuously terms it, see Vickers, *Appropriating Shakespeare*, esp. 214–71.

plays, are also in an important sense contemporary and, therefore, participants in the same circulation of energy and exchange. For Shakespeare and others the elephants' bones of Plautus' and Terence's plays still had plenty of life.

After surveying three hundred years of scholarship on Shakespeare and the classical tradition, John W. Velz predicted, among other things, future study of 'Plautine and Terentian themes in the mature comedies'.[34] Extending consideration beyond 'themes', this study fulfils the prediction by attempting a comprehensive assessment of form and structure. As has long been recognized in isolated studies, the plays of Plautus and Terence function as important sources and also as 'deep sources', as possessors of a comedic gene pool that shapes in various mediated ways succeeding generations. Exploration of these lineages can be rich and fruitful. The proof of direct paternity is often less important and less interesting than the establishment of ancestry, the tracing of complicated genealogy, the identification of inherited characteristics, the analysis of family resemblance and diversity. Assessment must be flexible enough, in other words, to consider New Comedy both as text and as tradition. It must also analyse New Comedic presence in light of larger Renaissance contexts, recognizing that sources and texts actively and reciprocally engage each other, often exhibiting the same harmonies and dissonances, continuities and discontinuities.

This investigation will focus largely on the evidence provided by dramatic theory and practice in a wide field of enquiry. Plautus and Terence themselves, we have already noted, descend directly from Greek New Comedy, which in turn appears after Greek Middle and Old Comedy. The immediate Greek ancestors of Plautus and Terence, as represented in Menander and the surviving fragments of other writers, merit consideration. After antiquity the discovery and propagation of New Comedy in Renaissance Italy deserves special attention. From the great variety of erudite comedies played between Ariosto and Oddi to the popular improvisations of the related *commedia dell'arte*, Italian dramatists produced and reproduced New Comedy with extraordinary fecundity and energy; they created the principal family lines that furnish later Renaissance adaptation in England as well as in France and Spain.

---

[34] *Shakespeare and the Classical Tradition*, 13.

Stephen Gosson, in fact, complained that Italian comedies were 'ransackt, to furnish the Playe houses in London'. At the end of the sixteenth century, and early in the seventeenth, Cambridge University regularly staged Latin versions of Italian comedies or independent compositions in Italian style.[35] Chapman casually mentions four Italian plays in the dedication of *The Widow's Tears*. Building upon the work of previous scholars like Lea, Herrick, and Salingar, Louise George Clubb's recent book, *Italian Drama in Shakespeare's Time*, advances cinquecento theatre to its rightful place of prominence among Shakespeare's formative traditions. She brilliantly demonstrates that Italian playwrights provided for Shakespeare and European theatre seminal 'units, figures, relationships, actions, *topoi*, and framing patterns, gradually building a combinatory of theatergrams that were at once streamlined structure for svelte play making and elements of high specific density, weighty with significance from previous incarnations'.[36]

From the eristic imitation of *The Comedy of Errors* to the eclectic recension of *The Tempest*, Shakespeare relies on New Comedy throughout his career. The plays of Plautus that loom largest in the following discussion are *Menaechmi*, *Amphitruo*, *Mostellaria*, *Captivi*, *Miles Gloriosus*, *Casina*, and *Rudens*; of Terence, *Andria*, *Eunuchus*, *Hecyra*, and *Adelphoe*. Some of these, e.g. *Menaechmi*, Shakespeare undoubtedly read directly, probably in Latin. Others he may have known only indirectly, as a deep source present in intermediary texts. *Captivi*, for example, lives in Ariosto's *I suppositi*, hence in Gascoigne's adaptation, the source for the Lucentio–Bianca plot of *Shrew*; *Hecyra* lives in Boccaccio's *Decameron*, hence in Painter's translation, a source for *All's Well*. More often the lines of transmission from antiquity are multiple and intersecting, horizontal and vertical, visible and invisible, impossible to trace definitively. The celebrated and widely imitated *Miles Gloriosus*, for example, created a prototype of comic *alazoneia* and exposure for later centuries; the seminal *Rudens* initi-

---

[35] Gosson, *Plays Confuted in Five Actions*, sig. D5v; on such Cambridge plays as *Hymenaeus* (1579), Forsett's *Pedantius* (1581), Fraunce's *Victoria* (1582), *Laelia* (1595), Ruggle's *Ignoramus* (1615), and the works of Brooke, Hawkesworth, and Randolph see Orr, *Italian Renaissance Drama in England*, 26–36; Bradner, 49–50; individual editions.

[36] p. 6. Clubb (49–50) concisely summarizes the evidence of direct theatrical connections between Italy and England, including mention of seven visits to England by Italian players between 1546 and 1578.

ated the subgenre of Plautine romance. Both directly and indirectly, New Comedy created a vast lexicon of theatrical possibility.

Like Plautus and Terence themselves, Shakespeare continually reformulates and interrogates his New Comedic heritage. Characters like the *senex*, *virgo*, *servus*, *miles gloriosus*, *parasitus*, *matrona*, *adulescens*, and *meretrix* undergo startling transformations. Likewise varied and, at times, subverted is the essential New Comedic structure—prologue, *protasis*, *epitasis*, and *catastrophe* with anagnorisis and peripeteia. Throughout his works Shakespeare creatively adapts New Comedic dramaturgy—the use of localities like the sea, brothel, and temple, the conventions of the enforced response and the surprise entrance, the art of construction by the pairing of opposite characters, the climactic use of *pistis*, or proof of identity. Dramatic devices like the lock-out, disguise, and eavesdropping appear in strange translations as do familiar New Comedic configurations: the blocking father, his daughter, her lover; the clever slave and master; the importunate lover and worldy courtesan; the reunion of parent and child. As always, classical elements, present in different degrees in different plays, combine with non-classical ones—the Bible, medieval literature, the Italian novella, contemporary fiction and drama—not in static coexistence but dynamic interaction.

This study organizes discussion of New Comedy's presence in Shakespeare into four broad and overlapping categories—New Comedic errors, intrigue, *alazoneia*, and romance. In his errors plays—*The Comedy of Errors* and *Twelfth Night*—Shakespeare translates Plautine confusion into moral folly, and romanticizes classical eros, particularly by expanding the roles of women. In *The Taming of the Shrew* and *Much Ado About Nothing* he delights in intrigue but also explores its limitations and darker potential. The *alazoneia* plays—*The Merry Wives of Windsor* and *All's Well That Ends Well*—hark back to the ancient conception of comedy as ridicule, while interestingly engaging other conceptions, traditions, and expectations. The romances—*Pericles* and *The Tempest*—fluently blend New Comedic motifs and configurations with other sources to produce a *comoedia sacra* and to effect a redefinition of comedic *tyche*. This study concludes by discerning New Comedic presence in Shakespearean tragedy, specifically in *Hamlet* and *King Lear*. Creating in these plays a kind of 'heavy Plautus', Shakespeare subverts comedic character and action to supply stunning tragic power.

2

New Comedic Errors

DONATUS and Evanthius, standard guides to classical comedy, analysed comic plot in terms of *errores*, i.e., mistakes of identity, resolved through recognition. Such errors could result from tricks or chance, 'per insidie altrui, o del caso', as Castelvetro put it, or from some combination of the two.[1] Two of Plautus' errors plays, *Menaechmi* and *Amphitruo*, bequeathed to following generations a prototypal *processus turbarum*, which playwrights adapted to raise laughter as well as searching questions about identity and the nature of the self in society. In both plays the *processus* reaches a climax in the lock-out, which threatens to deprive an exasperated, hitherto self-assured husband of wife, home, and very self. An opportunity for some raucous fun, the lock-out in *The Comedy of Errors* appears ironically reversed at the end of the play, where it occasions the cure of Adriana's jealousy. In *Twelfth Night*, grandly expanded, the lock-out becomes a symbol that richly betokens spiritual exclusion and occlusion as well as the problematics of desire.

The resolution of classical *errores* occurs variously through a chance that sometimes hints at larger design. Perhaps the earliest surviving New Comedic errors play, Menander's *Perikeiromene*, presents lost children with tokens, separated twins, confusions about identity, and a final recognition. This play shares deep affinities with *Amphitruo*: both feature a soldier who returns home to find his beloved with another, through no fault of her own; the soldiers become enraged; an eventual discovery exculpates the woman and resolves the problem. The Prologue/goddess in *Perikeiromene*, Agnoia, 'ignorance', or better yet, 'misapprehension', announces in a postponed prologue that she has orchestrated the misunderstandings ἀρχὴν δ᾽ ἵνα λάβηι / μηνύσεως τὰ λοιπά—τούς θ᾽ αὑτῶν ποτε / εὕροιεν (165–7, 'to get a start on the process of discovery and to enable these people to find their family').[2] Agnoia

---

[1] On Donatus, Evanthius, and Castelvetro, see Salingar, *Traditions*, 84 ff.

[2] 'Agnoia' provides the title for two lost New Comedies (one by Diphilus or

thus initiates a process of errors to a definite end, unambivalently forecast. Moreover, the goddess, neatly correcting the *agnoia* of the audience who have misinterpreted the lost opening scene, assures us that she has already been at work throughout the play and that she intends to turn evil to good, διὰ γὰρ θεοῦ καὶ τὸ κακὸν εἰς ἀγαθὸν ῥέπει / γινόμενον (169–70, 'for through the power of a god, evil itself turns to good, even as it occurs'). We recall similar divine prologues—*Tyche*, or Fortune, in Menander's *Aspis*, Arcturus in *Rudens*, and also Mercury in *Amphitruo*. These divinities assert their control of events and bring about resolution; the gods turn tragedy to comedy or to tragicomedy; the ancient errors play shades imperceptibly towards romance.

And towards the more or less providential world of Renaissance comedy. In cinquecento plays, especially the *commedia grave*, a divine pattern guides 'characters through innumerable *intrichi, inganni, labirinti*, and *errori* to perfect order'.[3] The universe of these plays resembles that of *Errors*, with the Abbess and Priory, and that of *Twelfth Night*, where tempests are kind and salt waves fresh in love. Of course, such plays are not allegories, homilies, or didactic expositions; we are, for example, a long way from Burmeister's revision of *Amphitruo* (1621), wherein Alcumena becomes the Virgin Mary. Here instead the intimation of providential design often serves in context to unsettle and to disturb, to challenge as well as to affirm orthodox pieties. Still, as has not been well recognized, Shakespeare's errors plays belong to the larger community of Renaissance comedy, exhibiting familiar structural designs and thematic emphases. Here, as elsewhere in the Renaissance, *error personae*, Cutberd and Otter's canonical impediment to marriage in *Epicoene* (v. iv. 208), does not lead to separation, but to marvellous unions and reunions.

The Comedy of Errors

The Comedy of Errors—title claims identity. Only this play in Shakespeare's canon so succinctly defines itself. The term 'comedy' implies identification with classical forebears, here realized by

Calliades, the other by Machon), and, in substantive form, for two plays by unknown writers. See Edmonds, *Fragments*, iiiA–B, 98, 182, 288, 1213.

[3] Clubb, *Italian Drama*, 62.

extended imitation of two Plautine plays. 'Errors', from *errare*, 'to wander', suggests mistakes rather than deceits, accidents rather than intrigues, humorous confusions rather than ridiculous vices. Appositely, Baldwin cites Lambinus' definition of 'error' as the state wherein one believes what is not true or does not believe what is, 'quo id credit, quod non est: non credit quod est'.[4] Since Lambinus' edition of Plautus was a standard schoolbook, it may well have provided Shakespeare with the title and conception of his play, as well as with several suggestive references to *Amphitruo*. Shakespeare's choice of *Menaechmi*, the main source, and *Amphitruo*, the ancillary one, for this early attempt at comedy was entirely orthodox: both attracted much imitation in later literatures, especially that of the early humanists in Europe and England.[5] Both plays, however, are unusual in Plautus, the one relying on chance not contrivance, the other, his sole surviving attempt at mythological travesty.

We do not know exactly how Shakespeare's company cast the original performances of *The Comedy of Errors*, but we do know that the challenge of finding look-alikes proved too much for Ben Jonson, who abandoned his errors play, a version of *Amphitruo*, because he 'could never find two so like others that he could persuade the spectators they were one'.[6] Cecchi solved the problem by cleverly contriving his version of *Menaechmi*, *La moglie*, so that the twins could be played by one actor, 'che uno stesso Strione può recitare il personaggio di Alfonso, e quello di Ricciardo, cambiando solo l'habito: però non accade pigliarsi fatica di trouar duoi, che si somiglino'.[7] Following the lead of another Italian, Ariosto in *I suppositi* via Gascoigne's *Supposes*, or that of *Amphitruo*, Shakespeare multiplies rather than divides: he doubles

---

[4] Baldwin, *Five-Act*, 692. Bullough (i. 3) notes other similar titles, *The Historie of Error* (1577) and *A Historie of Fferrar* (1583); there were also Giovanni Battista Gelli's *Lo errore* and Pietro Buonfanti da Bibbiena's *Errori incogniti*; see also Riehle, 101–4.

[5] See Baldwin, *Five-Act*, 668–70; Radcliff-Umstead, *The Birth of Modern Comedy*, 61–2. The clerics of San Lorenzo performed *Menaechmi* in 1488, complete with Angelo Poliziano's lively preface praising the play as 'Lepidam et jocosam et elegantem ut nihil supra' (*Prose volgari*, 282). According to Smith (*Ancient Scripts*, 138), *Menaechmi* was the first identifiable classical script performed in England, by Wolsey's men (1526). On the history of the Amphitruo legend see Sedgwick, ed., 2–10; Shero, 'Alcmena and Amphitryon in Ancient and Modern Drama'; Costa, 'The Amphitryo Theme', in Dorey and Dudley (1965), 87–122.

[6] 'Conversations with Drummond', ed. Herford and Simpson, i. 144.

[7] Cecchi, *La moglie*, 1(v).

the number of identical twins and nearly triples the incidents of error from seventeen to fifty.[8] The eristic impulse, the urge to outdo, to surpass the classical model is endemic to the age: Aretino's *Talanta* presents triplets (two female, one male), all cross-dressed; *The Birthe of Hercules* adds a second servant to the Amphitruo story and develops the miniscule part of Thessala; Lyly's *Mother Bombie* (1594) exceeds Roman models by presenting two pairs of changeling children, four old men, four servants, and three pairs of lovers. *Errors* also exhibits Shakespeare's characteristic eclecticism, his habit of combining disparate sources—here Plautus, the legend of Apollonius of Tyre, and a Pauline epistle—into strange new creations.[9] Apparent also is Shakespeare's interest in centring his comedies on love affairs: the merely functional Wife becomes the complicated Adriana, whose marriage to the citizen twin will be a focus of attention; the irascible and opportunistic Menaechmus of Syracuse becomes the bewildered lover, Antipholus, conveniently provided for by the invented Luciana.

Although no one would deny Shakespeare's general indebtedness to Plautus in this play, the specific tally of debits and credits has occasioned some dispute. Because the two Dromios, for example, sport Italian names and little resemble cheeky intriguers like Chrysalus, Pseudolus, Epidicus, and Tranio, some have thought them Italianate rather than Plautine.[10] But not every classical slave is *callidus*; many, including Messenio of *Menaechmi* and Sosia of *Amphitruo*, are humorous victims of abuse and misunderstanding. Moreover, the two Dromios continually replay jokes and routines from New Comedy. They voice the familiar complaint about having to obey orders (e.g. IV. i. 112–13), and they yearn for freedom; they show fondness for word-play, especially *equivoca* (II. ii. 82 ff., III. i. 81 ff.), and for an occasional exuberant catalogue (III. i. 32 ff.). Like Messenio, Dromio of Syracuse solicitously warns his master about the conniving courtesan. Playing the standard *servus currens*, Dromio of Syracuse arrives on stage with his news, breathless from

[8] *Menaechmi*, ed. Rouse, xiv.

[9] Baldwin (*Five-Act*, 670) also suggests *Miles Gloriosus* as a possible source. Several have suggested *Captivi*: Levin, *Refractions*, 141; Phialas, *Shakespeare's Romantic Comedies*, 7–9. Benham ('A Note on the *Comedy of Errors*') detects a hint for the character of Egeon in the broken-hearted father of the Prologue, *Men.* 34–6.

[10] See Lea, *Italian Popular Comedy*, 438; quoted approvingly by Herrick, *Italian Comedy*, 223–4. On general Italian influence, see Bond, *Studia Otiosa*, 46–50; Clubb, *Italian Drama*, 49–63.

running (III. ii. 70 *s.d.*). Another familiar comic routine is the enforced recitation of responses to the master. Menaechmus bullies Peniculus the parasite in animated trochaic recitative:

> MEN. dic hominem lepidissumum esse me.   PE. ubi essuri sumus?
> MEN. dic modo hoc quod ego te iubeo.   PE. dico: homo lepidissume.
> MEN. ecquid audes de tuo istuc addere?   PE. atque hilarissume.
> (147–9)

MEN. Say that I'm a very charming man.   PE. Where are we going to eat?
MEN. Just say what I bid you.   PE. I'm saying it: Hello, very charming man!
MEN. Won't you venture to add something of your own?   PE. OK: Hello, very cheerful man!

So Antipholus of Syracuse similarly demands a rhythmic series of responses from his servant:

> E. ANT. Din'd at home? Thou villain, what sayest thou?
> E. DRO. Sir, sooth to say, you did not dine at home.
> E. ANT. Were not my doors lock'd up, and I shut out?
> E. DRO. Perdie, your doors were lock'd, and you shut out.
> E. ANT. And did not she herself revile me there?
> E. DRO. Sans fable, she herself revil'd you there.
> E. ANT. Did not her kitchen-maid rail, taunt, and scorn me?
> E. DRO. Certes she did, the kitchen vestal scorn'd you.   (IV. iv. 68–75)

The reported conversation (II. i. 62 ff.) ripe for comic improvisation, may also derive from similar reports in New Comedy (e.g. Terence, *Eun.* 337 ff.). In addition, Shakespeare converts the common Plautine term of abuse, *mastigia*, 'one who deserves a whipping', into a stage prop. In IV. i Antipholus of Ephesus sends his servant to purchase a 'rope's end' (16); this Dromio returns with the item in IV. iv, just when Antipholus expects his bail money. The consequent beating causes Dromio to lament, 'I am an ass indeed' (IV. iv. 29 ff.), to voice the typical Plautine slave's concern about his vulnerable back (e.g. *Most.* 858 ff.).[11]

Characters and gags from Roman comedy exist in a new space, one Shakespeare creates by transforming convention and setting. Both *Menaechmi* and *Errors* begin with a *narratio* that recounts the past and supplies pertinent information about the present. But the facts of the parallel accounts conflict obviously, and there are also

---

[11] In view of this Plautine convention I find it hard to agree with those who treat the speech with high seriousness, e.g. Wyrick, 'The Ass Motif', 442.

important differences in style and emphasis, beginning with the different narrative voices themselves. Plautus' Prologue stands manifestly apart, creates distance between audience and play, strikes the appropriate note of unsentimental urbanity, introduces the theme of manipulation—both theatrical and financial. He begins and ends his narrative by pointing to the illusory nature of the unfolding drama. The opening lines chattily identify the author and the setting, Epidamnus, while referring to Athens, the usual comic locale: 'atque hoc poetae faciunt in comoediis: / omnis res gestas esse Athenis autumant' (7–8, 'Now poets always do this in comedies: they allege that all the business occurs in Athens'). At the end of the speech he again emphasizes the theatrical fiction: 'haec urbs Epidamnus est dum haec agitur fabula: / quando alia agetur aliud fiet oppidum' (72–3, 'This city is Epidamnus while this play is performed; when another play is performed it will become another city'). The speaker indulges in comic neologism (11–12) and word play: 'ingressus fluuium rapidum . . . rapidus raptori pueri subduxit pedes' (64–5, 'After he entered the rapid river . . . the rapids pulled the feet of the boy's raptor out from under him'). Throughout the short *narratio* he continually intrudes, first to assure us that he has never seen the twins (23), then to break the tragic momentum of the tale with a humorous recollection about the twins' grandfather (45–6), and, finally, playing again with the notion of theatrical illusion, to offer to transact business in Epidamnus for the audience, provided, of course, that they hand over the necessary funds (53).

In contrast with the Prologue, Egeon relates his part in the past action as he participates in the present. Arrested in Ephesus, he hears the Duke's sentence and obeys his command to speak. The *narratio* itself, beginning with an echo of Aeneas' woeful remembrance (*Aeneid* ii. 3), consists of finely molded, formal blank verse, marked by balance, antithesis, and repetition, lightened by strategically placed couplets in the beginning and the end. Some of the repetitions signify thematic concerns and, in so doing, mark the distance travelled from Plautus. Egeon laments the turns of 'Fortune' (105), his 'misfortunes' (119), his bad 'hap' (38; cf. 141). But Fortune, he admits, gave him and his wife something to delight in as well (106), namely survival, and hap can sometimes be good: it was the 'hap' (113) of the Corinthian fishermen to rescue him and the infants. Egeon inhabits a world he cannot understand, a

world which is inexplicably bad and good to him by turns, a world
in which he survives the storm only to hit a rock, then is rescued
again only to face in time Solinus' death sentence. Dimly, however,
Egeon senses a mysterious order beneath the apparent chaos. He
coins an unusual epithet, 'the always-wind-obeying deep' (63), for
the sea which ruins him and he recalls the phrase several lines
later, describing the survivors of the storm as 'floating straight,
obedient to the stream' (86). The hints of some unfathomable
chain of command and obedience, of some providential order, con-
tinue in other cosmological references. 'The heavens did grant' (66)
obscured light, he says, a warning of impending doom. Later, they
are more merciful: 'the sun gazing upon the earth, / Dispers'd
those vapors that offended us, / And by the benefit of his wished
light / The seas wax'd calm' (88–91). The focus on the beneficent
power of the sun and the religious tone here suggest the place of
the powerless, uncomprehending mortal in a strange but ordered
world and prepare obliquely for the resolution by the Abbess.[12]

As Segal has shown, Plautus' Epidamnus is the scene for the
archetypal Roman conflict between *industria* and *voluptas*, the
place where the citizen Menaechmus tries to act out a holiday fantasy.[13] Exiting from his house, Menaechmus of Syracuse
reproaches his wife in lyrical song and gleefully anticipates lunch
with Erotium, the *meretrix*. Bringing her a *palla* stolen from his
wife, Menaechmus looks forward to sensual delights—food, drink,
and sex. Epidamnus, however, proves to be an inhospitable place
for such wish-fulfilment. Messenio punningly observes the link
between *nomen* and *omen*: 'propterea huic urbei nomen Epidamno
inditumst, / quia nemo ferme huc sine damno deuortitur' (263–4,
'The city got its name, Epidamnus, for precisely this reason: practi-
cally no one stops in this damn place without paying damages').
This is the city of 'Ribaulds, Parasites, Drunkards, Catchpoles,
Cony-catchers, and Sycophants . . . [and] Curtizans' in Warner's
colourful rendition, of the merchant who originally stole
Menaechmus in the Tarentum forum.[14] And Erotium, it is clear,

---

[12] Others who observe providential order in the world of the play include
Baldwin, *Compositional Genetics*, 120–46, 270 ff.; Arthos, 'Shakespeare's
Transformation of Plautus'; and, most important, Kinney, 'Shakespeare's *The
Comedy of Errors* and the Nature of Kinds', who reveals the shaping influence of
Paul's epistle to the Ephesians, the mystery plays, Anglican liturgy, and homilies.

[13] Segal, *Roman Laughter*, 42–51.

[14] Ed. Bullough, i. 17. On this location see Baldwin, *Compositional Genetics*, 57–72.

like the typical courtesan in New Comedy, makes pleasure her business, 'amanti amoenitas malost, nobis lucrost' (356, 'A pleasant place means misfortune for a lover, a fortune for us'). The hard edge of her business ethic, 'opera pro pecunia' (*Asinaria* 172, 'work for wages'), as Cleareta puts it, undercuts the romantic pretensions and exposes the folly of the businessman's idyll. The would-be lover can only be *raptor raptus*, as the Prologue might have observed.

Shakespeare, of course, changes the setting from Epidamnus to Ephesus, a place which at first seems equally inhospitable. Ephesus, however, threatens not only one's wallet but also one's self and soul:

> They say this town is full of cozenage:
> As nimble jugglers that deceive the eye,
> Dark-working sorcerers that change the mind,
> Soul-killing witches that deform the body,
> Disguised cheaters, prating mountebanks,
> And many such-like liberties of sin.   (I. ii. 97–102)

Emphasizing witchcraft instead of Plautine thievery (see also IV. iii. 71 ff.), Shakespeare probably follows the lead of St Paul and his depiction of Ephesian sorcery. In so doing, the playwright restores the emphasis found in ancient folktales of this type, wherein a witch commonly lures the husband, but winds up with the travelling twin, who outwits her.[15] Of course, Adriana is neither witch nor courtesan, but wife, and Shakespeare's expansion of the *matrona* here, accords well with other instances of Renaissance *imitatio*. Bullough (i. 6–7) notes similar expansion in Italian adaptations of *Menaechmi* by Berrardo, Firenzuola, Trissino, and Cecchi; Rotrou likewise names the wife and endows her with jealousy and comic pathos in *Les Ménechmes*; and other English plays— Chapman's *All Fools*, for example—also feature wives expanded from their classical models. In her opening dialogue with Luciana (II. i) Adriana exhibits jealousy, a trait present in Plautus' *matrona* but developed here in a courtly debate. The touch is lighter than many have recognized: their conversation switches into rhymed couplets (10); Adriana wryly punctures Luciana's philosophical paean to male dominance, 'This servitude makes you to keep unwed' (26); the scene ends with Adriana's misinterpretation of Dromio's report

---

[15] See Hansen, 'An Oral Source for the *Menaechmi*'.

and her foolish display of jealousy and self-pity. Thus it sets up the
subsequent confrontation with the travelling twin, a comic error
which Adriana's earnestness only heightens. Still, the poetry of her
later complaint, insisting on a union 'undividable incorporate',
betokens more than merely comic exasperation:

> How comes it now, my husband, O, how comes it,
> That thou art then estranged from thyself?
> Thyself I call it, being strange to me,
> That, undividable incorporate,
> Am better than thy dear self's better part.   (II. ii. 119–23)

Shakespeare turns the Plautine predation into a scene that briefly
touches on the mystery of identity from another angle, that of two
selves becoming one in marriage. We hear echoes of Portia's memorable conversation with Brutus and, perhaps, of the Anglican
wedding service and homilies.[16]
   And Plautus too, as Adriana continues:

> For know, my love, as easy mayst thou fall
> A drop of water in the breaking gulf,
> And take unmingled thence that drop again,
> Without addition or diminishing,
> As take from me thyself and not me too.   (II. ii. 125–9)

The speech recalls significantly Antipholus of Syracuse:

> He that commends me to mine own content,
> Commends me to the thing I cannot get:
> I to the world am like a drop of water,
> That in the ocean seeks another drop,
> Who, falling there to find his fellow forth,
> (Unseen, inquisitive), confounds himself.
> So I, to find a mother and a brother,
> In quest of them (unhappy), ah, lose myself.   (I. ii. 33–40)

Both water-drop images derive ultimately from one of Plautus'
favorite similes: 'neque aqua aquae nec lacte est lactis, crede mi,
usquam similius / quam hic tui est, tuque huiius autem' (Men.
1089–90, 'No drop of water, no drop of milk, is more like another
in any way, trust me, than he is like you and, for that matter, you
like him'). Or Sosia in Amphitruo: 'Neque lact' lactis magis est

---

[16] See Baldwin, Compositional Genetics, 159–88; Hennings, 'The Anglican
Doctrine of the Affectionate Marriage'.

simile quam ille ego similest mei' (601, 'No drop of milk is more like another than that "I" is like me' (cf. *Bacc.* frag. V; *MG* 551–2; Heywood, *Works*, iii. 109)). The simile, a simple, proverbial exercise in visual comparison, might once have supplied the microsopic stylistics of parallel-passage hunting. Here, however, its real importance lies in its transformation. For Adriana the image becomes a symbol of incorporate, indivisible wedded love; for Antipholus, a symbol of longing and frustrated desire. Both metaphors suggest the universal need of people for each other and the threat of self-loss in the ocean of the world. They illuminate Egeon too, again venturing on the high seas, one who 'hazarded the loss of whom I lov'd' 'of a love to see' (I. i. 130–1). The paradoxes here and above, the complex play on losing and finding, tilt the farce of complication towards a comedy of identity and deliverance.

The significant contrast between the travelling twins also measures the difference between the two plays. Menaechmus of Syracuse says simply that he looks for his lost brother because 'ego illum scio quam cordi sit carus meo' (246, 'I know how dear he is to my heart'). In Epidamnus he decides to play along for fun and profit, 'adsentabor quidquid dicet mulieri, / si possum hospitium nancisci' (417–18, 'I'll agree to whatever the girl says, if I can get a warm welcome out of her'). 'Habeo praedam' (435, 'The spoils are mine!'), he declares later. Thus he, like the other residents, enters the game of false appearances for personal gain. Everyone's on the hustle, even the maid who tries to get gold added to her earrings, and the fun lies in watching the *ingenium* of the various players. Trissino deepened the character of the travelling twin in his adaptation of *Menaechmi*, *I simillimi* (1548), but even this traveller sought 'qualche guadagno' (sig. Biiii, 'some profit'), from the situation. In Ephesus, however, Antipholus of Syracuse wonders in asides about dreaming (II. ii. 181 ff.), about whether he is 'in earth, in heaven, or in hell? / Sleeping or waking, mad or well-advis'd?' (212–13). Designated 'Erotes' and 'Errotis' in the Folio, both terms suggestive of desire and wandering, he follows out the adventure, confused about his experience, uncertain of himself. The romantic melodies of Ovidian metamorphosis sound quietly in his confusion and more forcefully in the lyrical music of Antipholus' amorous declaration to Luciana (III. ii. 29 ff.).[17] Like Rotrou's later

[17] See Carroll, *The Metamorphoses of Shakespearean Comedy*, 63–80.

Ménechme Sosicle, thoroughly smitten by Érotie, his future wife, this traveller will fall not upon prey, but into love. And Shakespeare emphasizes the fall by extending the dinner sequence and by placing it in the centre of his play.

Adriana's entertainment of the wrong twin, of course, leaves the husband out in the cold. Arriving with Dromio, Angelo, and Balthazar (III. i.), Antipholus of Ephesus finds his doors locked against him, an ancient predicament appearing significantly in tragic, lyric, and comic refiguration.[18] In *Menaechmi* the husband comes up against his own door (668 ff.) locked against him and that of Erotium; he thinks himself 'exclusissumus' (698, 'utterly locked out'), or in Warner's translation, 'now I am everie way shut out for a very benchwhistler'.[19] In *Amphitruo*, probably the direct inspiration for Shakespeare's scene, Sosia meets Mercury who bars his entrance; later the wife innocently entertains an impostor while the husband fumes outside (cf. III. i. 1 ff. and 1009 ff.). He hammers on his door while someone who looks and sounds like his servant taunts him from within; he and another dinner guest go away disappointed. Though Shakespeare adds the Dromios, the prefatory discussion on good welcome, and the bouncing rhythm of doggerel fourteeners, he stays relatively close to the Plautine originals here, as he will not in plays like *Twelfth Night* and *Much Ado About Nothing*. Others, particularly the French, adapted the lock-out more expansively: La Taille's *Les Corrivaus* centres on the simultaneous entrance of rival lovers into the lady's locked house; Grévin's *La Trésorière* features the husband and rival lover locked out while a third within makes love to the wife, ironically named, Constante.[20]

Amphitruo also supplies Shakespeare with Alcumena, pious

[18] Euripides has Jason try to break down the door in *Medea* (1314 ff.); Greek and Latin lyrical poets arrange the lover and the locked door into the *amator exclusus* topos; Aristophanes grandly adapts the configuration to the comic stage in *Lysistrata*, where the locking out takes on sexual, social, and political dimensions. Menander uses brilliant variations of the lock-out in *Misoumenos*, which begins with the lament of an amorous soldier, Thrasonides, languishing rather than boasting, locked out of his own house; and in *Dyskolos*, where complicated lock-outs eventually lead to the climactic unlocking of Knemon's door. Plautus' *Curculio* begins with Phaedromus lyrically apostrophizing the shut door. See Copley, *Exclusus Amator*; Hunter, *New Comedy*, 63–4. The title of a play by Poseidippus, 'The Lady That's Locked Out', survives (Edmonds, iiiA, 230–1).

[19] Ed. Bullough, i. 28. The lock-out in *Amph.*, discussed below, survives only in fragments, though reconstructions were available in sixteenth-century editions. For a modern attempt, see Fantham, 'Towards a Dramatic Reconstruction'.

[20] If, as Peter Stallybrass has suggested, Renaissance patriarchy typically

matrona, a model who elevates Adriana beyond the merely dull or shrewish stereotype. The rhetoric of accusation and protest between husband and wife in *Amphitruo* inspires several confrontations in *Errors*.[21] Amphitruo hurls the name of husband in Alcumena's face (813), just as Adriana thinks Antipholus would have, had he found her unfaithful (II. ii. 134–5). Both wives protest against the perceived impudence of the servants (721–2; II. ii. 168–70); both innocently insist that they dined with their husbands at home (804 ff.; IV. iv. 65 ff.). The husbands wrongly accuse the wives of infidelity (818–19; IV. iv. 101 ff.) and seek outside adjudication. Shakespeare recollects a comic situation and several scattered touches, thus providing for character complexity and for raucous domestic fun. In their adaptations of *Amphitruo* both Molière and Dryden likewise emphasized marital discord, each providing Sosia with a wife who gets angry not because her supposed husband (Mercury) makes love to her but because he fails to.

In *Errors* Shakespeare practises an inventive *contaminatio*, or recombination of separate plays; here he also combines separate incidents from a single play. To form the Pinch episode he conflates two distinct confrontations in *Menaechmi*. First, the Wife and her father, a doddering *senex*, face the travelling twin, who decides to act mad: 'Quid mihi meliust quam, quando illi me insanire praedicant, / ego med adsimulem insanire, ut illos a me apsterream?' (831–2, 'Since they declare me insane, what is better for me to do than to pretend I actually am insane, so as to scare them off?'). Second, the father returns with a doctor who pompously examines the other twin, pronounces him insane, and summons four slaves to carry him off (899 ff.). In *Errors* wife and doctor, Pinch, along with Luciana and the Courtesan, declare Antipholus and servant insane, ordering them bound and removed.

Shakespeare's conflation reveals his transforming hand at work. Part schoolmaster, part conjurer, part doctor, Pinch combines the erroneous certainty of the Medicus with the arrogant pomposity of the Pedant, a type popular in Italian comedies. Spurred by the

controlled female eros by enclosing the body, closing the mouth, and locking the house, all these variations ironically and comedically invert the usual order; Stallybrass, 'Patriarchal Territories', in Ferguson (1986), 123–42.

[21] This observation is rarely made though Gill ('Plot-Structure', 34–7) has long since provided the evidence. See, contra, Baldwin (*Compositional Genetics*, 211): 'Certainly Adriana is in no way imitated from Alcmena.'

Courtesan's lie (IV. iii. 92 ff.), the only deliberate deceit in the play, Adriana confronts her husband. The sparks that fly from the confrontation of truth-telling spouses are brighter than those arising from the meeting of the wife and the travelling twin. Instead of an argument between two strangers, Shakespeare presents a domestic quarrel, each side corroborated. In addition, he changes the role of the servant considerably. Messenio mistakes Menaechmus of Epidamnus for his master, saves him from the Doctor and the slaves, extracts a promise of manumission for his services. Plautus thus continues the process of error and mistaken identity. Dromio of Ephesus, however, reunited with his master, undergoes Pinch's examination along with him. Together they stand united against the interrogators until the stories conflict and the front crumbles. Shakespeare marks the collapse by overturning the convention of the enforced response:

> E. ANT. Say, wherefore didst thou lock me forth to-day?
>   And why dost thou deny the bag of gold?
> ADR. I did not, gentle husband, lock thee forth.
> E. DRO. And, gentle master, I receiv'd no gold.   (IV. iv. 95–8)

The answering repetitions mockingly recall the former harmonies. Bound and led away, Antipholus and Dromio enact a visual tableau that recalls the opening scene with Egeon. The parallel lightens retrospectively the opening while darkening the present one with the hint of tragic possibilities.

Additionally, Shakespeare reshapes and revalues the false madness of the travelling Menaechmus. In Plautus this madness is merely another trick, a mask assumed in order to frighten away the questioners. Menaechmus grimaces and gapes, 'ut pandiculans oscitatur!' (833), and cries 'euhoe' (835), imitating Bacchic ravings, as Lambinus points out.[22] He threatens to burn his wife's eyes out with flaming brands, 'ut ego illic oculos exuram lampadibus ardentibus' (841), to break the limbs and bones and joints of the *senex*, 'huius membra atque ossa atque artua / comminuam' (855–6). Humorously and parodically, Menaechmus enacts here moments from well-known tragedies, including *Bacchae* and *Herakles*.[23] The

---

[22] Plautus, *Opera* (Paris, 1577), 635.
[23] On this mad scene see Leach, 'Meam Quom Formam Noscito', 38 ff.; on the use of tragic or otherwise serious elements in *Amphitruo* see Stewart, 'The Amphitruo of Plautus and Euripides' Bacchae'; Galinsky, 'Scipionic Themes in Plautus' Amphitruo'.

madness, of course, is fake, a species of literary allusion that draws
its charge from the distance between text and subtext. Adapting
precisely this strategy to different audiences, the inventive Italians,
Trissino and Firenzuola, used the idiom of demonic possession in
this scene, each changing the subtext to Dante and importing variously the names of devils from the Inferno—Draghignazzo,
Farfarello, Malacoda, and Barbariccia.[24] In Errors, as in the Italian
plays, the charge of insanity likewise modulates to that of possession; this time, however, it causes real anger, a passionate and irrational perturbation that appears as a brief madness. ('Ira est furor
brevis' ran the popular Renaissance proverb.) Antipholus turns on
his wife and, like Menaechmus, threatens her eyes: 'with these nails
I'll pluck out these false eyes / That would behold in me this
shameful sport' (IV. iv. 104–5). Menaechmus' burning brands ('lampadibus ardentibus') Antipholus uses later to revenge himself on
Pinch, 'whose beard they have sing'd off with brands of fire' (v. i.
171). Depending on the performance, Antipholus' anger may constitute simply a comic climax; threatening Adriana in a wail, the
Santa Cruz Antipholus (1988) leapt at her only to land ineffectively
and hilariously into the strong arms of the burly courtesan. But the
moment has deeper and richer potential: it suggests the dark side
of the confusions and errors, the lurking terrors of dislocation and
alienation, which Shakespeare will explore more fully in Twelfth
Night and elsewhere. Greenblatt has suggested that pre-Freudian
sensitivity to these terrors may be greater than our own; the literary and non-literary evidence (especially the interesting case of
Martin Guerre) strongly suggests that what mattered most in the
conception of identity were 'communally secured proprietary rights
to a name and a place in an increasingly mobile social world'.[25] So
it is that the play here may effectively draw upon the latent violence of Amphitruo, which Camerarius considered a tragic argument translated into a comic play, 'traduxit enim poeta Tragicum
argumentum in scenam comicam'.[26] Early Hellenic versions of the
story, Shero notes, feature the enraged husband attempting to slay

[24] Trissino, I simillimi (Venice, 1548), sig. D1v; Firenzuola, I lucidi (Venice, 1560),
sig. Di; on Elizabethan attitudes towards exorcism and possession, see Baldwin,
Compositional Genetics, 37–56; Greenblatt, 'Shakespeare and the Exorcists', in
Parker and Hartman (1985), 163–87.
[25] 'Psychoanalysis and Renaissance Culture', in Parker and Quint (1986), 210–24
(221).
[26] Comoediae XX (Basle, 1558), 111.

the innocent wife. Similarly, Amphitruo in *The Birthe of Hercules* seeks to confirm his identity through violence:

well, and if I put vp all this quietlie, yt was not I. I am not *Amphitruo*. But if I goe in, & hewe them all in peices wth my sworde for revenge, then twas I, I then am *Amphitruo*.

Thomas Heywood also expresses this darker potential in his reworking, *The Silver Age*, wherein Amphitruo beats his servants and Alcumena yearns melodramatically for death.[27]

Menaechmus' theatrical madness neatly contains tragic style in the safe boundaries of self-consciously parodic allusion. Shakespeare, however, more fully integrates tragic style, complete with its fury and passion, into the texture of the play. Of course, the touch is again light and lightening, but the distance travelled from Plautus clearly includes some frightening interior landscapes. In Plautus characters who misunderstand each other or merely disagree constantly charge insanity. Variants of 'sanus' and 'insanus', a stock rhetorical opposition, appear over forty times in *Menaechmi*, a play of 1162 lines. Here, however, Shakespeare briefly explores one version of insanity, suggesting subtly that the tenuous relations between self and self-image, between individual and communal perception, lie at the heart of comedy as well as tragedy. This suggestion, fully articulated and explored, will empower Shakespeare's later exercise in Heavy Plautus—*Hamlet*.

Plautus plays the resolution of errors, the *cognitio*, for laughs: the twins finally meet each other and Messenio unravels the mystery, thereby winning his freedom; the Menaechmi plan to auction off the citizen's goods (and wife) and return to Syracuse together. Shakespeare too emphasizes laughter, but creates a complex closing action with surprising twists and turns.[28] The *summa epitasis* occurs when Adriana stands before the Priory, now locked out herself. This second lock-out displays Shakespeare's fondness for mirror episodes that ironically reflect and illuminate each other. Adriana's lock-out initiates a re-examination of her identity and a re-evaluation of her moral self. Both occur, remarkably, through

---

[27] *The Birthe of Hercules*, ed. Bond, ll. 2314–18; Heywood, *Dramatic Works*, iii. 114.

[28] This complexity has not won universal acclaim, as witness Steevens (ed. Vickers, v. 521): 'the poet seems unwilling to part with his subject, even in this last and unnecessary scene, where the same mistakes are continued till they have lost the power of affording any entertainment at all.'

the replay of an earlier Plautine reversal. The Wife's father, we recall, turned her complaints about Menaechmus against her:

> SE: quotiens monstraui tibi uiro ut morem geras,
> quid ille faciat, ne id opserues, quo eat, quid rerum gerat.
> MA. At enim ille hinc amat meretricem ex proxumo. SE. Sane sapit,
> atque ob istanc industriam etiam faxo amabit amplius.   (788–91)

FATHER. How many times have I clearly told you to humour your husband and not to stick your nose into what he does, where he goes, and what business he engages in?
WIFE. Yes, but that man makes love to a courtesan right under my nose!
FATHER. He shows good sense, and he will make love to her more and more, I assure you, because of this diligent activity of yours.

The Senex humorously upsets expectations: he acknowledges the husband's philandering but scolds the wife for her jealousy. His sudden turn against the complaining wife inspires the Abbess' sudden turn against Adriana outside the Abbey in 'The venom clamors of a jealous woman's speech' (v. i. 69 ff.). Plautus' humorous reversal becomes in Shakespeare a moment of moral self-revelation about baseless jealousy. Unlike the Plautine husband, Antipholus never plans 'Furtum, scortum, prandium' (170, 'purloin, sirloin, her loin'), but visits the Courtesan with a friend and a gift to spite his wife for the lock-out.[29] Adriana's subsequent silence before the Abbess and admission, 'She did betray me to my own reproof' (v. i. 90), signifies realization of her folly.

This transposition of error from innocent confusion to culpable folly, from mere mistake to moral fault, well illustrates the contemporary hermeneutic abundantly evident in editions of Plautus and Terence, translations, and theatrical adaptations. In Lo errore, for example, Gelli similarly depicts a confusion of identity based on a simple misunderstanding: Mona Amieri is mistaken for Mona Tieri. Yet, the verses before Act v identify the main error of the play as the folly of Gherardo Amieri, namely that of an old, white-haired man becoming a slave of Love: 'Debbe ciascun hauer hormai veduto / Quanto sia graue errore, / Ad huom vecchio, & canuto, / farsi schiavo d'Amore.'[30] Spenser, of course, goes further in The Faerie Queene, Book i, where Error appears in the forms of

---

[29] In the notes to his translation, Segal (148) records this witty version of the Plautine triad.
[30] Gelli, 62.

the serpent-woman and labyrinthine wood, both of which imperil the soul of Redcrosse Knight. Less didactic, Shakespeare subordinates the moral episode to the main *catastrophe*, which occurs when the twins finally meet and recover their identities. He here employs the dramatic entrance to full effect and will recall this stroke in many later plays. As in classical comedy, the conclusion features an untying of knots and a clarification of confusion; the meeting of the twins resolves the plot rather than effects any moral lesson or occasions any substantial change in character. Shakespeare thus subscribes to an ancient conception of comedy, defined in the *Tractatus Coislinianus* as μίμησις πράξεως γελοίας καὶ ἀμοίρου μεγέθους ('an imitation of an action that is laughable and lacking in grandeur'). As in tragedy, plot takes precedence over character. The comedic *epitasis*, Evanthius clarified for later generations, consists of a 'nodus erroris' ('a knot of error'); the *catastrophe*, a 'conuersio rerum ad iucundos exitus patefacta cunctis cognitione gestorum' ('the turning of the situation to a happy ending through the discovery of facts made manifest to all').[31] Shakespeare surpasses the classical models here, adding to the joyful discovery of the twins that of the Abbess as wife and mother, thus providing an inclusive family structure that unites the other reconciliations.

Emilia, who presides over and participates in the *catastrophe*, herself embodies multiple traditions: she is the Roman *matrona* who scolds transgressors, dispenses justice, and ends the conflict (cf. Artemona in *Asinaria*, Nausistrata in *Phormio*); the lost wife of romance, the Lucina who survives the sea and lives a holy life in a temple; the *maga*, a person of 'dignified authority, in touch with forces and agencies apparently beyond the human'. Shakespeare infuses her language, Riemer observes, with the vocabulary of Neoplatonic medicinal magic.[32] The grand finale in public and the resolution that finally restores the time, previously perceived as bankrupt and thieving, differs from the private *cognitio* between three characters in Plautus.

The action here occurs at the Priory, perhaps opposing or

---

[31] *Tractatus*, ed. Janko, 24; Evanthius, *De Fabula*, in Donatus, *Commentum Terenti*, ed. Wessner, i. 22.

[32] Reimer, *Antic Fables*, 113 ff. Leggatt (*Shakespeare's Comedy of Love*, 16) notes that the Abbess' invitation to celebrate new birth looks ahead to the endings of Shakespeare's romances, especially *Pericles* and *Cymbeline*.

replacing the Courtesan's house on stage. Flexibly adapting the
binary capabilities of New Comedy, Shakespeare contrasts suggestively these localities.[33] Quietly substituting the Abbey for the
Ephesian temple suggested by Acts and the Apollonius story,
Shakespeare strikes general resonances with the religious tone of
the opening. These resonances effect a closer imitation of the spirit
and purpose of another source, *Confessio Amantis*, where the story
of Apollinius' reunion with his wife illustrates the rewards of a
love that is generous, patient, chaste, and self-sacrificing.[34] The vis-
itors to Ephesus, both father and son, and the long-lost wife, lose
themselves only to find and be found, all within the borders of a
benignly ordered world. The final untying of Egeon's bonds completes the process of untying that began with Antipholus and
Dromio's violent breaking of their bonds; their liberation from the
dark, dankish vault (v. i. 248), effects the liberation of their counterparts from the Priory and from their bewilderment, and culminates in the liberation of Egeon himself. Here freedom means not
independence but an acceptance of bonds, a reintegration into
extant social institutions and structures, marriage and the family,
specifically. This reintegration begins with self-understanding, with
the elementary distinction between self and not-self which becomes
peculiarly urgent and confusing in the case of identical twins.

Shakespeare's first encounter with New Comedy looks back-
wards and forwards. The method is competitive imitation of classical models, transformed by romance, Italian, Christian, and native
traditions. Shakespeare's creative *imitatio*, his aggressive appropriation of classical comedy to new ends, is entirely consonant with
European practice. Playwrights early and late transformed the
errors configurations of these classical comedies, variously exploring and redefining the phenomenon of the *Doppelgänger*. An early
adaptation of *Amphitruo*, *Geta* by Vitalis of Blois (twelfth century), turns the play into a satire on scholastic logic and philoso-
phy; confronted by his double, the helpless servant employs useless
and humorous syllogisms. The printed version of *Jack Juggler* ends
with some moralizing about the deluding of innocents by the

---

[33] On the possible staging see Foakes, Arden edn. (1962), xxxv ff.; Dorsch, New
Cambridge edn. (1988), 20 ff; Kinney, 43–4. A temple or altar, of course, sometimes
figures importantly as a locality in New Comedy. In *Abraham* and *Pafnutius*,
Hrosvit deploys the same locational contrasts more explicitly and didactically.

[34] See Gower, *Confessio Amantis*, ed. Peck, xxii ff.

deceitful and the powerful. Heywood depicts Alcumena as a moral paradox, 'honest in her worst dishonesty and chast in the super-latiue degree of inchastity'. Changing the mythological travesty, *Amphitruo*, into a domestic comedy, *Il marito*, Lodovico Dolce drops entirely the supernatural, claiming that the play demonstrates the sovereign power of love ('Amor fa perdere / Souente il senno e l'intelletto a gli huomini') and the importance of forgiveness.[35]

Like his predecessors and contemporaries, Shakespeare engages some larger issues in his first errors play, exploring here the themes of identity, jealousy, love, and family relationships. But the emphasis is on laughter, the darker potentialities being left for other days and other plays—*Twelfth Night*, for example, or Goldoni's more radical reworking of *Menaechmi*, *I due gemelli veneziani*, which features the murder of one twin before the recognition. Confronting his 'speculum' (*Amph.* 442), Plautus' Sosia may fear loss of self, but Shakespeare's Dromios rejoice in the coincidence; purposefully echoing *Men.* 1062, Dromio of Ephesus blithely dismisses the sinister possibilities of the double: 'Methinks you are my glass, and not my brother: / I see by you I am a sweet-fac'd youth' (v. i. 418–19).[36] When the Duke forgives the penalty and refuses the ransom, the process of reintegration stretches outwards to include the city. 'Twinship', Gail Kern Paster observes, becomes 'an intensified image of the new communal norm—a civic fraternity in which even Syracusans belong'.[37] Thus good, indeed providential, hap and good will conjoin to achieve the frequently wished-for deliverance and to create the echoing concord of the reconciled self, the reunited family, and the recreated city—all cele-

---

[35] Vitalis, ed. Crawford, 181–209; *Jack Juggler*, 37–40; Heywood, *Dramatic Works*, iii. 102; Dolce, *Il marito*, 24v. Baldwin (*Five-Act*, 669–70) notes an interesting non-dramatic adaptation: in his attack on transubstantiation Cranmer adduces *Amphitruo* and perhaps *Jack Juggler* as illustrations of the power of illusion on our senses; see also Axton (ed.), *Three Tudor Classical Interludes*, 19–20.

[36] On this incident Ruth Nevo (34) writes: 'The whole little episode is a deliciously comic forerunner of a Lacanian *stade du miroir*. But it is also a parody of self-discovery. And it punctures the whole grand remedial idea of regenerated, enlightened, separate, complete and viable personalities with the impermeable lunatic logic of its narcissism. Punctures, and yet reaffirms, since the contentment of Dromio with his inability to acquire a separate self at all is, our laughter tells us, the most reassuring antidote to insanity Ephesus could possibly supply.' On the phenomenon of doubling in comedy see also Levin, *Playboys and Killjoys*, 72–83.

[37] *The Idea of the City*, 194.

brated in the concluding gossips' feast. Safely contained or margin-
alized are the threats of alienation, eros, jealousy, madness, and
murder. Plautine comedy begins and ends as a comedy of doors—
doors opening and closing, doors blocking, dividing, concealing,
doors locking in and locking out. Shakespearean comedy, as will
be increasingly evident, is a comedy of thresholds, of entranceways
into new understandings and acceptances.

Twelfth Night

Twelfth Night, many have observed, is a most recapitulatory play,
gathering up and transforming much of what has gone before. One
finds here the contours of prose romance, the rhythms of
Petrarchan rhetoric (critically examined), the intrigues of Italian
comedy, the magic of Ovidian metamorphosis. The play also
recalls Shakespeare's earlier comedies, especially *The Comedy of
Errors*.[38] As John Manningham, the play's first critic, observed in
his notebook entry for February 1601 (i.e. 1602):

at our feast 2/. wee had a play called [mid *crossed out*] Twelue night or
what you will / . / / much like the commedy of errors / or Menechmi in
plaut*us* / but most like and neere to that in Italian called Inganni.[39]

Noting that *Twelfth Night* recalls the mistaken identities of *Errors*,
Manningham identifies the deep source, Plautus' *Menaechmi*.[40]
Moreover, Manningham astutely perceives the relationship between
Twelfth Night and cinquecento theatre, probably *Gl'ingannati* (1531)
rather than Secchi's *Gl'inganni* (1547).[41] He might just as well have
mentioned Bibbiena's *La calandria*, a capacious and seminal play
that resembles *Twelfth Night* in its innovative and sophisticated use

---

[38] See the Arden edn. of Lothian and Craik (1975), xlvii–l; Muir, *Sources*, 132;
Donno, New Cambridge edn. (1985), 7–8.

[39] Lothian and Craik (eds.), xxvi. Gerard Langbaine (*An Account of the English
Dramatick Poets*, 466) also observed that the confusion of Sebastian's and Viola's
identities 'was doubtless first borrowed (not only by *Shakespeare*, but all our succeeding Poets) from *Plautus*, who has made use of it in several Plays, as *Amphitruo*,
Maenechmi, &c'.

[40] Baldwin (*Five-Act*, 715–18) also identifies the structure as New Comedic, discerning in *Twelfth Night* the *Andria* formula for five acts - *protasis*, *epitasis*, and
catastrophe.

[41] Kaufman ('Nicolò Secchi as a Source of *Twelfth Night*') adduces some specific
parallels with two Italian comedies, *Gl'inganni* and *L'interesse*.

of convention, featuring specifically the cross-dressing of a female twin. As will be clearer later, *Twelfth Night* also recapitulates all of Shakespeare's previous encounters with New Comedy: the amatory intrigues in *Shrew*, *Merchant*, and *Ado*; the duping of the *miles gloriosus* in *Wives* and *All's Well*. It anticipates also both the problems and resolutions of those later Plautine romances, *Pericles* and *The Tempest*.

The revision of *The Comedy of Errors* in *Twelfth Night* shows Shakespeare reshaping Plautine materials, maturing in his comic vision. Plautus is a much lesser verbal influence on the later play. Salingar observes that Sebastian's mention of 'Messaline' (II. i. 18) owes to the corresponding scene in *Menaechmi* where there is notice of 'Massiliensis, Hilurios', or '*Massylia, Ilyria*' (tr. Warner).[42] There may also be vestiges of Plautine wit in various Latinisms, the comic formations of Quinapalus (I. v. 35), 'Pigrogromitus, of the Vapians passing the Equinoctial of Queubus' (II. iii. 23–4); and, perhaps, in Viola's self-conscious adaptation of an artificial rhetorical style and her quick switch out of it (I. v. 170 ff.). But if these be reminiscences they are slight and remote; the real influence, as Manningham divined, resides in the use of setting, convention, character, and μῦθος, or plot, τὴν σύνθεσιν τῶν πραγμάτων (*Poet.* 1450a4–5, the arrangement of incidents). Shakespeare resonantly refigures New Comedic localities, and provides two subordinate New Comedic actions—the duping of Malvolio and the mock-duel. He recasts Viola as a Plautine schemer without a scheme and superimposes the errors plot on Italianate intrigue.

The locale of the play is Illyria, a new version of the coastal city common in Italian drama.[43] *Twelfth Night* features the basic two-house setting of New Comedy. Lois Potter observes: 'If the play was written for a stage with two doors at the back' (as at the Middle Temple and probably the Globe) 'the entrances and exits would have been particularly noticeable. . . . *Twelfth Night* is unusual in the amount of attention that is paid to the business of getting in and out of these doors.'[44] The two-door arrangement does not, as before, suggest clear contrasts—the *industria/voluptas*

---

[42] Salingar, *Traditions*, 240–1; Warner, ed. Bullough, i. 17.

[43] Clubb, *Italian Drama*, 11–12.

[44] '*Twelfth Night*': *Text and Performance*, 25. On the symbolic use of doors in Greek New Comedy see Wiles, *Masks*, 43 ff.

conflict embodied in the houses of Menaechmus and Erotium, and those of Antipholus and the Courtesan; instead, Shakespeare chooses to stress ironic similarities: Olivia's house and Orsino's present variations of the same closed and enclosing abode. In *Errors* and its Plautine sources, especially *Amphitruo*, the focus is on exclusion, on locking out; here the focus is on occlusion, on the processes of obstruction, on locking in. In Illyria physical barriers largely betoken spiritual ones. Orsino languishes at home in dreamy melancholy. Curio's curative suggestion, 'Will you go hunt, my lord?' (I. i. 16), draws only the effete punning on 'hart':

> Why, so I do, the noblest that I have.
> O, when mine eyes did see Olivia first,
> Methought she purg'd the air of pestilence!
> That instant was I turn'd into a hart,
> And my desires, like fell and cruel hounds,
> E'er since pursue me.   (17–22)

Orsino intentionally misreads the healthful suggestion to get out and do something, exercising only his wit in literary introspection and self-pity. His revision of the Actaeon myth here reveals the predatory, self-destructive elements in all desire, the paradoxical insistence on both giving and taking. Orsino ends the scene imagining his 'love-thoughts' in beds of flowers, 'canopied with bow'rs' (40), thus supplying another image of his own indolence and self-enclosure. Luxuriating in his own thoughts and feelings, Orsino reveals the unhealthy egoism of obsession, the painful pleasure of locking oneself up in thwarted desire and self-dramatization. 'Having loved the image of Olivia for a month before the play opens', Donno observes, 'he continues to protest his love for three more months even before he has a chance to speak to her directly'.[45] Twice, ironically, Orsino refers to the sea, both times as metaphors for his all-devouring love (I. i. 9 ff.; II. iv. 100 f.). No mere figure for melodramatic rhetoric, the real sea in this play will bring resolution and deliverance in the persons of the shipwrecked Viola and Sebastian.[46]

Like Orsino, Olivia locks herself up at home. Valentine fails to

[45] New Cambridge edn., 9.
[46] See Lawry, '*Twelfth Night* and "Salt Waves Fresh in Love".' Zoë Wanamaker (Jackson and Smallwood (eds.), *Players*, 85) recalls the setting of the 1983–4 production, including the 'sound of the sea which was ever present, the giver and taker of life, dark and threatening yet at the same time mysterious and romantic'.

gain admittance (I. i. 22 ff.), and Orsino later dispatches his page: 'Be not denied access, stand at her doors' (I. iv. 16). Viola's subsequent confrontation with the locked door and with Olivia's rebuff presents the familiar Plautine configuration from the inside out. The audience's journey to the other side of the closed door, from outside the closed fora of Menaechmus and Antipholus into Olivia's household, behind her shut and guarded gates, suggests the change from slapstick situational farce to more complex comedy. Malvolio reports on the locked-out messenger and Olivia finally relents, donning a veil in grief for her departed brother. She would live as a picture of sorrow, frozen into the static posture of mourning, veiled like Mistress Mall. Her resolution to be a cloistress for seven years lasts only for a few moments; pretending to describe a portrait, she takes off the veil: 'but we will draw the curtain and show you the picture. Look you, sir, such a one I was this present. [*Unveiling.*] Is't not well done?' (I. v. 236–8). Here Olivia's actions belie her words; even as she pretends to be a lifeless portrait, she expresses her vanity and need for praise and conversation.

The conventional setting of Roman comedy thus suggests in *Twelfth Night* interior states of characters. Orsino and Olivia are locked-in, entrapped in self-absorbed vanities, confused about their desires and the nature of love. Those characters who travel freely between the houses accurately diagnose the problems and variously recommend treatment. Feste sings the *carpe diem* song, 'O mistress mine' (II. iii. 39 ff.), and then in response to Orsino's request for the song that 'dallies with the innocence of love' (II. iv. 47), the mournful 'Come away, come away death'. Here the images of death—the shroud, the black coffin without 'a flower sweet' (recalling Orsino's bower), the hidden grave—all mock Orsino's obsession and suggest its essential morbidity. Feste directly contradicts Orsino's pretension to constancy, 'Now the melancholy god protect thee, and the tailor make thy doublet of changeable taffata, for thy mind is a very opal' (II. iv. 73–5). He catechizes Olivia, and proves that she is a fool for mourning her brother (I. v. 58 ff.). Viola's invented tale about her sister suggests the dangers of unrequited and enclosed love, of the 'green and yellow melancholy' (II. iv. 113 ff.). And Orsino's ardent hyperbole about men's love, spoken to a woman he cannot see about a woman who won't see him, sounds childish and silly. Viola bluntly tells Olivia off, 'I see you what you are, you are too proud' (I. v. 250), a reproof originally aimed at the Viola character of *Gl'ingannati*, 'tu sei troppo superbo' (723), which Shakespeare pointedly redirects. The way to freedom and love for Orsino and Olivia must lead them beyond their private selves, beyond their constricting gates and doors to the unlocalized public places of Illyria where there can be true reciprocity and exchange, real giving and receiving.

Shakespeare further complicates the design of *Twelfth Night* by adding New Comedic actions.[47] The duping of Malvolio originates in the conflict between him and Sir Toby, an English version of the classical *parasitus*, a great gorger of food and drink at others' expense.[48] In Plautus and Terence the parasite serves various functions in the plot: sometimes he is an intriguer who resembles the clever slave, like Curculio and Phormio; at other times he is the butt humorously excluded from the feast, like Peniculus (*Men.*) and Gelasimus (*Stichus*). Shakespeare combines both functions in his parasite, Sir Toby, who merrily plots against Malvolio and Sir Andrew, but who misses the final party with a bloody coxcomb. In Sir Toby's plot against Malvolio, Shakespeare locates the New Comedic intrigue he will pointedly refuse to provide in the main action, playing again the Plautine opposition between *industria* and *voluptas*. Plautus' *Bacchides* features a character like Malvolio, Lydus the tutor, who scolds Pistoclerus for 'tua flagitia aut damna aut desidiabula' (376, 'your outrages, losses, idle resorts'). And *Mostellaria*, which Shakespeare probably used for *Shrew*, opens with the cranky, anti-festive Grumio berating Tranio for his carousing, for indulging in squabs, fish, game, wine, and girls, the Roman equivalent to Sir Toby's cakes and ale. Writing on Plautine comedy Segal explores the opposition in detail and discusses Malvolio as the Plautine agelast, the laughless blocking figure who gets a deserved comeuppance.[49]

---

[47] Pyle (' "Twelfth Night", "King Lear", and "Arcadia" ') argues persuasively that the Dametas episode in *Arcadia* inspires both the gulling of Malvolio and the mock-duel. As usual, native influences join classical and neo-classical ones; Hotson (*The First Night of 'Twelfth Night'*, 159 ff.) adduces the Christmas revels, comparing Maria to the Lord of Misrule, the sword dance or sham combat to the duel, the mumming to the Sir Topas scene.

[48] On the parasite see Duckworth, 265–7; Vandiver, 'The Elizabethan Dramatic Parasite'.

[49] Segal, *Roman Laughter*, 70–92. Simmons ('A Source for Shakespeare's Malvolio') well argues that this agelast embodies characteristics associated with Puritans.

On Malvolio's role in the play John Manningham again provides insight:

a good practise in it to make the steward beleeue his Lady widdowe was in Loue wth him by counterfayting a lettr / as from his Lady in generall tearmes / telling him what shee liked best in him / and prescribing his gesture in smiling his apparraile / &c /. And then when he came to practise making him beleeue they tooke him to be mad.

Manningham's obvious pleasure in recalling the 'practise' against Malvolio echoes throughout the centuries. Charles I wrote Malvolio next to the title of the play in his copy of the 1632 Folio. In 1640 Leonard Digges also testified to the stage popularity of Malvolio, 'that crosse garter'd Gull'. Nicholas Rowe (1709): 'there is something singularly Ridiculous and Pleasant in the fanatical Steward *Malvolio*'; Samuel Johnson (1765): 'The soliloquy of *Malvolio* is truly comick; he is betrayed to ridicule merely by his pride'; George Steevens (1772): 'first let us pay our Respects to that most consummate Coxcomb, that ridiculous Composition of stiff Impertinence and uncommon Conceit—*Malvolio*'; Francis Gentleman (1774): '*Malvolio*'s ridiculous self-sufficiency is displayed in a most masterly manner.'[50] This chorus subscribes to Aristotle's conception of the comic as the ridiculous, that which we laugh at.[51]

Ἡ δὲ κωμῳδία ἐστὶν ὥσπερ εἴπομεν μίμησις φαυλοτέρων μέν, οὐ μέντοι κατὰ πᾶσαν κακίαν, ἀλλὰ τοῦ αἰσχροῦ ἐστι τὸ γελοῖον μόριον. τὸ γὰρ γελοῖόν ἐστιν ἁμάρτημά τι καὶ αἶσχος ἀνώδυνον καὶ οὐ φθαρτικόν, οἷον εὐθὺς τὸ γελοῖον πρόσωπον αἰσχρόν τι καὶ διεστραμμένον ἄνευ ὀδύνης.   (1449a32–7)

Comedy, as we said, is an imitation of people common and low, though not, indeed, thoroughly bad. What is laughable, however, always derives in part from what is ugly. The laughable consists in some fault, error, or deformity that is not painful and not destructive. Clearly laughable, for example, is the comic mask—ugly and distorted, but not painful.

[50] For Manningham, see Lothian and Craik (eds.), xxvi; for Charles I, lxxix–lxxxn; for Digges, see Vickers (ed.), i. 28; Rowe (ii. 195); Johnson (v. 109); Steevens (v. 446); Gentleman (vi. 100). Levin (*Playboys and Killjoys*, 36–7) discusses Malvolio as the scapegoat whom comedy always seeks to expel.

[51] Heath ('Aristotelian Comedy', 352–3) well explains that Aristotle does not mean here to exclude the painful or destructive from comedy, but to distinguish comedy from tragedy. Cf. Sir Philip Sidney (ed. Smith, *Elizabethan Critical Essays*, i. 176–7): 'Comedy is an imitation of the common errors of our life, which he representeth in the most ridiculous and scornefull sort that may be; so as it is impossible that any beholder can be content to be such a one.'

This is a harsher conception of comedy than many now prefer, but one central to both Old and New Comedy, to Aristophanes as well as to Menander, especially to his *Dyskolos*, the earliest surviving New Comedy. Renaissance commentators on Aristotle like Castelvetro divided τὸ αἰσχρόν into uglinesses of the body and soul. In the latter category Trissino singled out 'la ignoranza, la imprudenzia, e la credulità . . . le quali spesse volte dipendeno l'una dall'altra' ('ignorance, imprudence, and gullibility, which often depend one upon the other'). Invoking Plato, Bonciani identified 'l'ignoranza' as the root of all comedy.[52] In this context one can fully appreciate Feste's comment: 'I say there is no darkness but ignorance, in which thou art more puzzled than the Egyptians in their fog' (IV. ii. 42–4). Malvolio's ignorance manifests itself in self-love and in that prideful, anti-festive δυσκολία that the play exposes and ridicules.[53] Olivia comments incisively: 'O, you are sick of self-love, Malvolio, and taste with a distemper'd appetite' (I. v. 90–1).

The exposure of Malvolio is New Comedic in its general outline if not in its specific details. Often the agelast is put on display while schemers spy and make sardonic remarks, as in the box-tree scene (cf. *Pseud.* 133 ff.). Sometimes the schemer, like Sir Toby, is a parasite; most often, however, a *callidus servus* plans and executes the intrigue. Maria, the *architectus doli* of *Twelfth Night* descends from a long line of witty Plautine servants, not from any hint in Riche or the versions of *Gl'ingannati*. Like Palaestrio (or Tranio, Chrysalus, Pseudolus, Epidicus, and others, for that matter), Maria calls her wits to council ('*consilia in animum*', *MG* 197), and hatches a plot (II. iii. 131 ff.). Like her Roman counterparts she is cheeky and utterly confident in her abilities:

For Monsieur Malvolio, let me alone with him. If I do not gull him into an ayword, and make him a common recreation, do not think I have wit enough to lie straight in my bed. I know I can do it.   (II. iii. 133–7)

Compare Pseudolus assuring his young master of his skill and his expression of ebullient confidence:

[52] Castelvetro, *Poetica*, fol. 50v. ff.; for Trissino, see Weinberg (ed.), *Trattati*, ii. 71; Bonciani (iii. 154).
[53] Δύσκολο̄ means 'peevish, grouchy, hard to satisfy with food'. In II. iii Malvolio breaks up the party and reviles the parasite. With sure instinct Sinden's Malvolio (1969–71) cleared the glasses and the drinks; Copley's (1979) took away the large frosted cake that Sir Andrew had been holding lovingly (Potter, 66).

(maiorum meum fretus uirtute dicam, mea industria et malitia fraudu-
lenta),
facile ut uincam, facile ut spoliem meos perduellis meis perfidiis.
(582–3)
I—relying on the excellences of my ancestors, so to speak, as well as on
my own industry and talent for tricky wickedness—easily shall conquer
and easily shall despoil my nemesis by my knavery.

Like a Plautine deceiver, Maria plays on the weaknesses and vices
of the victim, employing considerable dramatic and rhetorical
skills. Sir Toby and Sir Andrew look on in amazed admiration:

SIR TO. Wilt thou set thy foot o' my neck?
SIR AND. Or o' mine either?
SIR TO. Shall I play my freedom at tray-trip, and become thy bond-slave?
SIR AND. I'faith, or I either?   (II. v. 188–92)

Here they use the idiom of military conquest that characterizes
Roman intrigues; in a mythological fancy Chrysalus goes so far as
to compare himself to the conquerors of Troy (*Bacc.* 925 ff.).[54]
And here the gentry offer to change positions with the servant, to
extend to her the reward that slaves in New Comedy typically
seek—freedom. The promise is fulfilled, we hear, at the end as
Maria's unlooked-for elevation (if this be the word) to Lady Belch
precisely parodies Malvolio's wilful aspirations.

The generally Plautine shape of the plot acquires specific
definition in the mad scene. Sir Toby's and Sir Topas' ministrations recall Pinch's treatment of Antipholus of Ephesus who, like
Malvolio, suffers accusations of madness and then imprisonment in
a 'dark and dankish vault' (v. i. 248). Shakespeare transfers
Menaechmus' original deceit from the accused to the accusers, to
the revellers who pretend that Malvolio is mad to punish him for
his pride and arrogance; he also transfers Antipholus of Ephesus'
anger to Malvolio; the charge of demonic possession again colours
the scene.

Moreover, the scene with Sir Topas the Curate inverts the
Plautine lock-outs of *Menaechmi* and *Amphitruo* and presents a
lock-in. Malvolio's physical incarceration suggests the spiritual
incarcerations of Orsino and Olivia, their closed worlds now given
concrete stage representation in Malvolio's cell. Their desires—

---

[54] According to Fraenkel (223 ff.) such imagery is a Plautine innovation.

egoistical, self-aggrandizing, ridiculous—find crude but revealing expression in his yearning to be Count Malvolio. Eros again serves the politics of self-love, and this is indeed a kind of madness, one that cries out for comic exorcism. Feste, the self-confessed fool, appropriately administers the treatment to the superior wise man, switching his own identity to Sir Topas and back. Feste's quicksilver changes, his ability to create and destroy illusion, contrast with Malvolio's idiotic performance previously, his laborious and unsuccessful metamorphosis into a smiling lover. Feste, even more so than Viola, has the ability to act, to lose one self (but not one's self) and become another; Malvolio remains rigidly himself, even in cross garters and yellow stockings, a costume assumed for self-advancement not self-transformation. No wonder Feste quizzes him on the Pythagorean doctrine of metempsychosis, on the transmigration of souls into different bodies, probably familiar to Shakespeare from the master of metamorphoses, Ovid. And no wonder Malvolio stoutly denies the doctrine only to hear Sir Topas's affirmation in wise foolery, 'Thou shalt hold th' opinion of Pythagoras ere I will allow of thy wits' (IV. ii. 58–9). The fool, as Feste earlier prophesized, looks to the madman.

Unlike original audiences, if Manningham is indicative, some have followed Charles Lamb's powerful misreading of Bensley's performance and judged Malvolio's treatment to be excessively harsh.[55] Of course, a given production can easily illustrate these ideas and augment Malvolio's pathos. Such an interpretation, however, distorts the scene and exaggerates Malvolio's claims on our sympathy. Fabian's observation, 'If this were play'd upon a stage now, I could condemn it as an improbable fiction' (III. iv. 127–8), like similar remarks by characters in Roman comedy (MG 213, Bacc. 214; Rud. 1249 ff.; cf. Gl'ingannati, 1386–8), emphasizes the artificiality of the action and insures the appropriate comic perspective. Long ago Scaliger observed that comedies sometimes have unhappy endings for certain characters, 'infelices . . . fines . . . sic Miles Plauti, & Asinaria, & Persa, & aliae'. Speaking of Miles Gloriosus, Nicolò Rossi responded by justly distinguishing between a subordinate, ridiculous plot line and the main romance action:

---

[55] Barnet, 'Charles Lamb and the Tragic Malvolio'; Berry, 'Twelfth Night: The Experience of the Audience'. On staging see the interesting study by Astington, 'Malvolio and the Dark House'.

nondimeno, io sento che il soldato s'introduca per azione ridicolosa in essa comedia e non sia altra persona principale che Pleuside giovane e Filocomasia meretrice inamorata di esso Plauside, la cui tramutazione è fatta dall'aversa alla miglior fortuna.[56]

Nevertheless, I think that the soldier is introduced to create a ridiculous action in this comedy and that there is no principal person other than young Pleusicles and Philocomasium, the courtesan in love with this Pleusicles, whose change is made from adverse fortune to better.

Shakespeare observes precisely this balance between actions, as does Chapman in *Monsieur D'Olive*: there the main romance action accompanies a direct imitation of the plot against Malvolio, and the butt, Monsieur D'Olive, ends up in angry embarrassment. These are the revenges of comedy that the whirligig of time brings in.[57]

Modern misgivings with such revenge and the laughter of ridicule derive from a mistaken focus on character as individual personality instead of as functionary in plot. On the level of plot a playwright has two basic options for an agelast—inclusion or exclusion. (With characteristic, one might say Menandrian, inventiveness Shakespeare tries to use both with Shylock.) To effect the former, one can present last-minute conversions, like that of Euclio in *Aulularia*, of Truculentus in the play of that name, and of Oliver in *As You Like It*; these are sometimes satirical ploys, more often patently artificial concessions to the common wish for a final party that includes everyone. But what party ever does? Even that wisp of a play, Plautus' *Stichus*, gathers enough energy to exclude Gelasimus from the revel that constitutes most of its action. In *Twelfth Night* Shakespeare likewise exercises the second option, that of exclusion, but with a difference. Malvolio excludes himself from the final resolution and the other characters intend to 'entreat him to a peace' (v. i. 380). Malvolio's proud allegiance to his

---

[56] Scaliger, *Poetices*, 145; Rossi, ed. Weinberg, *Trattati*, iv. 33.

[57] Malvolio's fall, despite the handwringing, is not all that brutal, especially by the standards of classical comedy: at the end of *Dyskolos* a slave and cook manhandle Knemon, now crippled, and drag him to a noisy party, all in lively iambic tetrameter catalectic accompanied by music; in *Persa* Dordalus is done out of money and publically beaten, as is Pyrgopolynices in *Miles Gloriosus*. Malvolio is not even bound, as were Antipholus and Dromio; and he does not end up truly mad as does Sir Giles Overreach of Massinger's *A New Way to Pay Old Debts*. Moreover, watching the mad in Bedlam was a popular English amusement up through the eighteenth century; whippings and chainings were common along with the milder treatment of the dark room (cf. *AYL* III. ii. 400–2).

superior self contrasts with the humility and flexibility of the other principals—Orsino, Olivia, and Viola—who undergo ordeals and humiliations, who learn to let go of their fixated selves, to laugh and to trust in time and in each other. He leaves the play—arch, angry, δύσκολος—storming out of the final scene. His exit line, 'I'll be reveng'd on the whole pack of you' (378) is funny (the whole pack isn't responsible), though actors like Irving, Sothern (who tore up the forged letter), and Sinden (who thought the exit a prelude to suicide), played it for pathos.[58] On the contrary, the final tableau suggests that Malvolio's isolation is a self-imposed fit of pique: 'We do not know precisely where Malvolio is going when he walks offstage, but by the time the other characters go out, the door has become the door of Olivia's house—once so hard to enter—into which they are all invited.'

The other New Comedic intrigue in *Twelfth Night* is the mock-duel between Sir Andrew and Viola. The mock-duel, an Italian innovation which appears also in Jonson's *Epicoene* IV. v, springs from the New Comedic tendency to heap up confusions and counterplots.[59] It also provides a further variation on the folly of believing too much in one's mask, and another opportunity for exposure. Sir Toby and Fabian engineer the plot against Sir Andrew who is, besides a gull and a fop, a version of the New Comedic *miles gloriosus*. Maria clearly identifies Sir Andrew as a boasting soldier:

he's a great quarreller; and but that he hath the gift of a coward to allay the gust he hath in quarrelling, 'tis thought among the prudent he would quickly have the fit of a grave.   (I. iii. 30–3)

Sir Andrew brags that he could beat Malvolio 'like a dog' (II. iii. 141–2) and quickly agrees to awake his dormouse valour against Viola. The hatching of Fabian and Sir Toby's plot results in several moments of exposure and discomfiture: first, after the Thrasonical challenge, Sir Andrew tries to buy his way out of the duel, offering his horse, 'grey Capilet' (III. iv. 286–7); then there is the reluctant drawing of swords and the intervention of Antonio; Sir Andrew plucks up his nerve again only to face Sebastian and a beating, for which he threatens an 'action of battery' (IV. i. 34); in the fifth act he runs on to the stage crying for help and a surgeon. The action

[58] On these interpretations see Donno, 29 ff.; Potter, 40–2; Brockbank (ed.), *Players*, 66; the quotation below belongs to Potter, 33.

[59] Specifically, it may derive from *Truculentus*, according to Boughner, *Braggart*, 16–17; for other examples see Orr, 43.

reveals the truth about the *alazon*, ridiculous in his weakness and cowardice. The particular device employed here—the pretended threat which results in farcical humiliation—recalls similar episodes, the Gadshill adventure in *1 Henry IV*, the duping of Parolles in *All's Well*, the embarrassments of Captain Tinca in Aretino's *Talanta*, as well as those of Sheridan's hilarious variation, 'Fighting Bob' Acres in *The Rivals*.

In its conception and general shape such exposure is eminently classical as well as Shakespearean; yet *Twelfth Night* features interesting variations on the mock-duel. The ruse discomfits Viola, momentarily caught in her own wiles, helpless in the situation. The trick backfires on the tricksters, Sir Toby and Sir Andrew, who mistake Sebastian for Viola and get beaten off-stage. In this beating, Shakespeare suggests the excesses of the Carnival ethic, the immoderate and single-minded pursuit of pleasure, just as he had exposed those of Malvolio's Lenten one. In his own way Sir Toby the parasite is just as limited a character as is the killjoy or the gull, incapable of moderation, reflection, change, or surprise. This rigidity of self and self-image the play consistently seeks to break down, both in subordinate characters like Malvolio, Sir Andrew, and Sir Toby, as well as in the main ones, Orsino and Olivia. Opposed to this rigidity, this locking-in of identity, is the extroverted flexibility of Fabian, who remains reasonable but participates in the jests; of Maria, who scolds the revellers for 'caterwauling' before joining them against Malvolio; of Feste, who moves freely throughout Illyria, and, Viola notes, adapts his wit to the particular situation, 'The quality of persons, and the time' (III. i. 63). Of course, most important is Viola, witty enough to wear a mask but wise enough to remain distinct from it. Unlike many others, Viola self-consciously plays a comic role, one she will step out of in due time. She is always Cesario and herself.

But who is Viola/Cesario? The major figures of *Twelfth Night* first see Viola as a character from New Comedy, and all change their minds in the course of the play. Viola herself initially decides to take on the role of a 'eunuch' (I. ii. 56). Thus she plans a strategy similar to that of Chaerea, who disguises himself as a eunuch to gain entrance to a house in *Eunuchus*, one of Shakespeare's favourite Terentian plays, according to T. W. Baldwin.[60] Viola

[60] *Five-Act*, 544–76.

abandons this plan and enters Orsino's service as a page; to him she is the charming *puer*, in whom 'all is semblative a woman's part' (I. iv. 34). To Olivia, Viola is the *adulescens* Cesario, the youth whose perfections creep in at her eyes (I. v. 296 ff.). Neither eunuch, nor *puer*, nor *adulescens*, Viola will finally assume her true identity as *virgo*, a virtuous maiden, though one much more dynamic and interesting than any of her ancient counterparts. The general absence of those *virgines* from their plays, we recall, exasperated Dryden's Eugenius:

As for the poor honest Maid, on whom the Story is built, and who ought to be one of the Principal Actors in the play, she is commonly a Mute in it: She has the breeding of the Old *Elizabeth* way, which was for Maids to be seen and not to be heard; and it is enough you know she is willing to be married, when the Fifth Act requires it.[61]

Eugenius exaggerates (what of Saturio's daughter in *Persa*?) but rightly notices the general tendency in New Comedic characterization. This tendency Viola, in the good company of Lelia, Secchi's Ginevra and Lelio, Bibbiena's Santilla, Della Porta's Cintia, and other cinquecento heroines, defiantly reverses.

The Orsino-Viola-Olivia triangle composes a typical New Comedic configuration, present, for example, in *Casina* and *Pseudolus*: the unrequited lover employs a *servus* in order to win the lady. As usual, the *servus* uses his tongue, wits, and acting ability for the helpless master, sometimes working as an envoy to the lady, always inventing and executing schemes.[62] In return the master promises a reward, usually emancipation. So too, Orsino, right on cue:

> Prosper well in this,
> And thou shalt live as freely as thy lord,
> To call his fortunes thine.   (I. iv. 38–40)

Playing *servus*, Viola traverses that twilight space in New Comedy where reported fiction often expresses hidden truth.

---

[61] *An Essay of Dramatick Poesie*, 19. On the heroines below see Melzi, 'From Lelia to Viola'.

[62] Later playwrights vary interestingly the standard set-up: Calderón's amorous Federico refuses to confide in Fabio, the tricky servant who works against, not for, his master in *El secreto a voces*; Wycherley's Fidelia sets up her master, who substitutes for her with the lustful, hypocritical, and married Olivia in *The Plain Dealer*, a cynical replay of *Twelfth Night*.

Comedic characters often tell lies that are or become true unexpectedly. In *Andria*, for example, the lovers' confabulation about the girl's origins and Athenian citizenship corresponds literally to her actual history; in *Phormio* the parasite's fiction about Phanium's relationship to Demipho turns out to be fact. Oscar Wilde, of course, brilliantly refigured this classical pattern in *The Importance of Being Earnest*, where Jack Worthing discovers that his real name is indeed Ernest and that he has a brother: 'It is a terrible thing for a man to find out suddenly that all his life he has been speaking nothing but the truth.'[63] Similarly, Viola's *fabula* in II. iv, her story about her father's daughter who pined for one like Orsino, hints at her true identity while expressing her own desire and longing, eventually to be revealed. Unlike the deceivers in *Andria* or *Phormio*, however, Viola knows herself to be speaking the truth in a lie; thus Shakespeare further heightens the New Comedic play between fiction and truth, between the various levels of character and audience awareness.

Despite many resemblances, the differences between conventional New Comedy and *Twelfth Night* are large and striking. To begin with, there are no blocking characters in the main action—no money-grubbers, pimps, wealthy soldiers, irate fathers, or harsh laws to obstruct the course of love. Both military men—the ship Captain and Antonio—are giving and generous, in contradistinction to the lascivious captain in Riche and the blustering comic type. The older generation supplies no opposition either: Viola's father is dead (as is Olivia's), though his counterpart is very much alive in Riche's tale and *Gl'ingannati*, a play that also features Gherardo, a ridiculous *senex amans*. Far from being an authority figure, Duke Orsino himself acts like a lovesick *adulescens*. Shakespeare's careful avoidance of the usual external obstructions emphasizes the internal ones, the varieties of self-love conspicuously evident in Malvolio. His revision of New Comedy also displays the problematics of desire, especially the predatory and self-destructive impulses at its core. The Italianate variety of disguises and confusions, moreover, clearly suggests the delusive nature of desire, the radical instability of both its subject and object.

Viola's disguise, of course, culminates a long and distinguished

---

[63] Ed. Murray, 537–8.

dramatic history of cross-dressing.[64] The Italians, beginning with
Bibbiena's *La calandria*, varied to dazzling effect the spectacle of a
girl in boy's costume. *Gl'ingannati* and its descendants, including
Shakespeare's source—the tale of Apolonius and Silla in *Riche his
Farewell to Militarie Profession* (1581)—display the complication of
the disguised wooing for her own beloved and, in turn, being
wooed by the *innamorata*. Viola, however, differs from her disguised predecessors in important respects. Unlike Lelia, Silla, or
Shakespeare's own Julia and Rosalind, she has no clear reason for
assuming a disguise and serving the Duke, or as she originally
intends, Olivia:

> O that I serv'd that lady,
> And might not be delivered to the world
> Till I had made mine own occasion mellow
> What my estate is!   (I. ii. 41–4)

The difficult syntax and vague expression cloud Viola's thoughts.[65]
The idea of making one's occasion mellow paradoxically yokes
two incompatible attitudes, that of active involvement for change
and that of passive waiting for ripeness. Uncertain of purpose,
poised between action and inaction, Viola parts way with the
scheming slaves of Plautine comedy, master-planners like Epidicus,
about whom the Epilogue can finally say, 'Hic is homo est qui lib-
ertatem malitia inuenit sua' (732, 'Here is a man who managed to
get his liberty by his wickedness'). Viola has no such goal or character; she dons the disguise for no specific purpose, as part of no
scheme for tricking someone out of money (usually a specific sum),
or a girl (usually free-born anyway). Assuming her disguise, Viola
simply surrenders to the evolving amorous entanglements, trusting
in time. 'O time, thou must untangle this, not I, / It is too hard a
knot for me t'untie' (II. ii. 40–1).[66] An intriguer without an
intrigue, wooing where she would woo, Viola strikes a unique and
delicate balance between activity and passivity.[67]

[64] Henderson (in his edn. of Aristophanes' *Lysistrata*, 136), e.g., notes ancient
instances associated with Dionysiac revels.

[65] These lines led astray even so acute an observer as Samuel Johnson (ed.
Vickers, v. 108), who thought Viola 'an excellent schemer', who here forms 'a very
deep design' to supplant Olivia. White and Spedding (Variorum edn., 1901, 27–30)
refute this judgement.

[66] She embodies 'patience' - a virtue traditionally associated with 'Fortitudo'; see
Heckscher, 'Shakespeare in his Relationship to the Visual Arts', 38 ff.

[67] And, perhaps, between male and female. The girl in boy's costume is, in fact,

Clearly, Shakespeare writes against New Comedic practice, his sources, and his previous works in order to present a different kind of heroine. The disguised Viola differs also from Plautine deceivers in her attitude towards acting and towards her role. Women like Milphidippa or Acroteleutium, for example, wily characters in *Miles Gloriosus*, delight in deception and play their roles with verve, pride, and self-conscious style. Assured of their own skill in the theatrical arts, they boast and improvise, turning each challenge into greater triumph. Viola, however, 'continually strains against the disguise', observes Leggatt, pointing to her broad hints (I. v. 184; III. i. 141) and the indirect revelation of love (II. iv. 25 ff.).[68] She is at times a nervous actress who worries about gaining access to Olivia, doubts her own ability, memorizes a speech and throws it away, departs from her text (I. v. 232). During the course of the play she becomes frightened and befuddled, even though at other times plucky and confident. Her disguise is, in a sense, transparent, revealing the charm, vivacity, and vulnerability of the actress. Those around her perceive Viola's admirable traits: Orsino senses the maid in boy's clothes, Diana's lip and the small pipe of her voice (I. iv. 31 ff.), and praises her, 'Thou dost speak masterly' (II. iv. 22); Olivia, too, responds to Viola's eloquence (I. v. 276), as well as her boldness and spirit. Even Sir Toby recognizes her 'good capacity and breeding' (III. iv. 186). Unlike the acting in classical comedy, Viola's performance reveals her better qualities even as it exposes by contrast the false fronts of others. Orsino lives by striking a series of languorous poses, complete with musical accompaniment; and Olivia claims to be mourning, but puts on and takes off the veil at whim. Viola may fool others as Cesario, but not herself. 'I am not that I play', she declares (I. v. 184).

To resolve this tangle of adapted New Comedic action, Shakespeare superimposes the errors plot from *Menaechmi*,

---

a boy in girl's costume. Recent critics have argued that the play draws energy from the same-sex wooings presented, and that these presentations constitute part of a complicated early modern discourse on gender and sexuality. See Rackin, 'Androgyny'; Greenblatt, 'Fiction and Friction', *Shakespearean Negotiations*, 66–93; Orgel, 'Nobody's Perfect'; Howard, 'Crossdressing'; Traub, *Anxiety and Desire*, 130 ff.

[68] Leggatt, *Shakespeare's Comedy*, 235 ff. Wikander ('As Secret as Maidenhead') relates Viola's ambivalence towards role-playing to the tensions implicit in the profession of boy-actress.

complete with twins, cross-wooings, and mistaken identities.[69] The adventures of Antonio and Sebastian in Illyria reprise many of the earlier incidents in Ephesus and also in Epidamnus, the original Plautine setting. Messenio's mistaken intervention for Menaechmus inspires the intervention of Antonio, who jumps into the street fight to rescue Viola. The bewildered beneficiary can only give confused thanks. Facing the uncomprehending Viola, Antonio feels the anger of Antipholus of Syracuse, likewise arrested in the street, refused his own purse, and led away as mad (IV. iv). Antonio's plight recalls that of Egeon, also arrested and unrecognised by one he loves. Both *Menaechmi* and *Errors* conjoin here to create a scene that mingles the slapstick confusion of mistaken identity with the poignance of loss and betrayal.

Shakespeare replays the errors plot here with significant variation. Antonio is a man who falls in love with another man, Sebastian. The gratuitous detail that Sebastian called himself earlier 'Rodorigo' (II. i. 17) links this relationship to the other disguises and wooings, even as it insists on the homoeroticism. In accents reminiscent of Orsino, Antonio is spurred by 'desire / (More sharp than filed steel)' (III. iii. 4–5). And this image provides no easy access for an exclusionary moral schematic which would distinguish between such desire and love, selfless and generous. For Antonio is clearly generous and self-sacrificing, handing over his purse, risking his life to guard Sebastian from danger. His tale will in salient ways reverse the comedic story of the principals. His revelation of identity leads to imprisonment, not liberation, to separation, not matrimonial union. Yet his story provides another dimension to the various forms desire and love take in the play; and though he will be unrequited, he cannot be ignored.[70]

Like Antonio, Sebastian re-enacts a sequence of actions from *Menaechmi* and *Errors*. His arrival resembles that of his counterpart in Plautus: both travelling twins show a hot temper, meet a parasite, and accept gifts from a woman. And like Shakespeare's first adaptation of the Plautine twin, Antipholus of Syracuse, Sebastian arrives in a strange and threatening place with a com-

---

[69] Suggestion for this superimposition may have originated in the source tale: Riche speaks of the 'cupp of errour' from which all drink and of 'Dame Errour' who entangles the lovers; Bullough, ii. 345.

[70] See Smith, *Homosexual Desire*, 66 ff., 117 ff.; Traub, 130 ff.; Pequigney, 'Two Antonios'.

panion who leaves after the passing over of a purse (*Twelfth Night* II. iii; *Errors* I. ii). Beguiling the time in the city, both Sebastian and Antipholus of Syracuse encounter a servant sent from an amorous lady (IV. i; I. ii). Enter the lady, Olivia (IV. i. 44), and Adriana (II. ii), who leads off the bemused traveller, wondering about his own sanity:

> SEB. What relish is in this? How runs the stream?
> Or I am mad, or else this is a dream.
> Let fancy still my sense in Lethe steep;
> If it be thus to dream, still let me sleep! (IV. i. 60–3)
>
> SYR. ANT. Am I in earth, in heaven, or in hell?
> Sleeping or waking, mad or well advis'd?
> Known unto these, and to myself disguis'd?
> I'll say as they say, and persever so,
> And in this mist at all adventures go. (II. ii. 212–16)

Both Sebastian and Antipholus of Syracuse soon fall in love. Both appear on stage with drawn weapon, precipitously involved in threatened violence (IV. i; IV. iv); and both make a final entrance later to discover their missing twins and to resolve the complications (V. i; V. i). Sebastian differs from Lidio of *La calandria*, happy to cuckold the foolish husband; from Fabrizio of *Gl'ingannati*, who takes advantage of a locked door to make love to Isabella; and from Riche's Silvio, who impregnates Julina and then abandons her. Instead he resembles Antipholus of Syracuse, whose amorous adventure strikes the appropriate tone of light romance and courteous festivity.

The final resolution, in accordance with Aristotelean precept, combines *peripateia*, 'reversal', and *anagnorisis*, 'recognition', and arises from the plot, ἐξ αὐτῶν τῶν πραγμάτων (*Poet.* 1455a16–17, 'from the incidents themselves'). Preceding the final entry of Sebastian Shakespeare brings the action to the height of confusion, to *catastasis*.[71] The marital and commercial mix-ups of Ephesus expand into multiple charges of betrayal: Viola stands accused of violating Antonio's friendship, Orsino's trust, Olivia's love; Antonio voices an acute sense of injury; Orsino, more dangerous than Apolonius who casts Silla into a dungeon, threatens to kill his

---

[71] Scaliger, 15: 'Catastasis, est vigor, ac status Fabulae, in qua res miscetur in ea fortunae tempestate, in quam subducta est' ('The *catastasis* is the force or issue of the plot, in which the story is mixed and caught up in the tempest of fortune'). See Herrick, *Comic Theory*, 119–22.

unfaithful page; and Malvolio vents his anger and ill-will. Thus Shakespeare boldly intensifies the darker possibilities of the action, even at the expense of character and probability in Orsino's case, in order to make more dramatic the reversal, the change of a situation into its opposite, ἡ εἰς τὸ ἐναντίον τῶν πραττομένων μεταβολὴ (*Poet.* 1452a22–3). So doing, Shakespeare follows orthodox Renaissance theory and practice regarding the *catastasis*. Bibbiena, likewise, had Calandro's brothers capture and threaten to kill Lidio right before the resolution; Flamminio in *Gl'ingannati* plans a gory Senecan revenge on Fabio (2169–72). To striking effect tragic menace, not slapstick confusion, precedes comic resolution.

The reunion of long lost siblings occurs frequently in classical and Renaissance drama and the anagnorisis here is thoroughly conventional in form. As siblings confront each other and piece together their history, an onlooker expresses amazement in a homely simile. We recall Messenio's comparison of the twins to drops of water or milk (1089–90); Samia in *La calandria*: 'O, Dio, o miracolosa marauiglia, non è alcuno si simile a se stesso, ne la neue alla neue, ne l'uovo a l'uovo, come è l'uno a l'altro di costoro' (p. 40, 'O God, O miraculous wonder! There is nothing so like as these two, not snowflake to snowflake, or egg to egg, as this one to the other'). And the beleaguered Antonio in *Twelfth Night*: 'How have you made division of yourself? / An apple, cleft in two, is not more twin / Than these two creatures' (v. i. 222–4). Shakespeare advances in subtlety and complexity from the original recognition in *Menaechmi* and from his earlier effort in *Errors*. Having completed his personal metamorphosis from Rodorigo through Cesario, Sebastian finally takes on his (and his father's) rightful name. The artificial token of identity—the ring, birthmark, or necklace—Shakespeare playfully mocks in the superfluous exchange: VIO.: 'My Father had a mole upon his brow.' SEB.: 'And so had mine' (v. i. 242–3). The playwright needs no Emilia to restore losses this time and now both twins, not merely the traveller, look forward to a wedding and new life. In *Twelfth Night* the λύσις, 'untying', does not require undressing, as in Riche, nor the genital humour of *Gl'ingannati*. And whereas both these works separate the revelations of each twin's identity, Shakespeare combines them into a moving dramatic moment.[72]

[72] On the reunion see the testimony of Virginia Woolf (ed. Wells, '*Twelfth Night*': *Critical Essays*, 80–1), recalling a production at the Old Vic (1933): 'Perhaps

As in *Errors*, 'the catastrophe is a nuptial', to use Don Armado's phrase. Several nuptials, in fact, and the main ones—seen in the perspective afforded by predominant trends and conventions—have been carefully prepared for and arranged. Reacting against the occasional harshness of classical comedy, Italian adaptors romanticized plots and popularized the multiple wedding conclusion. Transforming *Menaechmi* into *I lucidi*, for example, Firenzuola has the wife's goods returned to her and omits the part about putting her up for sale; this kinder treatment, he claims in the epilogue, demonstrates the superior consciences of contemporary youth, 'gli hanno molto migliore conscientia i giovani dal di d'hoggi, che quelli del tempo antico' (sig. Dxi). In the last scene of *La calandria*, the twins are perfunctorily but happily matched with off-stage ghosts. The Orsino figure in *Gl'ingannati* hears the marvellous story of a page's disguised devotion and, before he recognizes her as his own servant, falls in love:

Oh virtuosa donna, oh fermo amore! Cosa veramente da porre in esempio a' seculi che verranno. Perché non è avvenuto a me un tal caso? (2412–14)

O virtuous lady! O constant love! A case worthy to be celebrated for centuries to come! Why hasn't such a thing happened to me?

Viola, however, loves Orsino from the beginning, and he gradually comes to trust and admire her. Sebastian encounters Olivia, who combines Erotium's allure and Luciana's chaste attractiveness, a dream woman who seems already to know and love him. As Newman observes, 'The epicene figure of Cesario can be compared to a *trompe l'oeil* perspectivist painting. When Olivia sees him from her point of view, she "sees" Sebastian; when Orsino looks at Cesario, he "sees" Viola.'[73] Shakespeare marks Olivia's progress from the proud and constricted figure of the opening scenes into a bold lover by carefully orchestrating her appearances. In I. v she is

---

the most impressive effect in the play is achieved by the long pause which Sebastian and Viola make as they stand looking at each other in a silent ecstasy of recognition'; also, that of Zoë Wanamaker, a recent Viola (eds. Jackson and Smallwood, 89–90): 'Just like a fairy story, indeed, that is what is so wonderful about it, the sudden appearance of Sebastian, the apple cleft in twain, the mirror of herself. It is a magical moment, the resolution of confusion, the meeting of self, of each other; the whirlpool and the tempest that brought them to Illyria die down and suddenly there is wholeness again.'

[73] Newman, *Shakespeare's Rhetoric*, 104.

locked-up, guarded, and veiled; in III. i she enters a more open playing space, a garden probably (92), in order to meet with Viola. Several scenes later, she leaves her house or garden to meet with Viola off-stage, 'I'll come to him' (III. iv. 60); later they return on-stage together (196 s.d.). Olivia enters the scene of the street brawl (IV. i) unattended, breaks up the fight, and brings Sebastian home. He calls attention to the outdoor scene of her next entrance, 'This is the air, that is the glorious sun' (IV. iii. 1), and she invites him to the 'chantry' (24) for the wedding. No longer a recluse, Olivia enters the final open-air scene of v. i for the revelations, where she meets the Duke, who likewise has left his courtly prison. 'Daylight and champian discovers not more' (II. v. 160).

The pairing off of the lovers, at least the main characters, provides a festive conclusion to the play. In Illyria as in Ephesus new bonds replace old confusions as 'Nature to her bias' (v. i. 260) draws the characters to their proper mates. Such errors as Olivia and Orsino commit answer to their deepest desires.[74] Audiences on- and off-stage may experience a wonder quite appropriate to the Feast of the Epiphany. This wonder, however, is not at all Christian or Plautine, but Ovidian, and several commentators have called attention to Ovid's significant presence in the play.[75] Two have cited the story of Iphis, a woman who changes into a man, as a parallel to Viola's transformation. Here, and in Lyly's courtly variations on the theme of magical sexual metamorphoses, the wonder arises from the sudden fulfilment of desire in a marvellous way. A closer Ovidian paradigm, perhaps, is the story of Pygmalion, which mingles erotic longing and mysterious resolution but which focuses on the spectator's emotions rather than on those of the transformed.[76] The sculptor kisses the statue and finds it warm to his touch, 'visa tepere est' (*Metamorphoses* X. 281).

---

[74] The same holds true for the errors in Piccolomini's *L'Alessandro* (imitated in Chapman's *May Day* about the time of *Twelfth Night*); Aloisio (dressed as a girl) and Lucretia (dressed as a boy) are mysteriously drawn to each other and eventually united.

[75] See Palmer, '*Twelfth Night* and the Myth of Echo and Narcissus'; Carroll, 80–102; Taylor, 'Shakespeare and Golding'; Bate, *Shakespeare and Ovid*, 144–51; for the Iphis analogy discussed below see the essay of Carroll, 'The Ending of *Twelfth Night*' and that of Lamb, 'Ovid's *Metamorphoses* and Shakespeare's *Twelfth Night*', in Charney (1980), 49–61, 63–77.

[76] Cf. *Measure for Measure* III. ii. 45; Marston's 'Pygmalion', ed. Bullen, iii. 258; Bate, *Shakespeare and Ovid*, 23, 234–8.

dum stupet et medio gaudet fallique veretur,
rursus amans rursusque manu sua vota retractat;
corpus erat: saliunt temptatae pollice venae.   (287–9)

He amazde stood wauering too and fro
Twene ioy, and feare to bee beguyld, ageine he burnt in loue,
Ageine with feeling he began his wisshed hope too proue.
He felt it verrye flesh in deede. By laying on his thumb,
He felt her pulses beating.   (tr. Golding, fol. 127v.)

The beloved ideal, dimly perceived, becomes flesh and blood.

But wonder and epiphanic joy need not be universal, as many productions and critics make clear. Orsino and Viola may appear ill-matched and the final union is deferred beyond the bounds of the play, pending the recovery of Viola's clothing; Antonio's devotion earns him pain and an uncertain future; Sir Toby and Sir Andrew exit from the party with cracked crowns; Malvolio leaves in a huff. Lois Potter observes that the ending of *Twelfth Night* is 'unlike most Shakespearean denouements', in which the main characters all share in the final revelations:

Twelfth Night leaves many of its characters as separate and isolated at the end as at the beginning, despite their brief intersection with other lives. Thus, Sir Andrew, Sir Toby and Malvolio do not know that Olivia has married Sebastian, or that Viola is Cesario; Maria, apparently, does not appear in the scene at all, and her marriage to Sir Toby is explained in what seems almost a throwaway line. No lines are provided for Fabian and Feste to take account of these facts.[77]

To conclude, Feste sings a mournful song, whose refrain suggests to Geoffrey Hartman the 'melancholy desire to be beyond desire' apparent in Orsino's opening call for music.[78] The mingled tonality of the ending suggests the darker side of New Comedic errors, the potential for dislocation and alienation, for journeys that do not end in lovers' meeting. The conventional happy ending, here deepened and qualified, may be played as desire's last delusion.[79]

[77] pp. 31–2; on the limitations to the festive ending, see also Summers, 'The Masks of *Twelfth Night*', in Dean (1967), 134–43; Barton, '*As You Like It* and *Twelfth Night*', in Bradbury and Palmer (1972), 160–80; Grief, 'A Star is Born'.
[78] 'Shakespeare's Poetical Character in *Twelfth Night*', in Parker and Hartman (1985), 37–53 (49).
[79] Other playwrights revise New Comedy to explore more fully this darker potential. Calderón's Lisarda witnesses her lover's marriage to another and must marry instead her father's choice; for her life goes according to the title, *Peor está que estaba*, 'from bad to worse'. Farquhar pairs a wedding and a divorce in the

As in *The Comedy of Errors*, Shakespeare adapts New Comedy in *Twelfth Night* fluently and coherently. The major innovations—the addition of two New Comedic actions and exposures, the presentation of Viola as a Plautine schemer without a scheme, the superimposition of the errors plot on an Italianate intrigue—all suggest the folly of schemes and intrigues. Those who plot and pursue their beloveds appear progressively more ridiculous in the play—Orsino, Olivia, Sir Andrew, Malvolio. To be sure, those who join in the nuptials at the end have been active: Viola puts on the disguise and engages Orsino in revealing and flirtatious conversation; Olivia woos Cesario; Maria concocts the plot against Malvolio. But in all cases, especially the principal two, the weddings result indirectly from such actions; they are blessings conferred in surprising ways, beyond the lovers' design, expectation, and comprehension. 'Bene è vero che l'huomo mai un disegno non fa, che la fortuna un' altro non ne faccia', says Fessenio in the opening lines of *La calandria*: 'It is very true that man never makes a plan but Fortune makes another one.' In Olivia's words: 'Fate, show thy force: ourselves we do not owe' (I. v. 310).

This idea is implicit in New Comedy, for all of its Byzantine plotting, where resolution often occurs by chance or providence. As Joel B. Altman, writing on Terentian resolutions, observes incisively:

And the truth is that no contention really exists, *sub specie aeternitatis*. For at the heart of things are unsuspected relationships that reason has not even considered. A father discovers that the woman who seemed to stand in the way of the profitable match he had been seeking is his own daughter; a husband learns that the unchaste wife he refuses to acknowledge is the girl he himself had seduced. The implications are disquieting. The joyful celebration of *dianoia* turns out to be also a humble acknowledgement of its ultimate inadequacy. And the final vision, while comic, implies that the desired unity of opposites that is achieved in the perception of relationship—the reconciliation of fathers and sons, the acquisition of both love and money—is a consummation not usually attainable by ordinary human means.[80]

---

ending of *The Beaux' Stratagem*; Aimwell and Dorinda rejoice to be joined, Mr and Mrs Sullen, to be parted. And Goldoni's revision of *Menaechmi*, *I due gemelli veneziani*, ends with a poisoning and a suicide.

[80] p. 146. Ordinary human means, however, prove amply sufficient in many classical and neo-classical intrigue plays. Lope de Vega's *El perro del hortelano*, for example, subverts the errors-play resolution by having the low-born Teodoro fake the discovery of his noble father.

This is the lesson of these errors plays as well, one that contemporary editions, translations, and adaptations of Plautus and Terence reified in more explicitly Christian terms. Here the great and simple coincidence of twins reformulates all plans and nullifies all plots. And here the wise course is to exercise patience—the virtue featured in the ancillary sources—*Confessio Amantis* and *Gl'ingannati* (Prologo 128–9). Not, finally, a Plautine intriguer, Viola is a romance heroine who acts and who trusts in time. In her and in the action of *Twelfth Night* Shakespeare looks ahead to *Pericles* and *The Tempest*.

3

New Comedic Intrigue

IN *The Taming of the Shrew* and *Much Ado About Nothing*
Shakespeare arranges New Comedic conventions, devices, characters, and situations into amatory intrigues, into tangles of disguise
and deception. Traditionally, of course, such intrigues feature a
central trickster.[1] In *Shrew* and *Ado*, however, Shakespeare departs
from this dominant comedic tradition by presenting several competing tricksters, instead of one. Like Jonson and Middleton on
occasion, he organizes these comedies into multiple planes of
intrigue action that run courses parallel, contiguous, and intersecting. The affair of Lucentio and Bianca, for example, complements
that of Petruchio and Katherina; that of Claudio and Hero, that of
Beatrice and Benedick. In both plays the intrigue action features
centrally courtship by disguise. And though these disguises encom-
pass a range of modes—from simple masks to complicated proxies
and impersonations—all twist the plot into pleasing coils.
Shakespeare's New Comedic intrigues raise questions about personal and social identity, while exploring the powerful, often subversive and destabilizing energies of the theatre and role-playing.

Together *The Taming of the Shrew* and *Much Ado About
Nothing* constitute a sophisticated critical response to New
Comedy. Like other Renaissance dramatists, Shakespeare exploits
possibilities implicit in New Comedic form, possibilities that had
already been put to brilliant, if other, uses by the Greeks and
Romans themselves. The earliest New Comedic playwright we possess in substantial volume, Menander, boldly experimented with
intrigue structures and conventions, creating a complicated interplay of ironies. In *Sikyonios* Act v, Theron is trying to bribe an

---

[1] We think of Aristophanes' Lysistrata and Pisthetairos, Plautus' clever Pseudolus,
Terence's Phormio, the Intronati's Lelia, Bibbiena's Fessenio, Molina's tragic varia-
tion—Don Juan, Molière's Scapin and Tartuffe, Corneille's mendacious Wily
Unbeguiled, Dorante, Beaumarchais's irrepressible Figaro; see also Salingar,
Traditions, 88–128; Beecher, 'Intriguers and Trickster', in Beecher and Ciavolella
(1986), 53–72.

elderly and poor Athenian to pretend to be Kichesias, father of missing daughters, so that one Philoumene, consequently, can claim Athenian citizenship. The old man, however, is the father of missing daughters, is in fact the very Kichesias he is supposed to pretend to be; Philoumene, consequently, is an authentic Athenian citizen. Exploiting different levels of awareness for comic and ironic effect, the playwright creates a fiction that is or becomes true in surprising or unexpected ways. During the attempt at the scam Kichesias, not fully comprehending the situation, says γέρων ὅς εἰμι γέγονα (354, 'I am become the old man I am').[2] This remark serves as a fitting epigraph for Lucentio, Bianca, Claudio, and Hero, as well as for Kate, Petruchio, Beatrice, and Benedick—all of whom, willingly or unwillingly, play in fictions that confirm or reveal identities. Furthermore, such fictions need not merely correspond to pre-existent facts; sometimes, through the magic of playing, they alter the very nature of reality, confer new identity, create new truth, at least for the moment. Depicting the processes of love and marriage, both *The Taming of the Shrew* and *Much Ado About Nothing* explore the dynamics of such fiction-making, exhibiting the festive potential of New Comedic intrigue as well as its darker possibilities.

The Taming of the Shrew

By now it is customary to note that this play embodies a patriarchal discourse on power and gender that subordinates women to men. Strong recoil from this subordination has prompted enlightening re-exploration of the play's literary and cultural contexts. Less helpfully, it has so dominated critical reaction as to marginalize the rest of the play, serving to reduce the complex stage interactions into one politically incorrect thesis:

For feminist scholars, the irreplaceable value if not pleasure to be realized by an historicized confrontation with Shakespeare's *The Taming of the Shrew* lies in the unequivocality with which the play locates both women's

---

[2] Other editors think that γέρων belongs to the preceding speaker, thus rendering Kichesias' line more simply, 'I am become who I am'. Plautus stages a similar scene, *Poenulus* 1099 ff. Gratwick (*Cambridge History of Classical Literature*, ii. 101–3) argues that Menander provided the source for Plautus.

abjected position in the social order of early modern England and the costs exacted for resistance.[3]

Here the complex polyvocality of the text is compressed into one (and that noxious) monologue. Even if the homiletic and social preachings of early modern England were univocal on these matters, the stage, as Renaissance anti-theatricalists well knew, was no pulpit. And as their descendants in Cultural Poetics and Materialism have well noted, plays did not merely propound official orthodoxies but enacted conflicting discourses, serving as charged sites for ideological testing and contesting. Analysis of the New Comedic elements in *Shrew* can illuminate these conflicts and bring some of the play's other voices into audible range. More specifically, Shakespeare's radical revision of New Comedic conventions in the Tranio-Lucentio-Bianca plot opposes the perceived paradigm of gender relations in the taming. Furthermore, a focus on New Comedic intrigue and role-playing usefully complicates our perceptions of the taming, especially as it occurs in the performance for Vincentio, the taming-school, and in the final wager scene.

The Taming of the Shrew boldly arranges various elements from New Comedy into festive intrigue. Notwithstanding Muir's curt judgement, 'the names of Tranio and Grumio, but nothing else, were taken from the *Mostellaria* of Plautus', several commentators have argued for the influence of *Mostellaria* on Tranio and on the play.[4] And, as is well known, Shakespeare modelled the Lucentio-Bianca story on Gascoigne's *Supposes*, itself a version of Ariosto's *I suppositi*, which frankly acknowledges indebtedness to *Eunuchus* and *Captivi* in its prologue:

et ui confessa l'autore hauere in questo & Plauto & Terentio seguitato, che l'uno fece Cherea per Doro, & l'altro Philocrate per Tindaro, & Tindaro per Philocrate, l'uno nello Eunucho, l'altro nelli captiui sopponersi, perche non solo nelli costumi, ma nelli argumenti anchora delle

---

[3] Boose, 'Scolding Brides and Bridling Scolds', 179.

[4] *Sources*, 22. For contrary opinions see Fay, 'Further Notes on the Mostellaria of Plautus', 245–8; Harrold, 'Shakespeare's Use of *Mostellaria* in *The Taming of the Shrew*'. Despite some spurious parallels, the accumulated evidence is in quality and quantity superior to that compiled for *Amphitruo* in *Errors*, a play accepted universally as a source despite the garbled text of the crucial scene. Among *Mostellaria*'s other descendants are Bentivoglio's *I fantasmi*, Jefferay's *The Bugbears* (through Grazzini's *La spiritata*), Heywood's *The English Traveller*, Larivey's *Les Esprits*, Jonson's *The Alchemist*, and Fielding's *The Intriguing Chambermaid*.

fabule uuole essere de gli antichi & celebrati poeti, a tutta sua possanza imitatore.[5]

And the author confesses to you that in this he has followed both Plautus and Terence, in that Terence substituted Chaerea for Dorus and Plautus, Philocrates for Tyndarus and Tyndarus for Philocrates, in *Eunuchus* and *Captivi*, respectively. Because the author wants, to the best of his ability, to be an imitator of the ancient and famous poets, not only in their customs but also in the arguments of their plots.

Whether one assigns priority in point of composition to *Errors* or *Shrew*,[6] both plays restage moments from *Amphitruo* and *Menaechmi*, namely, the lock-out scene and the scene of confused identity, false accusation, and arrest. To be sure, *Shrew* draws more on folk legend and on Ovid and creates a more complicated action than does *Errors*;[7] both, however, transform New Comedy into Elizabethan farce.[8]

As usual, a misplaced emphasis on verbal iteration has distracted attention from the larger, more important correspondences between *Mostellaria* and *Shrew*. Like his counterpart in *Mostellaria*, Grumio is a country servant who gets cuffed in his first appearance (*M* 9–10; *S* I. ii. 17 *s.d.*). Later he delivers the complaint typical of the beaten slave: 'Fie, fie on all tir'd jades, on all mad masters, and all foul ways! Was ever man so beaten? Was ever man so ray'd? Was ever man so weary?' (IV. i. 1–3). Like his double in *Mostellaria*, Shakespeare's Tranio is a *callidus servus*, a clever servant. Both Plautus' and Shakespeare's Tranio have been enjoined by an absent master to take care of the son, formerly a model

---

[5] *Gli soppositi*, sigs. Ai(v)–Aii.

[6] The chronology is not certain; some have argued well for the priority of *Shrew* to *Errors*, including Mincoff, 'The Dating of *The Taming of the Shrew*'; Morris, Arden edn. (1981), 50–65; Wells and Taylor, *William Shakespeare: A Textual Companion*, 109 ff. On links between these two plays see Thompson, New Cambridge edn., *Shrew* (1984), 6–8.

[7] On backgrounds see Bradbrook, 'Dramatic Role as Social Image'; Hosley, 'Sources and Analogues of *The Taming of the Shrew*'; Brunvand, 'The Folktale Origin of *The Taming of the Shrew*'; West, 'The Folk Background of Petruchio's Wooing Dance'; on Ovid, Carroll, 41–59; Morris, 133–6; Roberts, 'Horses and Hermaphrodites'; Bate, *Shakespeare and Ovid*, 118–29.

[8] There has been lively critical debate about the nature of the farce in *Shrew*. Heilman ('The *Taming* Untamed', 161) thinks the play 'suprafarcical'; Kahn (*Man's Estate*, 104–18) sees the farce as ironic; Bean ('Comic Structure', in Lenz (1980), 66) and Oliver (New Oxford edn., 51–2) believe that the farce elements in the play conflict with its characterization; Saccio ('Shrewd and Kindly Farce') redefines farce as a genre that can reveal the energy, resilience, and ingenuity of characters.

youth who applied himself to learning (*M* 133–4; *S* I. i. 1 ff.). Both
fulfil the parental charge (cf. *M* 25–8; *S* I. i. 210 ff.) by aiding the
son in costly merriment and amorous intrigue. The plots of
Mostellaria and *Shrew* feature the return of the absent father, who
knocks futilely at a locked door, thoroughly bamboozled by the
servant's lies. Both fathers eventually discover the truth, become
reunited with their prodigal and amorous sons, and let their servants off from condign punishment.

Thus the *Shrew*, like *Mostellaria* and its other descendants, features the conflict between young deceivers and old dupes.
Shakespeare again multiplies the possibilities, providing no fewer
than four seniors—Baptista, Gremio, the Pedant, and Vincentio—
all duly tricked or discomfited. Grumio comments aptly, 'See, to
beguile the old folks, how the young folks lay their heads
together!' (I. ii. 138–9). As in *Mostellaria*, Tranio emerges as the
architectus doli; ''tis plotted' (I. i. 188), he announces confidently, a
pithy version of the typically Plautine moment of inspiration (cf.
Most. 387: 'Habe bonum animum: ego istum lepide medicabo
metum' ('Courage! I'll cure that fear of yours in fine style.'). He
suggests Lucentio's impersonation of a schoolmaster (I. i. 191–2),
coyly agrees to the exchange of identities, plays the role of his
master with dash and swagger. Entering 'brave' (I. ii. 217 *s.d.*), he
speaks dignified blank verse and asserts his right to woo Bianca,
causing Gremio to comment, 'What, this gentleman will out-talk us
all' (I. ii. 246). At the end of the scene he magnanimously suggests
that the rivals 'do as adversaries do in law, / Strive mightily, but
eat and drink as friends' (I. ii. 276–7). Impudently, Tranio outbids
Gremio for Bianca, blithely offering his master's wealth for a
dowry (II. i. 363 ff.). Here he resembles the Tranio who tricks two
other old men, Simo and Theoproprides, in *Mostellaria* III. ii, 'ubi
ludificat una cornix uolturios duos' (832, 'where one crow makes a
sport of two vultures'). Both Tranios pretend that great danger
threatens an aged dupe and both draw the victim into the plot by
pretending to rescue him. Plautus' servant invents the macabre tale
about the haunted house (446 ff.); Shakespeare's tells the Pedant,
''Tis death for any one in Mantua / To come to Padua' (IV. ii.
81–2). Both servants congratulate themselves on their successes
with typical New Comedic enthusiasm: Tranio answers the exiting
Theopropides' prayer—'Hercules, ted inuoco' (528, 'Hercules, I
invoke you!')

> et ego—tibi hodie ut det, senex, magnum malum.
> pro di inmortales, opsecro uostram fidem!
> quid ego hodie negoti confeci mali. (529–31)

And so do I—that today he may make big trouble for you, old man. Great gods above preserve us! What a heap of monkey-business I've finished today!

Similarly, Shakespeare's Tranio dismisses the exiting Gremio, 'A vengeance on your crafty withered hide! / Yet I have fac'd it with a card of ten.' (II. i. 404–5). Tranio here makes one with those many classical and neo-classical servants who privately applaud their own cleverness.[9]

Shakespeare's portrayal of Tranio as classical *servus* illuminates his portrayal of the other comic schemer and manipulator, Petruchio. These two characters have the largest speaking parts in the play. Both Tranio and Petruchio act demanding roles in an amorous play of their own design. Like Tranio, Petruchio consciously decides to play a part, to woo Kate 'with some spirit':

> Say that she rail, why then I'll tell her plain
> She sings as sweetly as a nightingale;
> Say that she frown, I'll say she looks as clear
> As morning roses newly wash'd with dew;
> Say she be mute, and will not speak a word,
> Then I'll commend her volubility,
> And say she uttereth piercing eloquence. (II. i. 170–6)

Like Tranio, Petruchio assumes a role and fits a mask for another. In the course of the play both energetically manipulate a reluctant actor into a supporting role: Tranio casts the travelling pedant as Vincentio; Petruchio casts Katherina in the role of 'most patient, sweet, and virtuous wife' (III. ii. 195). These parallels do not evoke subtexts depicting the beating of shrews or bridling of scolds but ancient, theatrical, and comedic impersonations.

Whether or not one agrees with Dr Johnson, 'the two plots are so well united that they can hardly be called two without injury to the art with which they are interwoven', Shakespeare does deliberately parallel the two casting actions whereby Tranio's 'cunning'

---

[9] See, e.g., Heywood's Reignald, *Dramatic Works*, iv. 61–2; Bentivoglio's bragging Negro, *I fantasmi*, sig. Diiv. The *callidus servus* has enjoyed a long and varied stage life from Aristophanes' Xanthias (*The Frogs*) up through Beckett's Lucky (*Waiting for Godot*), whose dithyrambic monologue aply summarizes the existential plight of his betters, so-called.

gets him a temporary father (II. i. 411) and Petruchio's, a perma-
nent wife.[10] Tranio's instruction, 'Go with me to clothe you as
becomes you' (IV. ii. 121), immediately precedes the scene wherein
Petruchio shouts down the haberdasher and tailor for not clothing
Kate becomingly. The next two scenes are likewise paired: in IV. iv
the Pedant plays his role well in front of the aged Baptista; in IV. v
Kate plays her role well in front of the aged Vincentio. The contrast between the Pedant's dull and workmanlike impersonation
and Kate's brilliantly comic performance, 'Young budding virgin,
fair, and fresh, and sweet' (IV. v. 37), points up the essential differences in the two castings. Tranio's masking of the Pedant functions
as yet another suppose, a typical New Comedic knot of intrigue,
destined to be untied at the end. Petruchio's masking, however,
appears to be talismanic; it fashions a new Kate, transforming the
wearer into the mask, at least for the moment.

In many New Comedies—Plautus' *Mostellaria*, Terence's
Eunuchus, for example—the return of an absent father figures
largely in the intrigue and resolution of the plot.[11] Usually, a servant soliloquizes in comic anguish about the father's arrival (see
also *Most.* 348 ff.; *Supposes* IV. i). Shakespeare retains only a trace
of the usual panic in the aside of Biondello (an Italianate *puer*),
'Mine old master Vincentio! Now we are undone and brought to
nothing' (V. i. 43–4). He focuses instead on Vincentio as the object
of Kate and Petruchio's merriment: male and female intriguers join
forces against the befuddled patriarch. After playing the game of
supposes against each other, they now play on the same side. In
Padua they move from centre stage to the aisles, becoming spectators to Vincentio's humiliation and confusion.

The New Comedic door-knocking of Vincentio derives directly
from *Supposes* (IV. iii–iv. 7), where Philogano, searching for his
son, has someone knock on a door and finds impersonators of
himself and his son. Shakespeare modifies this incident by recalling
several touches from *Errors* and the Plautine deep sources—
Menaechmi, *Amphitruo*—and *Mostellaria*. Like Antipholus of

---

[10] Johnson, ed. Vickers, v. 110. The conventional nature of such casting misled
George Colman (1765) into identifying Plautus' *Trinummus* as a source for *Shrew*;
Farmer (1767), adducing *Supposes*, corrected the error (ibid.) v. 275–6.

[11] Other playwrights tried variations. Terence provides two such returns in
Phormio, as does Pierre de Larivey in *Les Esprits*; following Della Porta's *La sorella*,
Middleton contrives the pivotal return of the absent mother in *No Wit, No Help
Like a Woman's.*

Ephesus and unlike Philogano, Vincentio first invites his companions in for a drink before he gets the rude reception; the denial of admittance and of his identity becomes more embarrassing before an audience. And like Antipholus, Menaechmus, Amphitruo, and Theoproprides, he knocks on the door himself. In *Supposes* Philogano is left to sort out his problems and there follows a scene of self-pitying complaint. In *Shrew*, however, the troubles fall upon Vincentio thick and fast: Biondello denies him, Tranio faces and braves him, an Officer comes to arrest him. This rapid and escalating action recalls the similar sequence in *Errors* IV. iv, where Antipholus of Ephesus has the maddening encounters with his Dromio, Adriana, and Pinch before the arresting officer arrives.[12] With sure dramatic instinct Shakespeare complicates the entanglements right before the untying. And he sharply compresses the extended denouement of *Supposes*, encompassing eleven short scenes (IV. viii–v. 10) and some extraneous action, by reverting to the single stroke used so effectively in *Menaechmi* and *Errors* (and to be used again in *Twelfth Night*)—the dramatic entrance. Lucentio enters, kneels to his father, effects a reconciliation. Their meeting, like those of the separated relatives in Shakespeare's error plays, dissolves the intrigue into harmonious understanding, forgiveness, and reunion.

The principal intriguer in *Shrew*, Tranio, exits to avoid punishment. Unlike Gascoigne's Dulipo who fades permanently from the action, reunited off-stage with his long-lost father, Tranio has an advocate, Lucentio, and reappears at the final banquet, unpunished and unrepentant. In this, he resembles his classical counterpart in *Mostellaria*, who likewise has an able defender, Callidamates, and who gets off scot-free and impenitent.[13] Impudent as his namesake, Shakespeare's Tranio, formerly a master now a servant again (V. ii. s.d.), enjoys the fate of his cousins on later stages: Heywood's

---

[12] Cf. the similar sequence in *Every Man in his Humour*, V. i (Quarto); according to Baldwin (*The Organization and Personnel of the Shakespearean Company*, tables facing 229, 435), Shakespeare himself may have played both paternal roles—Vincentio and Lorenzo Sen. Cf. also the corresponding, less Plautine sequence in *The Taming of a Shrew*, sc. xvi.

[13] Fay (247–8) and Simpson (22) detect a similarity between *Most.* 1159, 'quidquid fecit nobiscum una fecit: nos deliquimus' ('Whatever he did, he did along with the rest of us. We're all at fault'), and *Shrew* (V. i. 129–30): 'What Tranio did, myself enforc'd him to; / Then pardon him, sweet father, for my sake.'

Reignald, who escapes punishment through the intercession of the
son; Jonson's Face, who not only escapes but swindles his former
cohorts and helps the returned master Lovewit win Dame Pliant;
Molière's Scapin, who gets a pardon by pretending to be gravely
ill.

Behind Shakespeare's Tranio flits the whimsical shade of his
classical namesake and also that of another classical *servus*,
Parmeno of *Eunuchus*, whose words to the lovelorn Phaedria echo
in the play: 'Redime te captum quam queas minimo' (I. i. 162,
'Ransom yourself from captivity as cheaply as you can').[14]
Eunuchus, popular in its own day, much imitated in the
Renaissance and after, is one of Ariosto's acknowledged sources
for the 'supposes' plot, hence a source of Gascoigne's translation,
and hence a deep source of Shakespeare's play.[15] In the action
most pertinent to *Shrew*, Chaerea, disguised as a eunuch, gains
access to Pamphila and rapes her; her long lost brother appears,
reveals that she is Athenian by birth, and arranges her marriage to
Chaerea.

Such action provoked the Bembine scholiasts to see in *Eunuchus*
love's *furor*, a madness that does not recognize limit or counsel.
The humanists likewise glossed the play's double action and particularly the disguise intrigue as illustrations of love's sovereign and
irrational power. According to Muretus, the opening dialogue,
reprised in Lucentio and Tranio's conversation, 'exprimitur
immoderati amoris insania, & quam difficulter cordatus etiam ani-
mus, ex tam impotente malo se eripiat' ('expresses the insanity of
immoderate love and how difficult it is, even for a reasonable
mind, to free itself from this ungovernable evil'). Chaerea's use of
disguise likewise shows 'Primos adolescentis ardores, & Venereos

---

[14] Samuel Johnson found the true source of the line in Lily's *Grammar*; Farmer
drew precisely the wrong conclusion: 'The quotation from *Lilly* in the *Taming of the
Shrew*, if indeed it be his, strongly proves the extent of his reading: had he known
Terence he would not have quoted erroneously from his *Grammar*.' The evidence of
a single slight misquotation cannot support so categorical an assertion; and in any
event, the exclusive focus on verbal iteration again precludes the possibility (here a
certainty) of mediated presence. See Vickers (ed.), v. 210–11; 261 (for the quotation); 275–6, 291–2; Baldwin, *Small Latine*, i. 577–8.

[15] Suetonius (ii. 456–7) reports that *Eunuchus* was performed twice in one day
and that it earned more than any previous comedy, 8000 sesterces. The play gives
the lie to Caesar's complaint about Terence's lack of *vis* (ibid., 462–3). The line of
descendants includes also Udall's *Ralph Roister Doister*, Shakespeare's *Love's
Labour's Lost*, Wycherley's *The Country-Wife*, and Sedley's *Bellamira*.

aestus, posthabita rei domesticae ac publicae cura' ('the first ardours of the adolescent and his erotic passions, overruling all concern for private and public responsibilities').[16] Both Ariosto and Gascoigne reflect this tradition in their versions, wherein Chaerea's descendants enjoy visitation rights for two years and finally impregnate Polynesta.[17]

The story of Chaerea's rape and marriage, replete with its representations of male lust and female valuation in a closed property system, provides a paradigmatic example of the sexual politics and patriarchal power now denounced in *The Taming of the Shrew*. And yet, Shakespeare's evocation of *Eunuchus* is pointedly adversative. Like all quotations, Tranio's 'points to an obligatory intertext, to a conscious manipulation of what Barthes calls the circular memory of reading'.[18] This manipulation is a self-conscious use of repetition to establish difference, a sign of the deeply eristic nature of the later text. In this play Shakespeare radically revises the New Comedic deep source, purposefully departing from the moralized gender readings urged variously by contemporary humanists and some modern feminists. Substituting bemused fascination for the censorious disapproval of the old and new commentators, Shakespeare places love at the epicentre of the action. He depicts this love not merely as dehumanizing phallic desire but as the powerful, irrational, and mutually shared *raison d'être* for comedic intrigue.

Shakespeare's focus on love, a romanticized version of New Comedic eros, generates a number of other important changes. First among these is the refiguration of the *virgo*. Italian innovators from Ariosto to Oddi had already prepared the way, of course, transforming the slight classical sketches into variously complex women. Bianca too emerges as a character more interesting and important than the *muta persona* of Terence's *Eunuchus*. Pamphila,

---

[16] Mountford, ed., *The Scholia Bembina*, 17; *Terentivs, in Quem Triplex Edita Est* (1560), 210, 248.

[17] Chaerea's disguised entrance became a standard trick in the comedic repertory, capable of diverse refiguration. Lodovico tries it in Chapman's *May Day* only to find the lady a disguised man and to receive a beating, thus literally and literally confounded by a motif from *Casina*. In *The Country-Wife*, Horner adapts the strategy more directly and successfully to facilitate several amorous affairs. The ruse brings Lionel both sexual satisfaction and reunion with his lost love in *Bellamira*. No wonder Beaumarchais' Count observes: 'The singing-master story is a very old trick—it has a stagey look about it' (*The Barber of Seville*, 78).

[18] 'Introduction', *Intertextuality*, in Worton and Still (1990), 10.

in fact, has no character at all but merely a function in the dramatic action. After briefly describing Chaerea's disguise, rape, and escape, Muretus writes, 'Hic turbae admirabiles concitantur'.[19] He observes the striking up of wondrous confusions, not any guilty or injured persons. Far from being the helpless, voiceless Pamphila or the 'abjected' woman of some feminist readings, Bianca, capable of wilfulness and surprise, takes charge of the wooing scene:

> Why, gentlemen, you do me double wrong
> To strive for that which resteth in my choice.
> I am no breeching scholar in the schools,
> I'll not be tied to hours, nor 'pointed times,
> But learn my lessons as I please myself.   (III. i. 16–20)

The student commands the teachers; the lady controls her suitors. From a subordinate position Bianca wields real power and contrasts directly with the insubordinate Kate, who variously asserts her strength and independence only to find herself continually overmastered. By the end of the play, however, Kate will learn what Bianca knows—namely, that the skilful playing of a social role can bring freedom, fulfilment, and power. Bianca's self-assertion achieves final expression in her spirited repudiation of wifely obedience in the wager scene.

Shakespeare's presentation of amatory intrigue plays against classical subtexts in another important way: the disguise creates a two-planed wooing action, one part performed by Lucentio himself, the other by Tranio as Lucentio. Since the disguised Tranio wins Bianca by outbidding Gremio, the odd binary arrangement has seemed to some superfluous and puzzling. Why doesn't Lucentio himself simply bid for and win Bianca, as Tranio does in his name? Shakespeare clearly wishes to portray love as involving personal choice and affection; this marriage will be more than a mere matter of social and financial arrangement. For this reason he splits the public and private aspects of courtship into parallel actions—one designed to satisfy societal requirements, the other, personal needs, in other words, one for Baptista, the other for Lucentio and Bianca. In classical comedy the emphasis is largely on the first plane only: the marriage action works to reveal or confirm blood lines and citizenship, to establish socio-economic identity.

Tranio's performance fulfils the equivalent prerequisites. Lucentio's performance, however, expands classical comedy in new directions. He seeks to win Bianca's love which, if not 'all in all' (II. i. 129), is important to them and to the play.

Accordingly, and as he had in *Errors*, Shakespeare changes the blunt sexuality of the subtext to emphasize courtship and romance. Unlike the rapist Chaerea, and his sexually active descendants in Ariosto and Gascoigne, the disguised Lucentio must woo and win the conspicuously chaste Bianca.[20] For the courtship Shakespeare chooses the unlikely expedient of a Latin lesson. The classical author is Ovid rather than Aristotle and his 'checks' (I. i. 32), but Lucentio here chooses to quote sober lines from *Heroides*, rather than a spicy passage from *Ars Amatoria* or the *Metamorphoses*. The passage quoted is highly significant as the original speaker is Penelope, model of the faithful and virtuous wife. Through such artifice Lucentio reveals his own subtext in a charming and civilized courtship scene. Both lovers *qua* grammarians misconstrue purposefully. The Latin exercise is actually an artful linguistic dance that deceives Baptista and the vigilant Hortensio while giving the lovers a chance to speak. That Lucentio teaches Latin rather than music (a surprising choice, given Shakespeare's usual portrayals of the two disciplines) illuminates the nature of their courtship. In their own way these two practise rhetoric, the art of civilized communication according to established laws and conventions. Though they forsake the rigours of declensions and conjugations, both work at a complex negotiation through language, one that ends appropriately with this later exchange, whose closing rhyme signals unity and harmony: 'BIAN. And may you prove, sir, master of your art! / LUC. While you, sweet dear, prove mistress of my heart!' (IV. ii. 9–10). Shakespeare's revision of New Comedy here creates a paradigm wherein both partners attain a measure of freedom and power while observing received codes and performing in social roles.

For the Latin lesson Petruchio substitutes the harsher curriculum of the taming-school. Here he adopts the humour of a shrew, but also, more importantly, the role of a wife, now properly or improperly Katherina's. In the Renaissance the wife, not the

---

[20] Observing a similar propriety, Dr Kelke transforms Euclio's pregnant daughter into a chaste heroine in the *Aulularia* played before Queen Elizabeth at Cambridge (1564); see Smith, *Ancient Scripts*, 157–9.

husband, had primary responsibility for household government. As Linda Woodbridge observes:

The Rev. William Gouge preached that 'affaires abroad do most appertaine to the man, and are especially to be ordered by him. That which the wife is especially to care for, is the businesse of the house.' . . . Robert Cleaver pontificated, 'the dutie of the husband is, to trauell abroad to seeke liuing: and the wiues dutie is to keep the house.' . . . William Whately hammered it home: 'He without doores, she within: he abroad, she at home.'[21]

Harassing the servants, the tailor and haberdasher, complaining about the cooking and the bed-making, railing and brawling, pretending that all is done 'in reverend care' (IV. i. 204) of the spouse, Petruchio does not exercise male prerogatives but usurps and parodies female ones. Eschewing the traditional, masculine methods of shrew-taming—the binding, beating, and bleeding—Petruchio instead plays bad wife instead of bad husband, forcing Kate to recognize his excesses. *Haec vir* matches and confounds *hic mulier*. After Petruchio strikes the servant, Katherina says, 'Patience, I pray you, 'twas a fault unwilling'; and after he overturns the table and beats the servants, she responds again, 'I pray you, husband, be not so disquiet. / The meat was well, if you were so contented' (IV. i. 156, 168–9). Petruchio's exuberant mismanagement of domestic economies draws Kate into correcting him, into, in other words, the opposite role of good wife. This theatrical method of behaviour modification, of course, has its risks: the role-playing here, as Karen Newman has observed of other instances, 'subverts the play's patriarchal master narrative by exposing it as neither natural nor divinely ordained, but culturally constructed'.[22] Nevertheless, if wifeliness is a culturally constructed role, so is shrewishness, the disadvantages of which become clear here, even to Katherina herself.

The other deep source of *Shrew*, Plautus' *Captivi*, contributes to Ariosto and Gascoigne the main 'suppose' of their plays, namely, the exchange of identities between master and servant. In Plautus' variation the master Philocrates tries to instruct the servant Tyndarus in the device (219 ff.); so does Lucentio, Tranio (I. i. 198 ff.). Agreeing to the imposture, both servants express their devotion to their master:

---

[21] *Women and the English Renaissance*, 172.   [22] *Fashioning Femininity*, 50.

TYND. Nam tu nunc uides pro tuo caro capite
carum offerre me meum caput uilitati. (229–30)

Indeed, now you see that for your dear head I offer mine, as a thing of no
worth.

TRAN. I am content to be Lucentio,
Because so well I love Lucentio. (I. i. 216–17)

In *Captivi* the exchange of identity suggests some of the ironies of
societal stratification, and explores again the dynamics of role-
playing.[23] Tyndarus admires Philocrates' performance, especially
his smooth adoption of lower-class talk, 'ut facete orationem ad
seruitutem contulit' (276, 'How cleverly he's picked up the speech
of a slave'), and his ability to philosophize and lie (284). Similarly,
Lucentio praises Tranio's assumption of mannered elegance and
authority, 'Well begun, Tranio' (I. ii. 227). In both plays the actors
cannot be distinguished from each other 'For man or master' (I. i.
201) by their faces or manners.[24]

In *Shrew* this change of identity becomes charged with meaning
and resonates throughout the play, uniting action in 'supposes'. It
echoes in part Sly's promotion from tinker to lord and that of page
to Madam wife, providing as well the 'down-side' of the switch,
Lucentio to Tranio. This exchange, alternating its fields of energy
between the poles of dominance and subservience, largely constitutes the main action of taming. Here the alternations between service and mastery flash and dazzle. We have observed Petruchio's
exaggerated solicitousness; and Kate, in her most imperious, domi-
neering moments, is most driven, most a slave to her passions,
most lacking in freedom and happiness. The play works towards
redefining mastery and service in a conclusion that transforms
rather than articulates the old dichotomy.

The transformation results specifically from Shakespeare's

[23] According to Cappelletto (*Lectura*, 74–5), Pontanus found *Captivi* especially
rich in moral sentences and memorable ideas; Lessing (quoted in Lindsay's *Captivi*,
5) praised it as 'the best comedy ever put on the stage'. Renaissance adaptations
include Rotrou, *Les Captifs*, and Jonson, *The Case is Altered*.

[24] This exchange of identity has a rich history as a comic premise, appearing
early in Aristophanes' *The Frogs*, in the Spanish *comedia de figurón*, and, to satiric
purpose, in many works, notably in Marivaux's *Slave Island*. Figaro's witty comment is pertinent to the entire tradition (*Barber*, 43): 'On the basis of the virtues
commonly required in a servant does Your Excellency know many masters who
would pass muster as valets?' Napoleon called the sequel, *The Marriage of Figaro*,
'the revolution in action' (Wood edn., 30).

innovative use of New Comedic disguise and deceit. Often in New Comedy, as we have seen in *Twelfth Night*, fiction becomes or reveals truth in surprising and unexpected ways. Tyndarus of *Captivi*, for example, pretending to be Philocrates, says to Hegio, 'tam ego fui ante liber quam gnatus tuos' (310, 'once I was as free as your son') and 'quam tu filium tuom tam pater me meu' desiderat' (316, 'as you long for your son, so my father longs for me'). Hegio swallows the lies and arranges the prisoner swap; but since the audience knows that Tyndarus is actually the long-lost son of Hegio, his fiction contains a truth unimagined by the teller. The revelation of this truth, with an emotion more characteristic of Terence than Plautus, constitutes the recognition of the play. Tyndarus' fiction corresponds to a pre-existent reality which the audience knows and which the play confirms.

Likewise, Petruchio's fiction about Kate as perfect wife becomes true in ways surprising and unexpected as Kate learns to play the game. The various other fictions in the play, particularly those in the amatory intrigue, provide an illuminating perspective on this one. There fictions require relatively simple masks and performances: people like Tranio, Lucentio, Hortensio, and the Pedant put on costumes, speak set lines, play well-defined roles. Their performances end and they resume their previous identities. Kate's performance is more complex, less a Plautine imposture than an Ovidian metamorphosis. The role becomes her as she ceremoniously, self-consciously, playfully, becomes the role—the patient, virtuous, obedient wife. Shakespeare's New Comedic action is not revelatory but performative: it concludes not by revealing a pre-existent, well-known truth, but by changing fiction into truth. At the end of the play Kate, both like and unlike Kichesias, might well say with him, ὅς εἰμι γέγονα ('I am become who I am').

Or has she really? This question is the crux for interpretation of Kate and of the notorious ending speech, which offers a wide range of theatrical and critical possibilities, including on one extreme the dark interpretation of Charles Marowitz. For him the play is a Gothic tragedy that illustrates the 'modern technique of brainwashing'; it shows a 'Grimm Fairy Tale world, a world of sinister archetypes and hopeless victims'.[25] Though tendentious, this reading conforms to the view now dominating critical discus-

---

[25] Marowitz, *The Shrew*, 20.

sion: the speech is a paean to male supremacy and expresses the abject surrender of the female self.

The dramatic context, however, is complex and works against simplistic interpretation. Kate's remarks do not, in fact, comprise a philosophical set-piece but are part of a contest, wherein she competes against Bianca, the model sister who proves herself to be wilful, and the Widow, who has just insulted her in public. This speech is a performance that continues the action of putting the Widow 'down' (v. ii. 35), a wrestling metaphor (and a bawdy pun), and that of putting down her sister, an activity which has engaged her since the opening scenes. Driving the ladies back to the banquet and lecturing them (and everyone else) on wifely duties, she is more the triumphant victor than humiliated loser. In the theatre her poetry—the music, imagery, rapid shifts in argument and in rhythm—expresses strength and control, not weakness and submission. The original Kate, in fact, was a boy-actress whose female costume might have suggested the artifice fundamental to all social roles, especially that of wife. For this actor the final speech provided a big moment, the premium showcase in the play for eloquence. As Juliet Dusinberre speculates: the apprentice's 'elation at his/her *stage* triumph silently colours the audience's reaction to the whole scene'.[26]

What is more, the open-ended imposture of the Sly scenes, which never end in the expected unmasking as they do in *The Taming of a Shrew*, now parallels the main action wherein the fiction goes on indefinitely, indistinguishable from fact.[27] This indistinguishability, of course, wonderfully cuts both ways and problematizes all simplistic readings. Do we witness fact or fiction, transformation or imposture? The page disguised as Sly's wife begins the play as the boy playing Katherina ends it, by saying, 'I am your wife in all obedience' (Induction ii. 107). Holderness queries shrewdly: 'Is the spectator of *The Taming of the Shrew* as much a victim of illusion as the tinker? Is every playgoer an "*hypocrite lecteur*", the "*semblable et frère*" of Christopher Sly?'[28]

---

[26] 'Women and Boys: Stealing the Show?', 4.

[27] Hosley ('Was There a "Dramatic Epilogue" to *The Taming of the Shrew*?') examines evidence which suggests that this open-endedness is intentional.

[28] *Shakespeare in Performance: 'The Taming of the Shrew'*, 11. Compare this ending with that of Fletcher's sequel, *The Woman's Prize or the Tamer Tamed*, wherein Petruchio's second wife, Maria, tames him. This play ends with Maria's similarly paradoxical assertion of triumphant submission in love and a kiss. Fletcher points

Whatever one's interpretation, Kate's climactic final speech constitutes on the level of plot a classical πίστις or proof. According to Aristotle (*Rhet.* 1355b35) and later commentators on Terence, proofs could be ἄτεχνοι, inartistic (oaths, ordeals, or signs merely adduced) or ἔντεχνοι, artistic (examples, signs, and enthememes requiring the art of the speaker).[29] Kate's speech clearly qualifies as the latter. In classical comedy *pistis* leads to anagnorisis, the recognition of true identity that resolves the plot. In New Comedies like *Eunuchus* the *virgo* proves to be an Athenian citizen, and recognition of her true identity makes possible a desired marriage. Similarly, in the *Shrew* Kate, through the magic of theatrical play, presents herself as ideal wife, no longer a shrew; proclamation of this new identity makes both possible and desirable her marriage, already performed, to Petruchio.

Shakespeare again reconstitutes the social anagnorisis of classical comedy into terms moral and personal; and by placing the fractured wedding of Petruchio and Kate, that zestful parody of social and dramatic forms, in the middle instead of at the conventional end of the play, he can focus on life after the wedding. The main plot of *Shrew* explores post-nuptial life, the rough and delicate processes whereby people come to be spouses, the slow, complicated, and ongoing negotiations, the long, shifting series of posings and exposings, postures and impostures. This interest also governs the conclusion of the Lucentio-Bianca plot. Along with Kate's speech, the final Lucentio–Bianca by-play grandly reformulates the conventional New Comedic conclusion, the wedding that simply dismisses the lovers to happiness; Shakespeare's conclusion, instead, explores the internal dynamics of love and marriage. Lucentio's belief in his wife's submissiveness is simply the first of many foolish misconceptions that marriage inevitably will correct; and Bianca's sharp response, often distorted by critical over-reaction, is just the first of the many surprises that any real marriage holds.

Curiously, the three plots of *The Taming of the Shrew*—the Induction, the Lucentio–Bianca story, the Katherina–Petruchio

the moral in the epilogue, stating that the play means not to encourage either sex to dominate but 'To teach both Sexes due equality; / And as they stand bound, to love mutually' (7–8).

[29] Cf. Quintilian, *IO* v. x. 1 ff.; Herrick, *Comic Theory*, 29–31, 179–89; Grimaldi, *Aristotle, Rhetoric* 1: *A Commentary*, 37–8, 349–56; Janko, 219–20.

taming—have each enjoyed separate and individual theatrical lives. The Sly story forms the basis of two eighteenth-century farces entitled *The Cobler of Preston*; Ariosto's and Gascoigne's original 'supposes' plays portray the Lucentio-Bianca courtship; Garrick's *Catharine and Petruchio*, the most famous and long lasting adaptation of Shakespeare's play, drops the Induction, the Sly episodes, and the other wooing. Shakespeare, however, unites the three actions by portraying them as variations of New Comedic intrigue: each features the classical device of courtship by disguise, proxy, or impersonation; each illustrates variously the New Comedic tendency of fiction to be or become true in surprising ways. Like descants, the actions resonate and play against each other, drawn into occasional harmonies by their common concern with the business of love and marriage. The four principal lovers here find themselves and each other, two of them experiencing varieties of New Comedic anagnorisis: Lucentio becomes Lucentio, restored and rightful son of a restored and rich father; Kate becomes a wife, flaunting her newly created self in playful and exuberant performance. These lovers, like Beatrice and Benedick, unite in marriage, not merely in matrimony; they find 'a way of being richly together with all their contradictions—and energies—very much alive and kicking'.[30] The allusion to *Much Ado* is pointed; for in that play Shakespeare again creates an amatory plot from New Comedic intrigue, again explores the powerful energies of theatre and role-playing.

Much Ado About Nothing

Like *The Taming of the Shrew*, Shakespeare's other comedy of intrigue, *Much Ado About Nothing*, features centrally courtship by New Comedic disguise, proxy, and impersonation. '*Much Ado about Nothing*', observes Kenneth Muir, 'may be regarded as a subtler version of *The Taming of the Shrew*, transposed from farce to high comedy—and, of course, Benedick needs to be tamed as well as Beatrice'.[31] In both plays the affair of relatively conventional lovers plays against the explosive and combative courtship of fuller individuals. And as before, this playing is more subtle and

[30] Daniell, 'The Good Marriage of Katherine and Petruchio', 28.
[31] *Sequence*, 78.

complex than many have allowed. Not arranged in simple counterpoint, the competing New Comedic plot lines draw on various
sources to create a rich and complex polyphony. Once again the
play looks beyond the comedic wedding to examine love and marriage.[32] And once again, a New Comedic fiction becomes true in
ways unanticipated by the principals, this time, Beatrice and
Benedick. *Ado* explores the delights and dangers of courtship by
disguise, role-playing, and New Comedic intrigue.

The influence of New Comedy on *Ado* does not derive from a
single discrete text—a direct or intermediated source—with a
recoverable itinerary. Instead, New Comedy provides structures
and principles by which Shakespeare organizes his novella material
and creates the ado in Messina. New Comedy is present here as a
complex legacy of character, convention, and form, deeply possessed and fluently manipulated. The dramaturgical principle of
paired opposites, operative in the contrasting siblings, Don Pedro
and Don John, organizes the main events of the play. The desired
and legitimated *virgo*, replete with Italian resonances, becomes
Hero, fit match for Claudio, a partially regenerated *adulescens*.
Classical precedents shape the courtship by proxy that begins the
play as well as the various eavesdroppings that come later. New
Comedic form governs much of the action: the play works towards
the false anagnorisis of Hero's infidelity and the fractured wedding;
these events set up the final recognition of Hero's innocence and
the true nuptials.

Structurally, *Much Ado About Nothing* departs from the
accepted sources, Ariosto and Bandello, in one important respect:
two half-brothers initiate the intrigues that constitute the play. One
brother, Don Pedro, is good; the other, Don John, is bad.
Shakespeare contrives the play to contrast the fraternal intrigues:
Don Pedro's humorous New Comedic deceptions oppose Don
John's perverse and potentially tragic deceits. Such opposition is a
perfectly orthodox piece of New Comedic dramaturgy. Minturno
notes generally that Terence often features 'in una medesima qual-
ità diuerse maniere di persone'; other commentators on Terence
specify the differences. Erasmus contrasts the pairs in *Adelphoe*:
bitter Demea and gentle Micio, urbane Aeschinus and boorish
Ctesipho, wily Syrus and dull Dromo. The Argument to Maurice

---

[32] On the redefinition of these concepts in the period see Stone, *The Family, Sex
and Marriage in England 1500–1800*; Rose, *The Expense of Spirit*, 12–42.

Kyffin's translation of *Andria* calls attention to various opposed pairs in that play: the *senes*—Simo, hot and testy, and Chremes, mild and moderate; the *adulescentes*—Pamphilus, staid and shamefaced, Charinus, harebrained and void of discretion; the *servi*— Davos, sly and subtle, Byrria, slothful and reckless. Kyffin also contrasts Mysis, the sober maid, and Lesbia, the drunken gossip.[33] The oppositions canvassed here suggest the moral contrast between Don Pedro and Don John, and, as we shall see, that between other siblings—Edmund and Edgar, Prospero and Antonio.

Much Ado About Nothing opens with a familiar Roman gambit, found, for example, in *Pseudolus*, *Poenulus*, *Eunuchus*, and in many other plays including Molière's witty recension of classical comedy, *Les Fourberies de Scapin*: a young man, helpless and breathless, falls in love; he reveals his passion, not to the lady, but to a faithful *servus*, who responds cynically; together they hatch a plot involving disguise and deception.[34] This gambit appears in *Shrew* I. i, where Lucentio falls for Bianca and confides in his servant:

> Tranio, I burn, I pine, I perish, Tranio,
> If I achieve not this young modest girl.   (I. i. 155–6)

Tranio asks, 'is it possible / That love should of a sudden take such hold?' (146–7), but decides to dispense with the usual cynical repartee, 'Master, it is no time to chide you now' (159). They then conspire to change clothes and identities. Like the pair in *Shrew*, Claudio and company arrive in town and Claudio catches sight of Hero, 'In mine eye, she is the sweetest lady that ever I look'd on' (187–8). Here two characters share the servant's role. Benedick zestfully plays the cynic who punctures the lover's bubble:

Why, i'faith, methinks she's too low for a high praise, too brown for a fair praise, and too little for a great praise: only this commendation I can afford her, that were she other than she is, she were unhandsome, and being no other but as she is, I do not like her.   (171–6)

Don Pedro plays the plotter, initiating the disguise and the practice:

---

[33] Minturno, *L'arte poetica*, 125; Erasmus, *De Ratione Studii*, tr. Thompson, 689; Kyffin, sig. Biii. See Robbins, 88 ff.

[34] Wright (131 ff.) contrasts interestingly Plautus' and Terence's handlings of this scenario.

> I will assume thy part in some disguise,
> And tell fair Hero I am Claudio,
> And in her bosom I'll unclasp my heart,
> And take her hearing prisoner with the force
> And strong encounter of my amorous tale;
> Then after to her father will I break,
> And the conclusion is, she shall be thine.   (321–7)

Shakespeare here distributes the part between two characters and, in addition, complicates the familiar intrigue; as befits a Prince, Don Pedro's disguise as Claudio is an enabling fiction, not merely a decoy (like Tranio's) or a ruse.

The New Comedic courtship by proxy arises from the smallest hint in Bandello, the mere mention of Timbreo's intermediary, 'vn gentilhuomo Messinese, con cui haueua molta familiarità'.[35] It develops into a New Comedic intrigue that will run its entire course—through confusion to resolution—in a discrete prefatory action. Though brief, the *processus turbarum* shows variety and complexity, proceeding by a series of conflicting reports that contradict our understanding in substance or detail. Claudio's initial talk with Don Pedro presumably occurs before Leonato's house. Having gathered the intelligence from one of his men who overheard a conversation in an 'orchard' (I. ii. 10), Antonio reports that the Prince himself intends to woo and wed Hero. Later, Borachio, reporting on an indoor meeting, says that Don Pedro plans to court Hero 'for himself, and having obtain'd her, give her to Count Claudio' (I. iii. 62–4), a possibly significant variation from the plan as announced. At the masqued ball Don John, who should know better, says to Borachio, 'Sure my brother is amorous on Hero, and hath withdrawn her father to break with him about it' (II. i. 155–7).[36] Unable to conceive of his brother as a disinterested friend, Don John projects on to him his own double-dealing personality. Benedick confirms the false supposition, 'the Prince hath got your Hero' (191–2).

A simple error thus begets confusion: the lover mistakenly thinks himself betrayed by his friend and erstwhile intermediary. This

[35] Bandello, *La prima parte*, fol. 151.

[36] Attempts to explain away this inconsistency have been unconvincing, e.g., the interpretation of 'amorous on' to mean 'amorous on behalf of Claudio' (Humphreys, Arden edn., 1981, 118) or the assumption that Don John has already recognized Claudio and directs the remark to him (Mares, New Cambridge edn., 1988, 72).

error appears in none of the accepted sources of the play but frequently in New Comedy. In Plautus' *Bacchides* (III. iii–iv), for example, Mnesilochus erroneously thinks his friend, Philoxenus, to be amorously involved with Bacchis; Terence's Charinus similarly misjudges Pamphilus in *Andria* (IV. i). Shakespeare's departures from Roman practice, however, are significant and revealing. In Plautus and Terence the error belongs to the main action of the play, not to its beginning scenes; one Terentian commentator, in fact, describes it as an 'elegans perturbatio'; another, as the 'epitasis vtriusque partis fabulae'.[37] Instead, Shakespeare places the error in the opening movement, thus creating a prelude to the graver error to follow. As Bullough (ii. 75) observes, 'Don Pedro's jesting approach to Hero when masked as Claudio anticipates the wicked approach of the disguised Borachio to Margaret.' Moreover, the error does not derive from the impersonal agency of plot, but from the interference of a malevolent malcontent. No Roman comedy features a Don John; nor do Ariosto or Bandello whose evil intriguers are frustrated lovers and clearly motivated. Shakespeare introduces a new kind of intriguer, a plain and simple villain who uses New Comedic plots and impersonations to evil ends. Finally, the New Comedic movement from desire through reversals and confusions to recognition and union here involves the audience, who, unlike the audiences in classical comedy, must doubt, pick their way through the maze of contradictions, and, at last, breathe some relief at Don Pedro's declaration:

Here, Claudio, I have woo'd in thy name, and fair Hero is won. I have broke with her father, and his good will obtain'd. Name the day of marriage, and God give thee joy!   (II. i. 298–301)

Shakespeare's sophisticated handling of the familiar error reveals some of the darker possibilities of courtship by disguise; depending on the production, it may elicit sympathy for Claudio, here befooled later crushed by a plot, or impatience with his gullibility.

Don Pedro and Don John represent respectively the good and evil potentialities of New Comedic intrigue. After Claudio and Hero are betrothed, the brothers immediately begin other practices. Both plan scenes of disinformative eavesdropping, wherein hidden listeners overhear conversations that are solely intended to deceive

[37] *Terentivs* (1560), 134.

them.[38] Those conversing put on miniature plays, sometimes commenting on the performance in their asides. Those concealed learn of secret, passionate, and unrequited lovers.

In his amatory intrigue, Don Pedro, like the typical *servus callidus*, plays author, producer, director, and chief actor. His practice recalls the similar scenes in Plautus' archetypal *Miles Gloriosus*, where disinformative eavesdropping dupes Pyrgopolynices, the braggart soldier.[39] In both plays the disinformative eavesdropping occurs in two parts. The successive performances of Milphidippa and Acroteleutium (IV. ii, IV. vi) parallel the successive performances of Don Pedro and company, Hero and his friends. In *Miles Gloriosus* IV. vi, two accomplished actresses confidently play their parts, pretending that one of them, Acroteleutium, loves the hidden *miles gloriosus*, Pyrgopolynices. Asides locate the target and begin the game:

> MI. Era, eccum praesto militem. AC. ubi est? MI. ad laeuam.
> AC. uideo. (1216)

> MI. Madam, there is the soldier all ready. AC. Where is he? MI. To the left. AC. I see him.

Compare the first eavesdropping in *Ado*:

> D. PEDRO. See you where Benedick hath hid himself?
> CLAUD. O, very well, my lord. (II. iii. 40–1)

Though not so ridiculous as Pyrgopolynices, Benedick is repeatedly depicted as a soldier (I. i. 43, II. i. 379, II. iii. 188 ff.), and, what is more, as a boaster.[40] He doesn't brag about military and amorous conquests but about his invulnerability to Cupid's arrows. Telling of the lady who suffers passionate and unrequited love for the hid-

---

[38] On 'Nothing' in the title as a homonym for 'noting', or eavesdropping, see Jorgensen, 'Much Ado About *Nothing*', 293–5; Slater (*Plautus in Performance*, 164–5) discusses what I call disinformative eavesdropping in *Persa*, noting also instances in *MG* and *Cist*. See also Duckworth, 109–14; Bain, *Actors and Audience*, 171–7.

[39] The main deception in *MG* springs from a girl's impersonation; the first 595 lines dramatize an onlooker's glimpsing of her making love to another in a closed house. Smith (*Ancient Scripts*, 138) mentions two Cambridge productions; Bolgar (532–3) notes Renaissance translations, Boughner (*Braggart*), the many dramatic descendants. Several have suggested Shakespeare's direct knowledge of the play, notably Baldwin, *Five-Act*, 670, 84; Lumley (citing Reinhardstoettner), 45–6.

[40] Newman (*Rhetoric*, 117 ff.) sees Benedick as a variant *miles gloriosus*; Traugott ('Creating a Rational Rinaldo', in Greenblatt (1982), 157–81) thinks that he parodies this stage figure. Humphrey's survey (33 ff.) suggests that productions have often emphasized the military aspects of the play.

den auditor, both sets of actors impute to the listeners an attitude of scorn and high disdain:

> MI. spero ita futurum, quamquam multae illum sibi expetessunt:
> ille illas spernit, segregat hasce omnis, extra te unam.
> AC. ergo iste metus me macerat, quod ille fastidiosust,
> ne oculi eiius sententiam mutent, ubi uiderit me,
> atque eiius elegantia meam extemplo speciem spernat.   (1231–5)

MI. I hope it will be so, although many women desire him for themselves. He spurns them all, however, denies the whole group, except you alone.

AC. And this is precisely the fear that vexes me, that his high disdain make his eyes change his mind, that his refined elegance spurn my kind of beauty at first glance.

D. PEDRO. She doth well: if she should make tender of her love, 'tis very possible he'll scorn it, for the man (as you know all) hath a contemptible spirit.   (II. iii. 178–81)

Acroteleutium threatens to commit suicide if rejected, 'si non quibo impetrare, / consciscam letum' (1240–1). So too is Beatrice in mortal danger, according to the report (173–6). Both performances are highly successful: Pyrgopolynices struts forward to grant magnanimous favour to the woman he has lusted for all along; so too Benedick says of Beatrice, whom he has obviously loved from the beginning, 'If I do not take pity of her, I am a villain; if I do not love her, I am a Jew' (II. iii. 262–3).

In III. i Hero, Ursula, and Beatrice replay a briefer version of the Plautine eavesdropping. As in *Miles Gloriosus*, the principal performers are a woman and her servant. Again one of them, Hero, spots the mark: 'For look where Beatrice like a lapwig runs / Close by the ground, to hear our conference' (III. i. 24–5). Like Acroteleutium and Milphidippa with their 'subdola perfidia' (943), Ursula expresses confidence in her artful wiles: 'Fear you not my part in the dialogue' (31). Like their Plautine counterparts and Don Pedro earlier, these ladies focus on the listener's scornful pride:

> HERO. But nature never fram'd a woman's heart
> Of prouder stuff than that of Beatrice.
> Disdain and scorn ride sparkling in her eyes,
> Misprising what they look on, and her wit
> Values itself so highly that to her
> All matter else seems weak.   (III. i. 49–54)

And Cupid's trap here, as before, works expeditiously.

In these scenes Shakespeare boldly adapts a Plautine routine to his own complex purposes. His intriguers obviously differ from those in *Miles Gloriosus*, who delight in trickery, fast money, and pompous victims. Don Pedro shows kindness and gentility as well as a love for teasing and sport. So too does Hero, who grows to relative complexity and fullness in the Plautine charade. Those who denounce Hero as flat and insubstantial, 'less a character than a cipher, or a mirror to the other characters', for example, ignore the wit and spriteliness she shows in this scene, not to mention the memorable interpretations of actresses like Helen Mirren in Trevor Nunn's 1968 production and Katharine Levy in the BBC version.[41] Hero plays the Plautine part with verve and style, lighting into her cousin for having 'coy and wild' spirits, for being 'so self-endeared' (35, 56). Off the cuff, she parodies Beatrice's famous wit in lively, jesting verses, outdoing her in spelling potential suitors 'backward':

> If fair-fac'd,
> She would swear the gentleman should be her sister;
> If black, why, Nature, drawing of an antic,
> Made a foul blot; if tall, a lance ill-headed;
> If low, an agot very vildly cut;
> If speaking, why, a vane blown with all winds;
> If silent, why, a block moved with none.
> So turns she every man the wrong side out,
> And never gives to truth and virtue that
> Which simpleness and merit purchaseth.   (61–70)

The capacity for improvisation and mimicry shows a quick wit and lively imagination. Also appealing is Hero's affectionate loyalty (a sharp contrast to the promiscuity of her counterpart in Pasqualigo), evident in the qualified praise of Benedick: 'He is the only man of Italy, / Always excepted my dear Claudio' (III. i. 92–3). Hero's modesty and charm here and in the rebato scene make the coming repudiation in church all the more disturbing.

The victims and consequences of the eavesdropping in *Ado* differ strikingly from those of the seminal scenes in *Miles Gloriosus*. There the eavesdropping is an elaborate con game designed to swindle the soldier of his money and girl and to expose him as a pretentious buffoon who deserves the final beating. The eavesdrop-

---

[41] Cook, 'The Sign and Semblance of Her Honor', 191; more interesting on Hero's limitations is Berger, jun., 'Against the Sink-a-Pace'. On some stage interpretations see Humphreys, 47.

ping confirms the soldier in his faults; it puffs him up to make more explosive the coming puncture. In Shakespeare, however, the eavesdropping itself works to correct faults, effecting a deflation which is immediate and personal. Both Benedick and Beatrice feel shame to hear themselves accused of pride and arrogance. He decides to change his ways (II. iii. 220 ff.); she, speaking for the first time in verse, bids adieu to contempt and maiden pride in a speech of complex emotion (III. i. 107 ff.)[42] Thus the eavesdropping works to opposite ends in Plautus and Shakespeare. And the ploy in *Ado* aims to unite lovers, not merely to defeat and expose an *alazon*. Of course, the Plautine eavesdropping, we should recall, likewise aims to unite sundered lovers—Pleusicles and Philocomasium—who wait in the wings. Shakespeare brings these lovers to centre stage, has them face obstacles from within rather than from without; Plautine farce here gives way to romantic comedy.

Unlike his brother, Don John presents the evil potentialities of New Comedic intrigue, in this anticipating Iago and, as we shall see, Edmund. Portraying him, Shakespeare departs significantly from Ariosto and Bandello, who depict the evil intriguer as sole inventor of the plot, and reverts to the example of New Comedy for the conspiracy. Borachio plays a sinister *servus callidus*: he sets up the practice, uses disguise and deceit, relies on 'cunning' (II. ii. 55). 'In Pasqualigo and Munday too', Bullough (ii. 72) comments, 'the suggestion of the central trick comes to the plotter from his assistant (Narciso in *Il fidele*, Pedante in *Fedele and Fortunio*) in the tradition of the clever slave'. So too in *Gli duoi fratelli rivali* (from Panimbolo to Don Flaminio, III. i), a *commedia* also based on Bandello's tale of Timbreo and Fenicia, and bearing many pointed resemblances to *Ado*.[43] Together Borachio and Don John constitute a wicked pair that corresponds perversely to the usual master-servant combination, adumbrated here, as we have seen, in the early configuration of Claudio, Benedick, and Don Pedro.

Borachio and Don John conspire to destroy rather than serve love. The eavesdropping they stage conveys a message exactly opposite to that of Don Pedro's second intrigue—namely, that the

---

[42] Witness Ellen Terry (*Four Lectures*, 88): 'Very difficult words for an actress; not very effective, but charged with the passion of a strong, deep heart! I have played Beatrice hundreds of times and never done this speech as I feel it should be done.'

[43] On these resemblances see Gordon, '*Much Ado About Nothing*: A Possible Source for the Hero-Claudio Plot'; Doran, 178–80; Clubb's translation, 30 ff.

lady is light not loving, unchaste not unrequited. The crucial assignation scene is not staged but described variously no fewer than five times.[44] These descriptions depict Hero as *meretrix*, as the courtesan who continually frustrates young lovers in Plautus and Terence by opening her door (in his case, her window) to others. The real or imagined visit of another man to the home of one's beloved is common in New Comedy, though the mood always differs, and the emphasis usually falls on the *naïveté* or confusion of the jealous lover.[45] To Hero's supposed Thais, Claudio plays Phaedria, the locked-out *adulescens* of *Eunuchus*, whose conversation with Tranio *Shrew* briefly recalled. Entrance into the woman's house also signified the sexual encounter, as commentators on *Eunuchus*, attending to the ambivalences of the Latin, duly noted.[46] We have already seen other variations of the device in *Menaechmi*, where the traveller replaces his brother in the visit to Erotium's house, and in *Amphitruo*, where the husband believed that another man has entered his house and enjoyed Alcumena. The outraged and jealous husband who castigates the innocent and slandered wife in *Amphitruo* becomes a central archetype of 'biting error', one that coalesces with other stories and exerts a fascination on Shakespeare early and late. *Othello*, of course, presents the greatest development of this topos; and in that later Italian intrigue play, not coincidentally, Iago will unite features from the eavesdroppings staged by Don Pedro and Don John in the excruciatingly comitragic eavesdropping of IV. i.

The intrigues of both Don John and Don Pedro converge and come to climax in the remarkable wedding scene. Neither Ariosto nor Bandello affords precedent for this scene: having left to commit suicide, Ariodant sends back a peasant to explain why; Timbreo, likewise, sends a messenger to Lionato's house to break off the match. As in *Shrew*, however, Shakespeare creates a frac-

---

[44] In Don John's promise only do we have the actual entrance mentioned, 'you shall see her chamber-window ent'red, even the night before her wedding-day' (III. ii. 112–14). Gilbert ('Two Margarets') explains this passage as an uncancelled vestige of Bandello before revision according to Ariosto.

[45] Recognition of the convention should qualify objections to its realism, beginning with that of Charlotte Lennox (ed. Vickers, iv. 140), who called the trick 'an improbable Contrivance', and the whole fable, 'mangled and defaced, full of Inconsistencies, Contradictions and Blunders'. Mixed with the highly inflammable Spanish sense of honour this visit is central to Calderón's *Casa con dos puertas mala es de guardar*, 'A house with two doors is difficult to guard'.

[46] *Terentivs* (1560), 293–4.

tured wedding to serve as an antitype to the conventional New Comedic nuptials. The usual *pistis* or proof of identity becomes here a false report that demonstrates the difficulties of perceiving, knowing, and 'noting' truly. The anagnorisis is likewise inverted: the typical discovery about the heroine, namely that she is a long-lost daughter or an Athenian citizen, therefore eligible for marriage, becomes here the false revelation that Hero is whore. This revelation shatters rather than enables the wedding. Tragic passion erupts in New Comedy, mocking expectation, 'This looks not like a nuptial' (IV. i. 68), exploding forms and conventions, disfiguring characters. Claudio, hitherto a typical Plautine *adulescens*—bland, yearning, and invertebrate—cruelly vilifies and rejects Hero, 'you are more intemperate in your blood / Than Venus, or those pamp'red animals / That rage in savage sensuality' (IV. i. 59–61).[47] Leonato, the good father, vehemently denounces his daughter and wishes her dead. Like Capulet before him, he becomes *senex durus* and *iratus*, that harsh, unreasoning figure who was already a comic stereotype in Terence's day (cf. *HT* 37). Here, however, Leonato is not comic at all but powerful in his suffering, disturbing in his mistaken anger. The gentle *virgo* becomes the pitiable victim, Innocence Slandered as well as a girl whose reputation and wedding suffer ruin. The broken ceremony recalls the parodic wedding in *Shrew*, but displays more fully the subversive and dangerous energies of New Comedic intrigue.

Balancing this display, of course, is the contrasted affair of Beatrice and Benedick. New Comedic intrigue leads these lovers to put aside pride and prejudice, and, like their witty descendants, Mirabell and Millamant, to move beyond the limitations of classical characterization and romantic convention. The movement proceeds in clearly marked stages, beginning with the merry skirmish of wits and advancing to parallel humiliations in the orchard scenes. Then Beatrice and Benedick must endure the quips, sentences, and paper bullets (II. iii. 240–1) that friends aim at mockers who themselves fall in love. Don Pedro and Claudio mercilessly ride Benedick, the newly-shaved, civet-smelling, lute-playing

---

[47] Spenser develops the tragic possibilities here: his Claudio figure, Phedon, kills the slandered fiancé, poisons the intriguer, and suffers captivity by Furor (*Faerie Queene* II. iv. 16–38). For evidence (though not conclusive) that Shakespeare knew this version of the tale see Thaler, 'Spenser and *Much Ado About Nothing*'. Cf. the outraged Fortunio (*Fedele and Fortunio*, IV. ii. 17–19).

courtier (III. ii); Margaret professes the apprehension that Beatrice
momentarily seems to have lost, teasing her wittily about taking
carduus benedictus for her sickness (III. iv. 73–4). The wedding that
separates Claudio and Hero unites Beatrice and Benedick, who
pledge their love in a moving and hard-won moment of tenderness:

BENE. I protest I love thee.
BEAT. Why then, God forgive me!
BENE. What offence, sweet Beatrice?
BEAT. You have stay'd me in a happy hour, I was about to protest I lov'd
you.
BENE. And do it with all my heart.
BEAT. I love you with so much of my heart that none is left to protest.
(IV. i. 279–87).

As is characteristic of New Comedy, the fictions of Don Pedro,
Hero, and Ursula here become true in surprising and marvellous
ways. Their story of mutually unrequited love corresponds to the
reality always evident in Beatrice's and Benedick's teasing and in
their noisy protestations. Like Petruchio's fiction, Don Pedro's
transforms as well as reveals; it initiates the difficult process
whereby lovers grow in understanding and commitment to become
spouses.[48]

The onrush of emotions and events in Shakespeare's wedding
scene hastens this process, forcing Beatrice and Benedick to confront each other and come to terms. Benedick chivalrously
promises to 'do any thing' (IV. i. 288) for Beatrice, momentarily
posing as romance hero, Petrarchan wooer, or gallant knight-
errant. To Beatrice's command, 'Kill Claudio', Benedick responds,
'Ha, not for the wide world!' (289–90), abruptly terminating the
imposture, leaving two troubled human beings to work out the
complex negotiations of the heart in an imperfect world.
Shakespeare here resists the temptation to represent these negotiations in the shopworn terms of love versus friendship, though there
was ample precedent in Bandello and in his own *Two Gentlemen
of Verona* and *Merchant of Venice*. And unlike J. P. Kemble and
many in the nineteenth century, he refuses to oversimplify the
dynamics here, to flatten out the painful conflicts and delicate

---

[48] Perhaps this explains why one dramatist, at least, yielded to the temptation to
envision Beatrice and Benedick in later years, Sir John Hankin, *Dramatic Sequels*
(1926) (cited by Muir, *Sequence*, 80).

uncertainties into broad humour or amorous swagger.[49] This business is simply too private and complicated for theatrical, New
Comedic, or romantic formulas. When Benedick finally decides to
challenge Claudio, there is a reflective seriousness, gritty realism,
and pained inconclusiveness about the decision, qualities that
charge the old configurations with new meaning.

Neither Benedick's plan, nor those of any other clever plotter,
however, can undo deceitful practices in Messina. Instead, the resolution comes unlooked for, brought about largely by the Friar and
Dogberry, who both show in different ways the limits of New
Comedic intrigue. The Friar relieves tension and initiates the
upward movement from the nadir of the church scene. By observation he declares Hero innocent and contrives the plan to conceal
her, all the while pretending she is dead, in order to 'change slander to remorse' (IV. i. 211). The Friar aims this plot at Claudio:

> When he shall hear she died upon his words,
> Th'idea of her life shall sweetly creep
> Into his study of imagination,
> And every lovely organ of her life
> Shall come apparell'd in more precious habit,
> More moving, delicate, and full of life,
> Into the eye and prospect of his soul
> Than when she liv'd indeed. Then shall he mourn.   (IV. i. 223–30)

In full clerical garb, invoking his 'reverence', 'calling', and 'divin-
ity' (168), Friar Francis precisely articulates Bandello's plan for a
providential resolution. Hearing of Fenicia's death, 'Timbreo com-
inciò á sentir grandissima doglia, con vn certo inchiauamento di
core' (fol. 156v., 'Timbeo began to feel the greatest sorrow, with a
certain locking of his heart'). Thus begins the process, emphatically
depicted as divinely inspired, that leads to recognition and reunion.

The Friar's plan, however, fails spectacularly. In direct defiance
of his counterpart in Bandello, Claudio remains callously indifferent to Hero and her reported death. To underscore this indiffer-
ence, Shakespeare stages successive scenes in which Claudio
obtusely fails to respond or responds inappropriately to aggrieved
parties. When Leonato and Antonio accuse Claudio of killing Hero
and angrily challenge him to a duel, Claudio says nothing of the
lady but seems annoyed by the bother, 'Away, I will not have to

[49] See Cox, 'The Stage Representation of the "Kill Claudio" Sequence', 34–5.

do with you' (v. i. 77). Later, he jokes with Benedick, who also confronts him to no effect, 'We had lik'd to have had our two noses snapp'd off with two old men without teeth' (115–16). There is no excuse for such sour jesting, or for Claudio's subsequent concern with his own 'high-proof melancholy' (123), or for his and Don Pedro's incongruous attempts to engage Benedick in clever raillery. And this is exactly the point, though directors from Garrick's time onwards have opted to cut the scenes or shorten them.[50] This sequence demonstrates the manifest failure of the Friar's plan and suggests the limitations of comedic intrigue. Mere disguise and deception cannot effect meaningful repentance in Messina nor reverse the tragic impetus of the action.[51]

For these ends Shakespeare provides instead the redoubtable constable Dogberry and his men. Drawn, perhaps, from Munday's 'Sbirri' or local observation, Dogberry functions as the antitype of the clever slave: he is a *servus ineptus* whose fumblings in language and action mysteriously nullify subtler intrigues and reveal the hidden truth. Instead of planning intrigues or masterminding complicated actions, Dogberry instructs his men to turn away from trouble and do nothing, to ignore the disobedient, to let drunks alone, to let thieves steal out of their company, to sleep out their watch (III. iii). Unlike the classical slave, he cannot change identities with quicksilver speed and consummate skill; but, rather like Bottom, Dogberry always plays himself, the noble constable, guardian of the commonwealth. Far from controlling language and manipulating others through its skilful use, Dogberry utters speech that constantly misfires, shooting off in the wrong direction, reversing itself in hypallage and acyron, exploding in malapropism.[52] He fails to communicate the facts about Don John's deception to Leonato before the wedding (III. v); he misunderstands these facts in the hearing, thinking Borachio and Conrade guilty of 'flat perjury' and 'flat burglary' (IV. ii. 42, 50). Were it not for the watch, who overhears and apprehends the criminals, the Sexton, who makes sense of the situation, and Borachio himself, who confesses

[50] See Mares, 26–7, 36.
[51] The failure of an authoritarian and moralistic attempt to manage fiction reflects darkly on the entire humanist project. Their texts likewise revolt against the didactic hermeneutic that would organize and contain them; their audiences, like Claudio, read independently and unpredictably.
[52] See Vickers, *Artistry of Shakespeare's Prose*, 189–91.

all clearly to Don Pedro and Claudio, things in Dogberry's Messina would remain hopelessly entangled.

Yet, despite his ineptitude, or perhaps because of it, Shakespeare's constable presides officiously over the denouement. 'What your wisdoms could not discover, these shallow fools have brought to light' (v. i. 232–4), aptly observes Borachio. The constable functions as a bumbling *deus ex machina*, as an external remedy for the confusions which the plot engenders. In him Shakespeare again departs purposefully from his sources, which employ internal remedies: Ariosto's maid (Shakespeare's Margaret) tells all; Bandello's intriguer (Shakespeare's Don John) confesses. As Leggatt comments, 'Shakespeare is at pains to see that Don John's mischief is undone not by a change of heart in the erring characters, or by the intelligent intervention of Hero's friends, but by the impersonal workings of the plot.' Dogberry is a character invented for the *catastrophe*, 'persona ad catastrophen machinata', in Donatus' phrase;[53] he functions like other late-entering agents of denouement in New Comedy—the long-lost relative or the returning father, for example. And like Shakespearean versions of these agents, the Abbess in *Errors* and Vincentio in *Shrew*, the late-arriving Dogberry lives apart from the main action of the play but holds the solution to its various difficulties; he possesses the significant information that restores identity, clarifies action, and unties the knots.

This untying requires Claudio's reclamation. To depict Claudio's repentance Shakespeare could find few helpful precedents in classical comedy where the action moves primarily to resolution of the plot, to, in the words of Riccoboni, 'deceptionis purgationem', and not to character reformation.[54] In fact both the classical theory and practice of characterization discouraged such portrayal, advocating instead the presentation of recognizable types with propriety and consistency. We recall three of Aristotle's four requirements for characters (*Poet.* 1454a22 ff.): τὸ ἁρμόττοντα, appropriateness to expectation; τὸ ὅμοιον, likeness to traditional characters; τὸ ὁμαλόν, consistency in representation. There were also Cicero's well-known instructions regarding the maintenance of decorum and Horace's influential prescription (*Ars Poetica* 119–20): 'aut famam sequere aut sibi convenientia finge, / scriptor' ('Writer, either follow tradition,

---

[53] Leggatt, 162; Donatus, as quoted by Herrick, *Comic Theory*, 129.
[54] Ed. Weinberg, *Trattati*, iii. 265.

or create things [plots and characters] which are consistent with themselves'). Achilles must be always active, wrathful, relentless, and fierce ('impiger, iracundus, inexorabilis, acer', 121), Medea, savage and unconquerable ('ferox invictaque', 123), Ino, tearful ('flebilis', 123), and so on. Such theory well accorded with the practice of using recognizable dramatic names, costumes, and masks (Julius Pollux lists about forty-four masks for New Comedy). Rather than create an individual in the modern sense, comments Wiles, 'the masks expressed êthos, a fixed moral disposition to undertake action x rather than action y in a given situation'.[55]

Renaissance theorists established more detailed guidelines for comedic characterization. Scaliger propounded broad categories: 'Personarum distinctiones in Comoedia sunt à conditione, à professione, ab officio, ab aetate, à sexu.' These received further subdivision. Discussing costume, Trissino, for example, extended the taxonomy to include nation, city, kind, age, fortune, disposition, and occupation. Carriero went further still, expanding to ten the number of signifiers, under the rubric 'la moralità'. Once a recognizable type appeared, he or she was to observe decorum, to speak and act in accordance with conventional expectations. Such a poetic naturally discouraged the portrayal of change. In one of the most important treatises of the age, Robortello restated Aristotle's criterion of τὸ ὁμαλόν:

aequabiles enim ubique mores sint in poemate oportet, ut si semel timidum, avarum, superbum, aliquem ostenderis, eundem talem semper ostendas, non aliquando timidum, aliquando audacem, aliquando avarum, aliquando liberalem: summum enim hoc vitium in poemate.[56]

For it is fitting that everywhere in poems morals be consistent, so that if you show someone at one time timid, avaricious, proud, you should show him always the same, not sometimes timid, sometimes daring, sometimes avaricious, sometimes generous: for this is the greatest defect in poems.

This conception of characterization, of course, did not prevent playwrights like Menander, Plautus, and Terence from working fascinating variations within their constraints, from creating char-

---

[55] On classical characterization see Herrick, *Comic Theory*, 130 ff.; Robbins, 38 ff.; on Horace, Brink, *Horace on Poetry*, ii. 197 ff; on masks, Webster, *Monuments*; on comic stereotypes, MacCary, 'Menander's Characters'. The quotation belongs to Wiles, *Masks*, 24.

[56] Scaliger, 20; for Trissino, see Weinberg (ed.), *Trattati*, ii. 63; Carriero (iii. 289); Robortello (i. 525).

acters who played against their masks, names, and costumes. It did, however, have enormous affect on literary history, wherein comic characterization, according to Harry Levin, has always seemed 'more spatially oriented, by contrast, more static and two-dimensional. If there is any alteration, it is brought about through metamorphosis rather than growth: through sudden conversion or unmasked disguise or magical enchantment.' The Aristotelian poetic, as interpreted by later commentators, clearly militated against the presentation of individual change, at least in terms likely to be satisfying to post-classical audiences, not to mention post-Freudian ones, familiar with novels and films.[57] For such presentation later playwrights, who understood both drama and human nature differently, had to seek other models.

Confronting the moral and dramatic limitations of New Comedic characterization, Shakespeare tries a new model for Claudio and a different idiom altogether. Benedick's jocular reference to 'Don Worm (his conscience)' (v. ii. 84), immediately before Claudio's penitential ritual, provides an appropriately moral frame of reference.[58] Claudio appears as the Penitent, sincere, humble, and reverent. The ceremonious procession with torches, the ritualistic stage reading and song suggest 'the depth of Claudio's emotional response'.[59] Adapted Plautine farce gives way to a religious rite that is solemn and stylized, one that expresses symbolically not naturalistically the internal dynamics of contrition.

The solemn and ceremonial mode does not last long. Reverting to classical prescription and practice, Shakespeare stages a *cognitio* that is a discovery of identity, but one with a difference. Hero

---

[57] The oft-discussed classical exceptions prove the general rule. Demea's supposed conversion in Terence's *Adelphoe* (observed, for example, by Riccoboni, ed. Weinberg, *Trattati*, iii. 267–8) provides for a new form of aggression against his brother at the close. The fourth-act conversion of Menander's Knemon in *Dyskolos* does not extend to the fifth, where he relapses into anti-festive *duskolia* and is soundly thrashed for it. The quotation above belongs to Levin, *Playboys and Killjoys*, 64–5.

[58] Hunter (*Comedy of Forgiveness*, 103–5) calls Claudio a *humanum genus* figure who undertakes the process of penance described by Aquinas. Lewalski ('Love, Appearance and Reality') reads this scene as a crucial part in Claudio's Neoplatonic progress from sensual desire to higher love; see also Ormerod, 'Faith and Fashion'. Hassel, jun. (*Faith and Folly*, 80–90) observes the parallels between Claudio's experience and liturgical patterns in the Homilie of Repentance and the *Book of Common Prayer*. But Shakespeare cuts Claudio from several different, sometimes incompatible, cloths.

[59] Mulryne, *Shakespeare: 'Much Ado About Nothing'*, 10.

enters the scene veiled, posing as her cousin, Antonio's daughter. Unmasking, she becomes again her chaste and loving self, *virgo* not *meretrix*. Hero does not discover a new identity, lost daughter or Athenian citizen, but, instead, recovers an old one. Original image and present reality coincide, as Claudio's earlier realization of her innocence suggests:

> Sweet Hero, now thy image doth appear
> In the rare semblance that I lov'd it first.   (v. i. 251–2)

This recognition precisely reverses the terms of the false *cognitio* earlier:

> O Hero! what a Hero hadst thou been,
> If half thy outward graces had been placed
> About thy thoughts and counsels of thy heart!   (iv. i. 100–2)

Hero shows herself in firm control of the paradoxes implicit here, distinguishing between the false self, who died 'defil'd,' and the living maid (v. iv. 63–4). Whereas the classical *cognitio* tends to be circumstantial, to reveal external facts, this one, like that of the earlier intrigue, *The Taming of the Shrew*, expresses internal realities, reveals moral, emotional, and psychological truths. Hero enacts the role of the Italianate *donna mirabile*, the wondrous woman who betokens larger mysteries and often returns from death.[60] Hero's reappearance looks ahead to the more transcendent presences of Helena, Isabella, and Imogen.[61]

Shakespeare's treatment of Claudio also revises New Comedic practices, though to a lesser degree. Often in New Comedy, though not always, the *adulescens* is, by modern standards, a shallow character. In *Eunuchus*, we recall, Chaerea, disguises himself, rapes a young girl, and then, upon discovering her to be a citizen, joyfully plans the wedding. In *Hecyra* Pamphilus puts aside his wife because she had been raped. Discovering that he himself was the rapist, he magnanimously accepts her again. To a modern eye, characters like these seem culpably unethical, intolerably egocentric, insufficiently penitent, and unjustly rewarded. So precisely has

---

[60] See Clubb, *Italian Drama*, 65–89.

[61] And perhaps to the less transcendent one in Ionesco's parodic *Jack or the Submission*. Lifting her veil for the astonished fiancé, Jack, Roberta I reveals her two noses; responding to Jack's demand for a wife with three noses, she exits and returns as Roberta II, triply endowed. 'Sweet, let me see your face', indeed.

seemed Claudio, critical history amply attests, not to mention Shakespeare's other *adulescentes*—Proteus, Angelo, and Bertram.[62]

And yet, Shakespeare plans Claudio's reunion with Hero to suggest, in some limited sense, his own awakening. After noting Hero, trusting what he sees, according to Don John's advice (III. ii. 119), rejecting her on the basis of false appearances, Claudio finally accepts Hero sight unseen; he pledges his love before viewing her face. The gesture is histrionic and symbolic: ignoring appearances altogether, Claudio mends the ceremony he fractured earlier by giving the daughter back, this time taking another daughter from the hand of her father, now in total trust. Bevington comments, 'Stage picture answers stage picture in a theatrical motif of rebirth'.[63] Claudio's silence in this scene has long disappointed critics and audiences, who believe that Shakespeare, like Della Porta (*Gli duoi fratelli rivali*, pp. 274–5), for example, ought to provide some appropriate rhetoric to mark the magical moment. Yet, Claudio's silence on stage is meant precisely to express wonder and a 'gioia infinita colmo'. Shakespeare here takes his cue from Bandello's description:

A l'hora, alhora à queste parole s'apersero gli occhi de l'amoroso Caualiere, e gettatosi al collo de la sua Fenicia, quella mille fiate basciando, e di gioia infinita colmo, senza fine con fisi occhi miraua, e tutta via dolcemente piangeua, senza mai poter formar parola, chiamandosi tra se stesso ceco.   (fol. 16v.)

Then, at that time, at these words the eyes of the amorous cavalier were opened and, throwing himself on the neck of his Fenicia, kissing her many thousand times and full of infinite joy, he stared and marvelled at her incessantly. Still weeping softly, unable to form a word, he thought that he had been blind indeed.

Like *The Taming of the Shrew*, *Much Ado About Nothing* depicts New Comedic intrigue, especially courtship by mask, proxy, and impersonation. Stating and restating this theme, the plays create complicated music, replete with multiple phrasings, counterpoints, and harmonies. Both plays conclude with playful

---

[62] An exception to the chorus of disapproval is Neill, 'More Ado about Claudio'. Branagh's recent film version (1993) attempts to rehabilitate Claudio by heavy use of the camera: we see Claudio witnessing the supposed betrayal and—through focus on Robert Sean Leonard's young, innocent, and tearful face—his later sorrow and repentance.

[63] *Action is Eloquence*, 145.

variations on the theme for all the principal lovers: Lucentio discovers that Bianca will not always act the role of submissive wife; Kate transcends the role by zestful impersonation; Hero's unmasking concludes the various episodes of disguise and proxy that compose the play; and Beatrice and Benedick, struggling against their predestined roles even to the end, experience a final exposure: the familiar Petrarchan and courtly convention of sonnet-writing finally unmasks them, irrefutable proof that they live and sigh like other lovers. This conclusion may suggest to some the radical instability of the self, the contingency of all subjects as constructed by their cultures and immediate situations. More specifically, it shows that marriage will be an ongoing series of such posings and exposings, a constant putting-on and taking-off of those masks that define our identities to the world, to the spouse, and to ourselves. As such, it requires patience, trust, and forgiveness. Ariosto's English translator, John Harington, read the source tale tellingly as a story that persuades 'to concord in matrimonie'; he glossed the episode by extolling the virtue of kindness in marriage.[64]

Much Ado About Nothing clearly demonstrates the darker potential of New Comedic intrigue. Adeptly manipulating familiar devices, Don John turns the game of disguise and deceit into a tragic coil. His malice and his method anticipate the later machinations of Claudius, Iago, and Edmund. The play also explores the limitations—dramatic and moral—of New Comedic characterization and action. Shakespeare departs from the traditional *adulescens* figure, drawing upon other traditions for Claudio's penance scene. He also revises the classical *virgo*, enlivening Hero with charm, providing for a wondrous rebirth. The intrigue action, especially its privileging of human wit (*ingenium*) receives throughout critical scrutiny and adaptation. In other Renaissance revisions of New Comedic intrigue, Jonson's *The Alchemist* and Marston's *The Dutch Courtesan*, for example, deceptions cross and multiply in dazzling succession, and only the cleverest intriguers win at the end. In *Much Ado*, however, clever plotting often backfires, and it takes a Dogberry, with a little help from his friends, to set things right.

How different all this—especially the resolution—is from the sources and adaptations must give us pause. Commentators on the

---

[64] *Orlando furioso* (1591; repr. 1970), 39.

original tale in Ariosto read the story as an illustration of providential justice. For Ieronimo Ruscelli the tale demonstrated 'che Iddio giustissimo non lascia mai lungamente lieti gli sclerati nel mal far loro, nè oppresi i buoni nella loro innocentia' ('that the most just God does not leave for long the wicked joyful in their malice, nor does He forsake the oppressed good in their innocence'). Aluigi Gonzago likewise concluded that God always defends the innocent, 'sempre la innocenza e difesa da Iddio'; Tomasso Porcacchi also thought that the tale 'ci fa conoscere quanto la giustitia sia grata alla Maestà di Dio' ('makes us know how pleasing justice is to the majesty of God'). 'In Geneuras accusation and deliuerie,' wrote John Harington, we may see 'how god euer defends the innocent'; 'in Polynessos death, how wickednesse ruines it selfe'. Bandello insistently preserves this emphasis as does Della Porta in *Gli duoi fratelli rivali*, whose Eufranone thanks the God who has arranged everything and who 'ha fatto che le disaventure diventino venture e le pene allegrezze' ('has so wrought that misfortunes become good fortune and sorrows become joys').[65]

Shakespeare never preaches so blatantly, but depicts here instead the workings of a benevolent comedic *tyche*, or chance. Of the three crucial eavesdroppings in the play (Claudio on Hero, the setups of Benedick and Beatrice, the Watch on Borachio), R. Levin observes, the last is the only chance encounter.[66] This depiction of chance harks back to the ancient *tyche* that arranges accident and brings order from confusion.[67] *Tyche* is the tutelary goddess and prologue of Menander's *Aspis*, πάντων κυρία / τούτων βραβεῦσαι καὶ διοικῆσαι (147–8, 'the master of all these things, the one who arbitrates and controls'). Given local habitation and a name in the bumbling constable and his men, *tyche* converts sounds of woe in this world to 'Hey nonny, nonny'. The ritualistic repentance scene, the rebirth of Hero, the final Friar-led procession to the chapel, and Beatrice's exclamation, 'A miracle', lightly suggest that such chance, here as in Greek New Comedy, is part of providential

[65] Ruscelli, *Orlando furioso* (1585), 37; Gonzaga, *Orlando furioso* (1542), fol. 19v.; Porcacchi, *Orlando furioso* (1580), 19; *Orlando furioso* (1591; repr. 1970), 39; Della Porta, tr. Clubb, 280–1.

[66] Levin, *Multiple Plot*, 90–1.

[67] See Täubler, *Tyche*; Gomme and Sandbach, 73–4; Zagagi, 'Divine Interventions and Human Agents in Menander', in Handley and Hurst (1990), 63–91.

design.[68] These suggestions of larger mysteries, and they are the slightest of suggestions, find development in later plays, especially the romances. Here it is enough to bring the lovers together in a final dance that answers to the earlier confusions of the masked ball, joyfully symbolizing individual happiness and social concord.

[68] See Lloyd-Jones, *Greek Comedy*, 24. Frye (*Anatomy*, 183) perceives in this design 'the mythical outline of a Proserpine figure'.

4

New Comedic *Alazoneia*

IN addition to errors and intrigues, New Comedy contributed to Shakespeare and Renaissance drama the *alazon* or boaster, one of the three principal comedic characters named in *Tractatus Coislinianus* (xii). Ἀλαζών signifies in Greek a range of meanings that include pretender, impostor, charlatan, and braggart. Aristotle defined the *alazon* as a boaster who 'pretends to creditable qualities that he does not possess or possesses in a lesser degree than he makes out' (*Nicomachean Ethics* 1127a22–3, tr. Rackham). Theophrastus (*Characters* 23) contributed a full character sketch. Such a figure, along with his opposite number, the *eiron*, appeared in comedy from its beginnings.[1] Probably remembering the braggarts of the comic stage, in fact, Plato had identified pretentious self-ignorance as fundamental to the ridiculous (τὸ γελοῖον); we laugh at those who pretend to wealth, strength, or beauty, who consider themselves superior in moral or intellectual qualities, without really being so, ἀρετῇ δοξάζοντες βελτίους ἑαυτούς, οὐκ ὄντες (*Philebus* 48e9–10). Again pertinent is Aristotle's influential formulation: ἀλλὰ τοῦ αἰσχροῦ ἐστι τὸ γελοῖον μόριον. τὸ γὰρ γελοῖόν ἐστιν ἁμάρτημά τι καὶ αἶσχος ἀνώδυνον καὶ οὐ φθαρτικόν (*Poet.* 1449a33–5, 'what is laughable, however, always derives in part from what is ugly. The laughable consists in some fault, error, or deformity that is not painful and not destructive.'). *Tractatus Coislinianus* viii refined Aristotle's definition by explaining that such faults were of two types—those of the soul and those of the body (ἁμαρτήματα τῆς ψυχῆς καὶ τοῦ σώματος). Italian commentators on Aristotle, we have already noted, likewise understood τὸ αἰσχρόν in two senses, as ugliness of the soul and of the body: 'la bruttezza é duplice, cioè dell'anima e del corpo'.[2] They routinely

---

[1] On *alazoneia* see Ribbeck, *Alazon*; Cornford, *Origins*, 115 ff. Janko, 216–18; Lloyd-Jones, *Greek Comedy*, 26. On Plato below, see Webster, *Studies in Later Greek Comedy*, 57.

[2] For Trissino, see Weinberg (ed.), *Trattati*, ii. 71; cf. Maggi (ii. 93–125); Pino (ii. 635–40); Castelvetro, *Poetica*, fols. 50v. ff.

placed *alazoneia*, variously translated, in the former category. By the time of the Renaissance then, *alazoneia* was one of the recognizable uglinesses of soul that comedy ridiculed. Translating *alazoneia* as 'ostentatio', Riccoboni identified a literary *locus classicus* in Terence's *miles gloriosus*, or braggart soldier. Among the general deceptions that please in comedy, he noted the following:

Quae ex falsa opinione, cum quis falso putat se excellere in artibus quibusdam et in viribus corporis aut animi, atque in his inaniter se iactat, qualis ostentatio Thrasonis apud Terentium.[3]

That which derives from false opinion, as when someone falsely thinks that he excels in certain arts or in strength of body or mind, and so shows himself off hollowly in these things, such as the boasting of Thraso in Terence.

Many centuries after Terence, John of Salisbury could appropriate Thraso's *ostentatio* as a symbol for every species of professional vanity: 'omnis professio suos Trasones habet'.[4]

As the above quotations suggest, Latin New Comedy supplied later ages with prototypal depictions of *alazoneia* in the characters of boasting soldiers.[5] The two central texts, of course, are Plautus' *Miles Gloriosus* (based on an anonymous *Alazon*) and Terence's *Eunuchus*, both favourites of Renaissance translators and adaptors. Typically the New Comedic *miles gloriosus* brags about prowess in war and love, appropriating the two discourses into a patently false rhetoric of power. The ancient concentricity of military and amorous impulses charges the action of Renaissance stages in Italy, France, Spain (especially the *comedias de capa y espada*, 'the cloak-and-sword plays' of the Golden Age), and England.[6] Shakespeare's Armado, Falstaff (as he appears in the history plays and in Windsor), Pistol, and Parolles bear an obvious family resemblance and draw dramatic strength from the bloodlines.[7] This great comic tradition Richard Steele confronted directly in his dissident varia-

---

[3] Weinberg (ed.), *Trattati*, iii. 275.

[4] As quoted by Theiner, *The Learned and the Lewed*, ed. Benson, 242.

[5] As ever, ancient dramatists worked skilful variations on the type; Menander's *Perikeiromene* and *Misoumenos*, for example, feature relatively modest soldiers, sympathetically portrayed. On soldiers in New Comedy see Duckworth, 264–5; Hunter, *New Comedy*, 66–71.

[6] See Boughner, *Braggart*; Hanson, 'The Glorious Military', in Dorey and Dudley (1965), 51–85. See also Lucian's clever variation, *Dialogues of the Courtesans*, xiii.

[7] *Pace* Maurice Morgann, who argued notoriously for Falstaff's courage, *An Essay on the Dramatic Character of Sir John Falstaff* (1777; rev. 1789–90).

tion, *The Conscious Lovers*, a revision of *Andria* that features the chaste and modest Bevil Junior pointedly avoiding a duel in the scene 'the whole was writ for' (Preface, 18–19). Whatever the worthy *exempla* illustrated by Bevil Junior, neither the scene nor the play is very funny.

The *Merry Wives of Windsor* and *Much Ado About Nothing* variously anatomize *alazoneia*. Both prominently feature boasting soldiers, whom Shakespeare employs variously, creating riotous confusions, exploring the relations between military and amorous impulses. Both plays present multiple variations on the braggart soldier, his central *alazoneia* echoed in diverse characters and situations. Both define the imposture as an overestimation of self and an underestimation of others, particularly women. Both feature a *cognitio* that takes the form of humiliating exposure, the prescribed ridicule. The articulation in each case, however, is quite different. *The Merry Wives of Windsor* depicts *alazoneia* in an English Windsor that is largely shaped by another Plautine deep source—*Casina*—and by its Italian descendants. *All's Well* owes to the novella, Boccaccio's *Decameron*, and to Terence's *Hecyra*. In both plays classical, neo-classical, and non-classical elements engage each other dynamically, creating multiple accommodations, striking diverse balances. *Wives* features an *alazoneia* that is an important but subordinate element in a larger intertextual mix. *All's Well* centres its action on *alazoneia*, presenting variations that resemble, engage, and contest each other.

The Merry Wives of Windsor

Lacking a clear main source, this play combines eclectically folklore, contemporary prose fiction, the Italian novella, medieval antecedents, and classical traditions, the last elements appearing as the least in most discussions of sources.[8] Yet, *Wives* draws on *Miles Gloriosus*, *Eunuchus*, and on enormously popular descendant traditions to depict Falstaff and his exposure. Moreover, and more pervasively, the play draws on configurations and conventions

---

[8] Additionally, Gurr ('Intertextuality at Windsor') demonstrates the influence of contemporary theatrical fashions and conditions, including rivalries between repertories.

originating in Plautus' *Casina* to depict Windsor and its citizens. Though Forsythe overstated the case, he set forth persuasive evidence for this influence, well observing that both *Casina* and *Wives* feature a husband and wife who support different suitors to a young girl, that this girl loves a third person and eventually marries him, that both sets of wives similarly conspire against a foolish husband, that both dramas work to the climax of a mock-wedding in which the bride is discovered to be a male.[9] Here we need not succumb to the fallacy of misplaced specification to recognize important affinities.

As elsewhere, Shakespeare adapts his New Comedic heritage in Italian style. Campbell notes the Italianate triple wooing of Anne Page and observes the *pedante* in Falstaff and Sir Hugh Evans, the *zanni* in the Host, the *medico* in Dr Caius, and the *fantesca* in Mistress Quickly. Salingar remarks Shakespeare's use of the Italianate double plot 'with its confusions of identity and crossed complications', his preference for multiple marriages and subordinate deceptions (like *beffe*), and concludes: 'paradoxically, the play in which he comes nearest to a wholesale adoption of Italian methods and an Italian manner is *The Merry Wives of Windsor*, his only comedy set in England'.[10]

These observations suggest an approach that can justly evaluate Shakespeare's wide-ranging neo-classicism in this play. The central *alazon*, Falstaff, descendant of Pyrgopolynices and Thraso, resides in a world created by Italian dramatists. *The Merry Wives of Windsor* belongs specifically to that family of plays that adapt *Casina* eclectically, mixing in other contemporary and classical elements, often a braggart soldier. Beatrice M. Corrigan first noted the common elements and variations in this group of plays— Machiavelli's *Clizia* (1525), Berrardo's, *La cassina* (1530, a translation of Plautus), Dolce's *Il ragazzo* (c. 1541), Della Porta's *La fantesca*, Lanci's *La ruchetta* (1584), Cecchi's *I rivali*, and the anonymous and unpublished Sienese *Il capriccio* (1566–8).[11] To this

[9] 'A Plautine Source of *The Merry Wives of Windsor*'. Forsythe did not take into account the possibility of intermediation; the feature of three rival suitors, for example, is an Italian innovation already put to good use in *Two Gentlemen of Verona* and *Shrew*. See also Frye, *Anatomy*, 167; Salingar, *Traditions*, 173; Bullough, ii. 9.

[10] Campbell, 'The Italianate Background of *The Merry Wives of Windsor*'; Salingar, *Traditions*, 190; see also Clubb, *Italian Drama*, 24–5.

[11] '*Il capriccio*: an Unpublished Italian Renaissance Comedy and its Analogues'.

list we may also add a descendant of *Clizia*, Gelli's *Lo errore*
(1556). Offering a wide range of dramatic and interpretive possibilities, these plays represent a related series of ingenious adaptations
rather than a coherent group; together they gather contemporary
responses to a seminal classical play and present a lexicon of theatrical possibilities. Shakespeare need not have studied this lexicon
directly to have picked up the language; in this regard traditions
speak much louder and longer than individual texts. Shakespeare's
reworking of *Casina*, *The Merry Wives of Windsor*, freely recom-
bines all the important constituents of the Italian versions: the
emphasis on jealousy, sometimes embodied in a scheming wife; a
ridiculous *senex amans*; a boasting soldier; romantic young lovers;
and, the signature motif, a male disguised as a bride. (There are
also echoes in *Wives* of other Italian innovations—an impudent
boy and a Latin-speaking *pedante*.) *Wives* arranges the standard
elements into new configurations: the jealousy appears in the husband Ford, not the wife, and motivates a parallel action; the wife
becomes the merry wives who control the major intrigues of the
play, a transformation that recovers the original dynamic of
Casina. The *senex amans* and *miles gloriosus*, along with various
other medieval and classical figures, conjoin in the stuffed figure of
Falstaff. Eros turns into romance Italian style: the lusty *adulescens*
becomes the loving Fenton, the silent and absent Casina, the win-
some Anne Page. The boy disguised as a bride, doubled, provides a
climax to a subordinate plot and accompanies the other humiliating exposures in the play. Shakespeare brilliantly redefines and
rearranges traditional elements to create an English comedy that is,
paradoxically, both classical and Italianate as well.

Annotating Plautus' *Casina*, Lodovico Castelvetro opined that
the son's love affair was 'senza niun valore, che bastava che la
moglie si fosse aveduta, che il marito fosse inamorato della serva'
('without value; it was sufficient that the wife be jealous and the
husband be in love with the servant').[12] Castelvetro's identification
of jealousy as an essential plot element echoes in the Italian adaptations, which often portray this passion. Della Porta's *La fantesca*,
for example, features Gelosia as the prologue and this passion
motivates the major actions of the play. Transferring the jealousy

---

These plays engendered others, thus extending the family lines; Dolce's *Il ragazzo*,
for example, found new life in Pierre de Larivey's *Le Laquais*.

[12] Castelvetro, 'Parere', 68.

from the wife to Ford, Shakespeare depicts it as another form of the *alazoneia* that overestimates the self and underestimates a woman. The wives' battle against the tendency to reduce them to sexual objects, possessions carefully guarded but easily stolen, has actually two fronts, one without and one within Windsor; Falstaff's noisy narcissism finds reflection in Ford's obsessive jealousy. Like a braggart soldier, Ford congratulates himself on his own percipience and vigilance, 'God be prais'd for my jealousy!' (II. ii. 309). He mocks the trusting Page as 'an ass, a secure ass' (300–301), and delights in his own invention, his plot to expose his wife, whom he misprizes as 'a false woman' (292).

Ford's jealousy motivates a subordinate action that mirrors the main action of *Casina*, namely the exposure of a foolish husband by a smart wife. To portray Ford's folly, Shakespeare reverts to his earliest experiment with Plautus, *The Comedy of Errors*. Like Antipholus of Syracuse who wonders whether he is 'Sleeping or waking, mad or well-advis'd' (II. ii. 213), Ford ponders his state, 'Hum! ha? Is this a vision? Is this a dream? Do I sleep? Master Ford, awake!' (III. v. 139–40). Here Plautine bewilderment results not from the simple error of mistaken identity, but from more complex misjudgement of his wife and self. Moreover, like the other twin, Antipholus of Ephesus (III. i), Ford angrily storms his house in the company of restraining friends (III. ii–iii, IV. ii). And both times he, like the town twin, leaves dissatisfied, convinced that his wife has been unfaithful. This scenario, deriving partly from *Amphitruo* as well, we have already observed in more disturbing form in *Ado*. Here Shakespeare works a new variation on the dramatic situation, this time portraying the jealous husband as a complementary fool to the braggart soldier-lover. (Jonson used essentially the same strategy with Thorello and Bobadilla in *Every Man in his Humour*.) In contradistinction to Falstaff, however, Ford moves from ostentatious self-love to the humble trust of another in marriage, a progress which recalls similar developments in *Errors*, *Shrew*, and *Ado*. Ford repents in verse, in lines dignified and convincing:

> Pardon me, wife, henceforth do what thou wilt.
> I rather will suspect the sun with cold
> Than thee with wantonness. Now doth thy honour stand,
> In him that was of late an heretic,
> As firm as faith.   (IV. iv. 6–10)

Together husband and wife plan the final exposure of the other *alazon*, Falstaff, bedecked, appropriately, in horns.

Shakespeare's striking transformation of the classical *matrona* into Mrs Page and Mrs Ford has rarely been noted or appreciated. Though these wives differ markedly from their unchaste counterparts in the novella tales frequently adduced as sources, critics have been reluctant to consider classical precedents. Most, in fact, subscribing too closely to the notion of stock characters, have seen the wives as anti-classical; witness, for example, Ruth Nevo: 'Shakespeare's New Comedy inverts traditional feminine roles, thus transforming a male-oriented, male-dominated perspective into its antithetical opposite.'[13] Such a generalization, though commonly held, ignores the demonstrable diversity of women and their roles in New Comedy, not to mention the dominating females of Aristophanes' *Lysistrata*, *Ecclesiazusae*, and *Thesmophoriazusae*. Plautus depicts the chaste and virtuous *matrona* Alcumena (*Amphitruo*) as well as the *virago* Artemona (*Asinaria*). Terence's Sostrata, instead of scolding her husband, gets scolded by him and is wrongly held responsible for her son's problems throughout *Hecyra*.

Of course, we need look no further than *Casina* itself to find precedent for Shakespeare's merry wives. As Forehand has shown, Plautus presents here a highly individualized *matrona* who outmanoeuvres her husband through clever tricks; he also presents a unique *senex*, one whom lecherous passion totally dominates.[14] Shakespeare, likewise, features sharp and witty wives practising against a passionately jealous husband. In both cases the wife relies on her neighbour and good friend (Myrrhina/Mrs Page). The action in both plays proceeds through humorous reversals and culminates in the husband's apology, the wife's forgiveness, and the final reconciliation. Reconstituted *matronae*, these wives take their place with Shakespeare's other variations on this classical figure— the Abbess in *Errors*, and the Countess of Rossillion.

[13] *Comic Transformations*, 160. The play resists the schematic gender readings now in fashion. Backing the suit of Dr Caius, Mrs Page, no less than Mr Page, plays a comic blocking figure whom the young lovers outwit. Frantz (*Festum Voluptatis*, 230–45) discusses the play in the context of Renaissance erotica.

[14] 'Plautus' *Casina*: An Explication'. Forsythe aptly compares both first scenes in the second act, wherein wife meets friend on the way to each other's house. The arrival of Lysidamus breaks off one conversation, 'uir eccum it' (213, 'Look, my husband's coming'), just as the arrival of Ford breaks off the other, 'Why, look where he comes' (II. i. 102).

It is a long way from Cleustrata to Mistress Ford, but some of the distance had already been travelled by Italians. The two playwrights who follow *Casina* most closely, Lanci and Machiavelli, expand the roles and characters of the *matrona*. In the conclusion of *La ruchetta* Cassandra pardons her erring husband, at the request of her friend, Gostanza ('Horsu Cassandra perdonategli per amor mio'); the husband gratefully responds, 'Non credo che sia al mondo huomo, che habbia la piu piaceuol moglie della mia' ('I don't think there is a man in all the world who has a more pleasing wife than mine').[15] Discussing *Clizia*, Radcliff-Umstead notes the major changes in Machiavelli's portrait of the wife, Sofronia:

Whereas Plautus' Cleostrata is always finding fault with her husband, insulting him at every occasion, Sofronia attacks Nicomaco only because of his failure to preserve the dignity of his age and because of the bad example he has set for his son. Sofronia is never jealous; Cleostrata is jealous even when there is no cause. . . . Cleostrata forgives her husband only because of the technical necessity of ending the comedy, but Sofronia pardons her husband because of her affection for him. All the efforts of the wife in Machiavelli's play are made to shock Nicomaco out of his amorous madness; Sofronia has to use brutal means to wake him from his dream of sensual delight. When he surrenders, she is ready to forget everything. Machiavelli has depicted this woman as a thoughtful and loving wife.[16]

In Gelli's reworking of this play, *Lo errore*, Mona Francesca likewise humiliates her husband then grants him forgiveness, but not before she forces him to agree to their son's marriage. Mrs Ford makes one with this good company of women: all defend themselves and their marriages from the crazed passion of the husband; all use for a principal weapon a remarkable *astuzia*; and in the end, all are loving and forgiving wives in reconstituted partnerships.

The *matrona* is not the only classical precedent for Shakespeare's witty wives; in their duping of Falstaff they strongly resemble the wily courtesan and maid of *Miles Gloriosus*. Shakespeare's adaptation of these crafty women, perhaps recalled as well in *Ado*, here proceeds by converting the courtesan to wife, a process first performed in *Errors*. Mrs Ford is an English descendant of Acroteleutium, while Mrs Page, like Milphidippa, plays an ancillary role in the deceit.[17] The women in Plautus' play and the wives

---

[15] *La ruchetta* (1584), 92, 93.   [16] *Birth*, 137.

[17] Their ancestors may also include Phronesium and Astaphium from

in Shakespeare's merrily lead the braggart on, remarking his fatuity, delighting in their own abilities to act and deceive. Both pairs inveigle the soldier into the house of a jealous husband (a pretended one in Plautus). Both pairs contrive and enjoy his exposure and ridicule.

Plautus' *meretrix* and Shakespeare's wives use sex and deceit as weapons against those men who would reduce them to objects of lust or to mere possessions. Their methods recall Menander's clever Habrotonon in *Epitrepontes*, who likewise uses shrewd insight and theatrical ability to trick men. Acroteleutium and Milphidippa are allied literally and figuratively to Palaestrio, the clever slave who marvels at feminine cunning and who tricks his way into freedom and power. Living by their wits, the powerless achieve comic triumph by rebelling against roles that are servile and by turning the social order upside down. Mrs Ford and Mrs Page also achieve comic triumph: they prove that wives can be chaste and merry too.[18] Unlike those disadvantaged sharpsters in Plautus, however, the wives are privileged, respectable members of a healthy community that repeatedly concerns itself with the ordinary particulars of everyday living—laundry, school lessons, birding, eating, drinking, wooing, and wedding. And instead of turning the social order upside down, they actually confirm the status quo, uniting against an impoverished outsider, a courtly intruder in the bourgeois setting, a would-be predator on the domestic harmonies that compose the world of Windsor. The wives' virtue, of course, has larger implications: it supports conventional morality and safeguards the transfer of property in a patriarchal system. Moreover, in a play celebrating the Order of the Garter, the wives' domestic conflation of chastity and power mirrors the national situation

Truculentus, as well as the forceful females from English drama, e.g., Dame Christian Custance who sternly rejects and beats the amorous braggart, Ralph Roister Doister; the captured woman who overpowers her conqueror in *Horestes*; and Mistress Meretrix, who routs Huff, Ruff, and Snuff in *Cambyses*. But these use physical strength not wit. Some appreciation of classical, Italian, or native traditions might have modified Parker's ('*The Merry Wives of Windsor* and Shakespearean Translation') reading of *translatio* and the female in the play as secondary, accessory, or defective.

[18] In this achievement they contrast with other wives in Renaissance drama: Grévin's Agnes (*Les Esbahis*), for example, mistress to three men, expert in the art of love, justifies her actions by mocking her husband's 'decroissance' (2401); Cervantes' Mistress Lorenza (*The Jealous Old Husband*), in action resembling that of *Wives*, dupes her husband while entertaining a lover.

under Elizabeth, at least as theorized by poets and by the Queen herself.[19]

Falstaff too embodies and transforms New Comedic classical characters, expanding them well beyond the boundaries, however spacious, of any single type.[20] Primarily, he is a *miles gloriosus*, that boasting soldier/lover who descends from Euripides' Herakles, Aristophanes' Lamakhos, down through Menander's soldiers and those of Plautus and Terence, through Italian and English ancestors as well.[21] Here too he resembles the familiar *senex amans*, the old man who presumes to be a lover, but is found to be 'Old, cold, wither'd, and of intolerable entrails' (v. v. 153–4). These two classical types were traditional targets of much Italian comedy including those plays descending from *Casina* (Della Porta's *La fantesca* features two braggarts, Capitano Dante and Capitano Pantaleone). Freely adding other types and traditions, Shakespeare combines them into one enormous figure, drawing all into coherence by the fat rogue's 'admirable dexterity of wit' (IV. v. 117–18).[22] In his mixed ancestry Falstaff resembles Molière's great comic creation Harpagon of *L'Avare*, direct descendant of Plautus' miserly Euclio,

---

[19] See Erickson, 'The Order of the Garter, the Cult of Elizabeth, and Class-Gender Tension in *The Merry Wives of Windsor*', in Howard and O'Connor (1987), 116–40; Neely, 'Constructing Female Sexuality in the Renaissance', in Levin and Robertson (1991), 1–26; Berry, *Of Chastity and Power*.

[20] See Duckworth, 416; Draper, 'Falstaff and the Plautine Parasite'; Doran, 159: 'the discomfited Falstaff of the *Merry Wives* is far nearer the type of amorous old man of Plautine and Italian comedy than is the more complex Falstaff of the history plays.' Barton ('Falstaff and the Comic Community', in Erickson and Kahn (1985), 131–48) finds precedents in Aristophanes.

[21] For other antecedents see Hunter, *New Comedy*, 163 n. 18. Aside from his earlier incarnation in the history plays, the Windsor Falstaff's most important ancestor is the Italianate Spaniard Armado (see Campbell, '*LLL* Re-studied'). Both soldiers engage in a *senex–puer* dialogue with a page; both are compared to ancient heroes and mythological figures (*LLL* I. ii. 63 ff; 173 ff., the show of the Worthies; *Wives* I. iii. 6 ff.). Both pursue unreceptive women by a letter which is derisively read aloud (*LLL* IV. i; *Wives* II. i). The pursuits culminate in a pageant or 'sport', wherein each suffers exposure and mockery. After the pageant there are some motions of reintegration: Armado vows to 'hold the plough' (v. ii. 883–4) for Jaquenetta for three years; the abashed Falstaff gets invited to dinner at Page's house (v. v. 170–3).

[22] Mrs Page calls him 'a Herod of Jewry' (II. i. 20) thus evoking the blustering tyrant from the miracle plays. As always, Falstaff resembles the Vice, the Prodigal Son, and the Lord of Misrule. Several have seen him as the scapegoat or the central character in folk rituals: Roberts, *Shakespeare's English Comedy*, 77–83; Bryant, jun., 'Falstaff and the Renewal of Windsor'; Parten, 'Falstaff's Horns'; Gallenca, 'Ritual and Folk Custom in *The Merry Wives of Windsor*'.

simultaneously the *senex amans* in rivalry with his son, and the blocking father who opposes his daughter's marital plans.

Prominent in Falstaff's genealogy is Terence's Thraso. This famous *miles gloriosus* Shakespeare honours several times in the adjective 'thrasonical' (*LLL* v. i. 12; *AYL* v. ii. 31), which in context implies vanity, affectation, and ridiculous military pretension. Recalling the 'kind of knowledge of Terence which would be drilled into every third-former in grammar school', T. W. Baldwin declared, 'I believe it is certain that the Falstaff of *Merry Wives* has been evolved from the source story under the influence of *Eunuchus*'.[23] Both plays feature the same configuration of characters: a love triangle consisting of a much-desired woman (Thais) who coolly commands the attentions of two men—one a jealous fool, the other a bragging soldier. The action results in satisfaction of the first and humiliation of the second, proceeding, 'through the conventional one, two, three stages from *epitasis* to *catastrophe* of the five-act formula'. Like Thraso, Falstaff gets invited to the final feast.

Baldwin also points to verbal parallels between the two plays, recollecting at one point Malone's citation of *Eunuchus* 550–2 as a gloss for *Othello*, a parallel also observed by Whalley and Colman.[24]

> CHAEREA: iamne erumpere hoc licet mi gaudium? pro Iuppiter,
> nunc est profecto interfici quom perpeti me possum,
> ne hoc gaudium contaminet vita aegritudine aliqua.   (550–2)

Now may this joy of mine break out? O God! Now is the time I could endure death so that life would not contaminate this joy with some sickness or woe.

> OTHELLO: If it were now to die,
> 'Twere now to be most happy; for I fear
> My soul hath her content so absolute
> That not another comfort like to this
> Succeeds in unknown fate.   (ii. i. 189–93)

To these passages Baldwin compares Falstaff's protestation to Mrs Ford: ' "Have I caught thee, my heavenly jewel?" Why, now let me die, for I have liv'd long enough. This is the period of my

---

[23] *Five-Act*, 559; the quotation below is from *Literary Genetics*, 456.
[24] *Five-Act*, 556 ff. The passage appears in Udall's handbook, *Flowres for Latine Speaking*, fol. 71r.

ambition. O this blessed hour!' (III. iii. 43–6). Baldwin notes that the speeches of Chaerea and Falstaff occupy parallel positions, one immediately after the satisfaction of desire, the other immediately before, that they express the same sentiment, that both speakers in the course of action resort to an absurd disguise. Ludicrously Falstaff here adopts the famous idiom of a famous young lover, the impetuous and passionate Chaerea, in order to loosen Mrs Ford's lace and her husband's purse strings.

Malone adduced for himself the other parallel Baldwin rehearses, namely the remembrances of Jove's heavy descensions into mortal form for love. In a notorious passage Chaerea excuses his rape of Pamphila by describing a picture he saw:[25]

> ibi inerat pictura haec, Iovem
> quo pacto Danaae misisse aiunt quondam in gremium imbrem aureum
> egomet quoque id spectare coepi, et quia consimilem luserat
> iam olim ille ludum, inpendio magis animu' gaudebat mihi,
> deum sese in hominem convortisse atque in alienas tegulas
> venisse clanculum per inpluviam fucum factum mulieri.
> at quem deum! 'qui templa caeli summa sonitu concutit.'
> ego homuncio hoc non facerem? ego illud vero ita feci—ac lubens.
>   (584–91)

In there was a painting, showing how Jove sent down a golden rain onto Danae's bosom, just as the story goes. I began to stare at it, and because that one had already played a similar game long ago, my spirit rejoiced all the more greatly. A god had turned himself into a man and come secretly on to another's roof-tiles! Through the rain hole he deceived a woman! And what a god! 'He who shakes the temples of heaven with his mighty thunder!' Was I, a mere mortal man, not to do likewise? I did so do likewise—and gladly!

Compare Falstaff anticipating his rendezvous in Windsor forest:

The Windsor bell hath strook twelve; the minute draws on. Now, the hot-bloodied gods assist me! Remember, Jove, thou wast a bull for thy Europa, love set on thy horns. O powerful love, that in some respects makes a beast a man; in some other, a man a beast. You were also, Jupiter, a swan for the love of Leda. O omnipotent love, how near the god drew to the complexion of a goose! A fault done first in the form of a beast (O Jove, a beastly fault!) and then another fault in the semblance of

---

[25] *Five-Act*, 554–5. See Augustine's objections to the passage, *Confessions*, bk. i, ch. 16; these are rehearsed by Gambara, ed. Weinberg. *Trattati*, iii. 222–3.

a fowl—think on't, Jove, a foul fault! When gods have hot backs, what shall poor men do? (v. v. 1–12)

We note the similar questions, 'ego homuncio hoc non facerem?' and 'what shall poor men do?'.[26] Marsus glossed the Terentian passage by citing Cicero: 'Luxuria vero cum omni aetati turpis est, tum senectuti foedissima est' ('Lust, indeed, is base in every age, but most foul in the old'). Thus, Baldwin remarks, the Terentian tradition, specifically the commentaries on *Eunuchus*, may have initially suggested the idea of a *senex amans* ludicrously looking to Jove's example.[27]

The force and fun of both recollections derive from the incongruity of the young lover's words in the old knight's mouth; together they characterize Falstaff as *senex amans*, the traditional target of the Italian plays derived from *Casina*. Discussing the scene in *Eunuchus*, Donatus notes how *adulescentes* are lead by 'calore iuvenali'; so too Muretus: 'Annota hinc inhonestis picturis iuuenum animos ad nequitiam incitari' ('shown here is how the souls of young men are incited to evil by shameful pictures').[28] Such passion appears grossly ludicrous in the aged, corpulent knight, decked out with stag's horns. Furthermore, no picture inspires Falstaff's mythological reverie; it is self-generated, an invocation and prayer to Jove for success in seduction. Pondering the transformations of beasts, men, and gods, reflecting on the power of eros and on the instability of identity, Falstaff imbues the Terentian passage with distinctly Ovidian colours.[29] Ironically enough, he does not attend to the darker possibilities of metamorphosis, the threat of punishment or retribution. And he discovers too late that his own attempt to play the divine lover will result in a transformation reminiscent of Bottom's, 'I do begin to perceive that I am made an ass' (v. v. 119).

Plautus' *Miles Gloriosus*, a play deeply important for Shakespeare both early and late in his career, also contributes to this portrayal of the Windsor Falstaff. Stoll noted that Falstaff, like the strutting Pyrgopolynices, is both a recruiting officer and a

---

[26] Shakespeare's phrase catches the sense of 'homuncio' better than the contemporary one, 'feloe of no reputacion' found in Udall, *Flowres*, fol. 73v., and, essentially, in R. Bernard, *Terence in English* (1598), 151.

[27] *Five-Act*, 555. [28] *Terentivs* (1560), 285, 290.

[29] Such colouration is entirely typical of Shakespeare's remembrance of Jove's amours; see Root, *Classical Mythology*, 81–2.

rebuffed suitor. Salingar extended the discussion, arguing that Shakespeare wanted to produce a rapid, complicated intrigue, similar to the early comedies of Chapman and Jonson, and naturally turned to *Miles Gloriosus* for a model. Plautus provided the essentials for the play: 'the boaster, inordinately vain about his sexual charm, who is lured into an intrigue with a married woman (a pretended married woman in Plautus), steals into his neighbour's house, is soundly thrashed and is terrified into avowing his fault.'[30] Salingar also notes that both plays emphasize the craft of women and feature good-natured bachelors—Periplectomenus and the Host; both have a static opening scene that delineates the character of the boaster; both feature an intrigue concerning a heroine who exits, finally, with her true lover in disguise.

Falstaff's military braggadocio appears throughout the play. He woos like a 'soldier' in 'soldier-like phrase' (II. i. 11–13); he promises to stare Ford 'out of his wits' (II. ii. 279), thus boasting of the basilisk eye that was stock weaponry in the braggart's arsenal; he threatens to awe Ford with the cudgel: 'it shall hang like a meteor o'er the cuckold's horns' (280–1). Moreover, both *Miles Gloriosus* and *Wives* use the conventional dialogue with the parasite to reveal the vanity of the boasting soldier. The importance and flexibility of this pairing, first appearing in Greek Middle comedy, is amply attested by Francesco Andreini's collection of *commedia dell'arte* dialogues between Capitano Spavento and Trappola.[31] In Plautus' *Miles Gloriosus* Pyrgopolynices converses with his parasite Artotrogus; Falstaff converses with the equivalents, Pistol, Nym, and Bardolph. There are, however, important dissimilarities in presentation. The classical boaster usually has his illusions fed by a wily parasite who encourages him for selfish purposes, ridicules him in asides, and gleefully plots the final puncturing of the balloon. In I. iii Falstaff himself fantasizes about Mrs Ford's 'leer of invitation' and Mrs Page's 'judicious iliads' (45–6, 60–1), expounding the dream of his own sexual attractiveness that motivates the entire action. He is as vain as Pyrgopolynices but needs no flatterer to puff him up. Falstaff feeds his own illusions as well as his own belly. His attendants, far from inflating the foolish fantasy, seek to deflate it:

---

[30] Stoll, 'Falstaff,' 212; Salingar, *Traditions*, 231.
[31] See Webster, *Studies in Later Greek Comedy*, 64, 174; Andreini, *Le bravure*.

FALSTAFF: Sometimes the beam of her view gilded my foot, sometimes my portly belly.
PISTOL: Then did the sun on dunghill shine.
NYM: I thank thee for that humour.   (61–4)

Pistol and Nym indignantly refuse to bear Falstaff's letters to the ladies. Whereas Pyrgopolynices sees himself by reflection, by the false images that others are only too happy to provide, Falstaff creates his own self-image and acts accordingly. This invention, of course, argues a kind of wit in Falstaff, a poetic fancy that sets him apart from the merely gullible and stupid prototypes. But this difference also isolates the fat knight in his illusions, making him solely responsible for his folly and its consequences.

The action of both plays leads to the boaster's entrance into the lady's house. Milphidippa assures Pyrgopolynices that the husband will be absent (1277). Mistress Quickly twice tells Falstaff that the husband will be out and that Mrs Ford awaits him (II. ii. 83–4; III. v. 44–6). We recall the humorous stage play and resonant symbolism of the locked door in *Amphitruo, Menaechmi, Errors, Twelfth Night*, and *Ado*, as Shakespeare stages two variations of the device here. Twice entering the woman's house, twice unlocking the locked door, Falstaff re-enacts the other entrances, real and feigned, in full expectation of the sexual reward. Like Plautus' courtesan, the merry wives, however, have wittily revised the New Comedic script. He who fancied himself a sexual imperialist, an extravagant voyager in love, trading with the East and West Indies of Windsor wives (I. iii. 71–2), gets locked in a laundry basket and, the second time, beaten in women's clothes. The ignominious adventure in the suffocating and odorous laundry basket has some precedent in *Il pecorone* and other novella tales, but similar enclosures regularly extinguish the ardours of foolish lovers in neo-classical comedy: the *senex amans* in Piccolomini's *Alessandro* gets locked in a bathroom ('in quella camera del necessario') where he suffers from the horrendous stench ('il puzzo horrendo');[32] the scene changes to a coal-house in Chapman's adaptation of *Alessandro, May Day*; in *La calandria* the amorous old fool gets stuffed into a large trunk that is about to be dumped in a river; and in *Les Fourberies de Scapin*, the wily servant tricks Géronte into a sack and then beats him.

[32] Piccolomini, 36.

The main *catastrophe* of the play, Falstaff's comeuppance, recapitulates an ancient comedic ritual—the taunting, costuming, and expulsion of an oldster by women. More specifically, it draws upon Plautus as well as Lyly, folk customs, and Ovid.[33] Like Pyrgopolynices at the end of *Miles Gloriosus*, Falstaff suffers humiliation: irate husbands (a pretended one in Plautus) and company abruptly frustrate both braggarts' amorous desires just at the moment of fulfilment. In addition, both soldier/lovers suffer financial penalties, the one required to pay 'minam auri' (1420), 'a mina of gold', the other to recompense 'Brook' fully (v. v. 166–9). (In Terence's inventive variation Thraso is encouraged as a rival who can support the lovers financially.) Pyrgopolynices is clubbed, Falstaff, à la Corsites in Lyly's *Endimion*, pinched by revellers disguised as fairies. The cruellest part of both punishments is public exposure and the painful anagnorosis: Pyrgopolynices realizes that he is a fool who has been tricked, 'uae misero mihi / verba mihi data esse video. scelu' uiri Palaestrio, / is me in hanc inlexit fraudem' ('O wretched me! I see that I've been hoodwinked. That wicked man Palaestrio! It is he who lured me into this trap'). Falstaff, likewise, perceives that he is 'made an ass' (v. v. 119). Falstaff's Ovidian metamorphosis into a beast, ass, or horned stag, well concludes the sequence of his humiliations. Terence's Jovian seducer becomes finally an overage Actaeon, suitably anglicized and rendered bathetic.[34]

New Comedy influences the larger design of *The Merry Wives of Windsor* as well as its characters. According to Hanson, Plautus continually structures his plays through a 'parallelism of roles, the thematic repetition in other characters of the traits of the braggart warrior'.[35] This repetition often occurs in a *servus* like Chrysalus

---

[33] See Aristophanes, *Lysistrata*, ed. Henderson, 146–7; John Lyly's *Endimion* (IV. iii. 25 ff.). Frye's (*Anatomy*, 183) observation is, yet again, irresistible: 'Falstaff must have felt that, after being thrown into the water, dressed up as a witch and beaten out of a house with curses, and finally supplied with a beast's head and singed with candles, he had done about all that could reasonably be asked of any fertility spirit.'

[34] See Steadman, 'Falstaff as Actaeon'; Roberts, *Shakespeare's English Comedy*, 114–15, 125–6; Barkan, 'Diana and Actaeon'; on Ovidian elements see Salingar, *Traditions*, 236–8; Carroll, 183–202; Bate, *Shakespeare and Ovid*, 164–7. Campbell ('Italianate Background', 96–7) notes the similar fate of another horned and exposed lover in a later Italian comedy, *Atalanta* (1610). Those who think Falstaff's treatment too harsh might recall that Baïf lengthened the end of his adaptation of *Miles Gloriosus*, *Le Brave*, to expand the humiliation.

[35] 'The Glorious Military', in Dorey and Dudley (1965), 62.

(*Bacc.*) or Palaestrio (*MG*). Couching intrigues in military language, they are the real field generals, the soldiers merely impostors. Renaissance dramatists, likewise, presented various and reflecting images of the soldier in other characters. Jonson's *Every Man in his Humour* (1598), for example, features the *miles gloriosus*, Bobadilla, along with the genuinely choleric Giuliano, and the clever Musco, who disguises himself as a soldier. Shakespeare likewise multiplies perspectives on Falstaff by portraying military swagger in the other characters. Pistol, a well-appreciated comic part in his day, is a preposterous *miles gloriosus*, a thundering boaster who rants in 'red-lattice phrases' and 'bold-beating oaths' (II. ii. 27–8).[36] He speaks fustian composed of stiff-jointed verse and scraps from tragedies, misquoted in grotesque parody. To a lesser degree, such another is the humorous Nym: he blusters in front of Slender, 'Slice, I say! *Pauca, pauca*. Slice, that's my humour!' (I. i. 133), and later promises to revenge himself on Falstaff 'By welkin and her star!' (I. iii. 92). Shallow provides a nostalgic variation on the military theme, yearning for the days when he ended disputes by 'sword' (I. i. 41), when his 'long sword' could make four tall fellows 'skip like rats' (II. i. 228–9). Even Slender brags of taking the great bear Sackerson by chain (I. i. 294 ff.; cf. Simple's praise, I. iv. 25–7). And the choleric Dr Caius bullies his servant Jack Rugby, challenges Evans to a duel wherein he promises to cut 'troat', and swaggers through much of the action.

These figures provide a revealing perspective on Falstaff. Like him, most of the other military swaggerers are lovers, or would-be lovers. Slender boasts of his courage while trying to impress Anne Page. Shallow's greeting, 'Would I were young for your sake, Mistress Anne!' (I. i. 260), shows that, to his mind at least, the young fighter and lover were one and the same man. Pistol, revealingly, announces his attention to woo Mistress Quickly:

> This punk is one of Cupid's carriers.
> Clap up more sails, pursue; up with your fights;
> Give fire! She is my prize, or ocean whelm them all! (II. ii. 135–7)

---

[36] Taylor (Oxford edn., *Henry V*, 1982, 64) remarks that Pistol appeared prominently on the title pages of three Elizabethan quartos (2 *Henry IV*, *Wives*, *Henry V*) and remained a celebrated part into the nineteenth century.

The conflation of martial and amorous ardours evident here clearly shows the twin delusions rampant in Windsor—the overestimation of the self as a soldier for all seasons, and the underestimation of the woman, here reduced to the status of a military objective, a thing to be lost or won. Dr Caius, another 'Hector' (II. iii. 33), presents an extreme and illuminating case of both delusions. He woos Anne arrogantly and ineffectually with his sword, mistaking his competition (he seems to be unaware of Fenton), misdirected to the duel, that Italian innovation which here, as in *Twelfth Night*, exposes the folly, usually cowardice, of the braggart. Dr Caius works through agents like Mrs Page and Mistress Quickly, and not once speaks directly to Anne in the play. Consequently, he is perpetually in the wrong place at the wrong time. His fortunes, running through swaggering folly to public humiliation, clearly mirror Falstaff's progress from Windsor boaster to country gull.

Opposed to the military lovers in the play is the young Fenton. Shakespeare's transformation of the absent youths of *Casina* into young lovers perfectly accords with Italian theory and practice. Castelvetro, as we have seen, complained that the classical lovers were extraneous. Italian playwrights expanded their roles and integrated them into the action, as did later adaptors, including John Dennis, who made 'everything Instrumental to Fenton's Marriage', as well as Boito and Verdi in their opera.[37] On the Italian plays Corrigan observes: 'the characters who assume paramount importance in the Renaissance versions are precisely those of the young lovers, particularly of the men.' Similarly adapted is Shakespeare's *adulescens*, Fenton, who also resembles a Chaucerian 'clerk': 'He capers, he dances, he has eyes of youth; he writes verses, he speaks holiday, he smells April and May' (III. ii. 67–9). Unlike the others in the play, Fenton actually woos the lady in person and, though rejected by her father, shows faith in her, 'Why, thou must be thyself' (III. iv. 3). He does not see Anne as a military objective or as merchandise to be fought for or bargained over, the prevalent attitude typified, for example, by Evans: 'Seven hundred pounds, and possibilities, is goot gifts' (I. i. 65). He pointedly disavows materialistic motives in the wooing, stung by Mr Page's accusation that he views Anne 'but as a property':

---

[37] *The Comical Gallant*, sig. A2v. On Boito and Verdi's work see Schmidgall, *Shakespeare and Opera*, 329–30. The quotation below belongs to Corrigan, 82.

No, heaven so speed me in my time to come!
Albeit I will confess thy father's wealth
Was the first motive that I woo'd thee, Anne;
Yet wooing thee, I found thee of more value
Than stamps in gold, or sums in sealed bags;
And 'tis the very riches of thyself
That now I am at.   (III. iv. 12–18)

Fenton's use of a military metaphor later in this scene, his promise
to 'advance the colours' of his love 'against all checks, rebukes,
and manners' (III. iv. 80–1), measures the difference between him
and the other suitors. War is a mere metaphor for the hostile circumstances and for his own steadfast persistence. He doesn't actually boast of soldierly prowess, woo with the sword, or consider
Anne a military prize. Instead, he takes the trouble to win her
heart and sends a ring (III. iv. 100). The letter he receives from her
later, a direct contrast to the presumptuous epistles of Falstaff,
'mutually' answers affection (IV. vi. 10); together Fenton and Anne
plot to outwit parents and foolish suitors. Those who come to
wive by swaggering, in Windsor as in Illyria, never thrive.

Similarly, the classical *virgo*, often silent and absent, becomes
Anne Page. Plautus' Philocomasium, the artful *meretrix/mulier* of
Miles Gloriosus, may supply some precedent here, but Italian dramatists largely prepared the way for the transformation. Corrigan
observes like changes in Machiavelli's *Clizia*, still absent but good
and beautiful, in Dolce's *Livia*, a 'gentildonna fanciulla' who recip-
rocates love, in Cecchi's *Persilia*, who appears briefly on stage, in
Lanci's *Ruchetta*, who asks for time to find her parents (with the
help of 'il cielo') before beginning an undesired marriage. Berrardo's
translation of *Casina* likewise expands the *virgo*'s role, encouraging
the fuller portrayal of Antoinette in yet another adaptation, Belleau's
La Reconnue.[38] Shakespeare continues the trend with Anne Page,
who, like his other *virgines*, Bianca and Hero, has more stage presence than her small part suggests and than many commentators
allow. Anne tolerates the idiotic Slender with kindliness and grace;
she protests vigorously against her mother's choice for her, Dr
Caius: 'Alas, I had rather be set quick i' th' earth, / And bowl'd to
death with turnips!' (III. iv. 86–7); going Ruchetta one better, she
chooses and plays her role in the final marital pageant.

---

[38] Corrigan, 82–3; Belleau, ed. Braybrook, 10, 15. Corrigan describes another
variation, the bawdy Giglietta of *Il capriccio*.

This pageant features the substitution of boys for brides, a multiplied replay of Chalinus' imposture in *Casina*. Plautus plays this substitution for bawdy slapstick as the chagrined lover gets his comeuppance.[39] Machiavelli, Dolce, and Lanci follow suit, reprising the raucous tone and genital humour. There were other interesting variations: *La fantesca* has no girl at all, but a boy, Essandro, in disguise throughout the play; Aretino's *Il marescalco* features a duped suitor who, preferring men to women, is delighted with the trick. Jonson's adaptation, *Epicoene*, derived partly from *Il marescalco*, makes the switch a surprising stage trick that culminates a scene of legal satire and comic confusion. Shakespeare, more simply, focuses on the deceivers deceived, on Slender who says in shock and surprise, 'she's a great lubberly boy' (v. v. 184), and on Caius, who exits for the last time, as we might expect, huffing and puffing, 'Ay, be-gar, and 'tis a boy. Be-gar, I'll raise all Windsor' (209–10).

The Merry Wives of Windsor presents an Italianate appropriation of New Comedic characters, conventions, and plays. Like the errors plays, it multiplies incident and character into complicated design, romanticizes classical eros, dramatizes mistaken identity. Like the intrigue plays, *Wives* focuses on marriage, featuring many tricks and deceits, in Evans' judgement, 'the greatest accumulation of practices in any play of Shakespeare's except *Cymbeline*'.[40] And, like *Shrew* and *Ado*, the play exhibits in one of its plots (the wooing of Anne Page) a Plautine romantic configuration that plays off another more eclectic story line. This line, the duping of Falstaff, reprises significant New Comedic elements as well, liberally combining them with other traditions. And yet, as always Falstaff finally transcends the classical types he subsumes. Speaking a lively prose much different from the usual Thrasonical huffe-snuffe,[41] he narrates the adventure of the buck-basket in hilariously vivid detail

---

[39] MacCary and Willcock (eds. *Casina*, 37) note that the false bride scene may have been popular in Atellan farce and has a prototype in comic treatments of the marriage of Herakles and Omphale; see also Webster, *Studies in Later Greek Comedy*, 161.

[40] *Shakespeare's Comedies*, 99.

[41] Compare for example the outrageous bluster of Huanebango in Peele's *The Old Wives Tale* (1595): 'Phylyda phylerydos, Pamphylyda floryda flortos, / Dub dub a dub, bounce quoth the guns, with a sulpherous huffe snuffe: / Wakte with a wench, pretty peat, pretty love, and my sweet prettie pigsnie, / Just by thy side shall sit surnamed great Huanebango' (646–9).

and is capable of occasional *eironeia*, of, for example, the witty sally he directs at himself:

QUICK. Alas the day! good heart, that was not her fault. She does so take on with her men; they mistook their erection.
FAL. So did I mine, to build upon a foolish woman's promise.

(III. v. 38–41)

Shakespeare's *Wives* explores the moral and psychological complexities behind classical comic action. The *miles gloriosus* here, seen variously in Falstaff, Pistol, and Caius, continually overestimates himself and underestimates others, particularly women. To such delusions the wives apply stringent corrective. Falstaff's *cognitio*, consequently, differs from the standard classical recognition of identity by token or the neo-classical variant brilliantly exploited in Italian comedy and in Shakespeare himself, the throwing off of disguise or unmasking. Instead, he discovers the folly of his misconceptions, of his evil thinking. The fairies berate him for 'sinful fantasy' (V. v. 93), the onlookers mock him as 'A puff'd man' (153). The *processus turbarum* illustrates in a comic way the truth of the Garter motto, '*Honi soit qui mal y pense*' (69, 'Evil be to him who evil *thinks*' [italics mine]).

Few today would argue that *Wives* is a seamless success for all of its rambunctious fun. Earlier critics, however, focusing on plot and on the comic unities, thought the play one of Shakespeare's purest comedies. The line of praise includes John Dryden, Nicholas Rowe, Charles Gildon, and culminates in Samuel Johnson's comment, 'perhaps it never yet had reader or spectator who did not think it too soon at an end'.[42] But to our eyes even the plot seems flawed. The revenge on the host, the business with the horses, is badly garbled, and in the present state of the text, entirely extraneous. Nor are Falstaff's subordinates, Bardolph, Pistol, and Nym, well integrated into the action. To be sure they amplify exploration of *alazoneia* and provide some comic colour, but the revenge plot against Falstaff, like Pistol's suit to Mistress Quickly, simply evaporates as the wives take over the play. In fact, Pistol and Nym themselves disappear as the play moves on; they do not reflect on the main action and characters as consistently and tellingly as they do in 2 *Henry IV* and *Henry V*. Here Shakespeare works with

---

[42] See Vickers, ed., i. 137, 255 (Dryden); ii. 195 (Rowe); ii. 221 (Gildon); v. 521 (Johnson).

comedic traditions which he will use with greater skill and subtlety in *All's Well*. There Pistol will reappear as Parolles, and the subordinate *miles gloriosus* figure will bear a relationship to the action and main characters that is important and purposeful.

All's Well That Ends Well

All's Well That Ends Well bears interesting similarities to Shakespeare's *Wives*, his earlier exploration of *alazoneia*. Both plays blend Roman comedy and folk tale. Both balance the exposure of the braggart with an inset New Comedic love affair, namely, the wooings of Anne Page and Diana Capilet. Both revise a New Comedic deep source as mediated through Italian traditions: *Casina* and the cinquecento adaptations behind *Wives* here give way to Terence's *Hecyra* and Boccaccio's *Decameron*.[43] Underlying the tale of Giletta, *Hecyra* shapes the infrastructure of *All's Well*; it features the conflict between a father and son that results in a forced marriage, the son's refusal to consummate the marriage, and the repudiation of the innocent wife. In both plays the son has a sexual encounter with a woman he thinks is someone other than his wife; a good courtesan figure with his ring provides for recognition and resolution.

Both *Wives* and *All's Well* anatomize *alazoneia* in the form of the *miles gloriosus*. The later play, however, divides military and amorous pretensions into separate but related incarnations— Parolles and Bertram. Inserting Parolles into Boccaccio's tale, Shakespeare defines and clarifies the exposure of Bertram, who, like the traditional *miles gloriosus*, overestimates himself and underestimates others, particularly women. *All's Well* represents a more complex treatment of *alazoneia* than does *Wives* and, whatever its shortcomings, a more purposeful matching and contrasting of braggart soldiers. In fact, its descent from *Hecyra*, its construction according to the *Andria* five-act formula, its use of double action and rhetorical argument (the discussions of virginity and of honour), its daring and skilful handling of traditions, and its thor-

---

[43] *Hecyra* is a well-recognized antecedent of the tale of Giletta; see Branca's edn., iv. 1185; Lee, *Decameron*, 102.

oughgoing inversion of New Comedic elements make it Shakespeare's most Terentian comedy.[44]

Discussing an archetypal comic pattern in which a *senex iratus* opposes and finally gives way to a young man's desires, Northrop Frye observes: 'The sense of the comic norm is so strong that when Shakespeare, by way of experiment, tried to reverse the pattern in *All's Well*, in having two older people force Bertram to marry Helena, the result has been an unpopular "problem" play, with a suggestion of something sinister about it.'[45] Though many variations appear in New Comedy and Shakespeare, there are still enough blocking and irate fathers in both to validate Frye's perception of the norm. Here Shakespeare violates this norm by portraying a different older generation, one sympathetic to young love, at least to Helena's. He introduces the Countess and Lafew, without precedent in Boccaccio or Painter, and expands greatly the role of the King. Remembering her own youthful fancies—'this thorn / Doth to our rose of youth rightly belong' (I. iii. 129–30)—the Countess comforts the lovelorn Helena and promises aid. The old Lafew likewise reverses conventional expectations, supporting poor maidenly virtue against titled arrogance. He praises Helena's 'Wisdom, and constancy' (II. i. 84), shows his admiration in the selection scene (II. iii), and, supposing Helena dead, remembers her 'dear perfection' (V. iii. 18). The King, old friend of the dead Count, formally and legally (I. i. 6–7) acting as Bertram's father, forces the match.[46]

Equally innovative in the opening scenes is the portrayal of Bertram, the *adulescens*. Cast by others in the familiar role, he pointedly refuses to play the part. Unlike those amorous young men so typical of New Comedy, the yearning Philolaches (*Most.*), Alcesimarchus (*Cist.*), Charerea (*Eun.*), or Pamphilus (*Andria*), Bertram is cold, unmoved, and to temptation slow. In classical and

---

[44] On the construction see Baldwin, *Five-Act*, 728–36. On non-classical sources see Lawrence, *Shakespeare's Problem Comedies*, 32–77 (folk tales); Godshalk, '*All's Well That Ends Well* and the Morality Play'; Neuss, 'The Sixteenth-century English "Proverb" Play'; Dessen, *Shakespeare and the Late Moral Plays*, 113–33.

[45] *Anatomy*, 180. Noting the sympathetic older generation, the callow Bertram, and the complex Helena, Riemer (50) calls the play 'Shakespeare's most surprising and most thorough experiment with comic form'.

[46] On the King's responsibilities here, the legal and social background, see Zitner, *All's Well That Ends Well*, 40 ff. Shakespeare's portrayal is not wholly without precedent in the ancients, who occasionally depicted parents indulgent of the amorous young. See, for example *Bacc.* 409–10.

neo-classical drama a young man's reluctance to marry an appointed bride usually derives from illicit attachment to someone else, to a pregnant neighbour in Menander's *Georgos*, for example, to the courtesan Bacchis in Terence's *Hecyra*, to a secret wife in Ariosto's *Il negromante*. In the opening scenes, however, Bertram neither loves nor desires anyone else. Terence's Pamphilus refuses to consummate the unwelcome marriage out of regard for his wife's reputation; Bertram denies Helena a kiss out of regard for his own. His hauteur, moreover, diminishes whatever sympathy he might, in similar circumstances, rightfully claim.

Bertram's prototype, Beltramo, 'tutto sdegnoso', all disdainful, rejects Giletta because he thinks her 'non esser di legnaggio che alla sua nobilità bene stesse' ('not to be of a stocke convenable to his nobility').[47] Making Helena poor not rich, Shakespeare goes one step further to emphasize the rejection as motivated by concern with social class. This concern, of course, regularly impedes matches in classical comedy and its descendants.[48] Here, however, Shakespeare overturns conventions by locating the concern in the *adulescens* himself. Bertram's objection to Helena's social status contrasts pointedly with the ardency of classical youths, who fall for every species of the unprivileged—lowly flute girls, courtesans, foreigners, and foundlings. His later desire for death or exile also inverts tradition, these being typically the desperate options of the unrequited *adulescens*, not the requited one.[49] Subscribing to an inflated notion of himself and his aristocratic blood, Bertram refuses to look upon Helena, to regard her much-praised virtue and beauty and her near-miraculous powers. He never sees the woman herself, but only 'a poor physician's daughter' (II. iii. 115). Bertram's overestimation of himself and underestimation of Helena, here contrasted to the courteous responses of the other nobles, evidence the same folly that will prize Parolles and misprize Diana. In both amorous and military endeavours, Bertram values too highly external trappings and pays too little mind to that which passeth show. To use Harry Levin's terms, this playboy is a killjoy.

[47] Boccaccio, iv. 324; tr. Painter, Bullough, ii. 391.
[48] Note the rich variations in the Spanish Golden Age, e.g. Lope de Vega's *El Perro del Hortelano* and Calderón's *Secreto a voces*, as well as Goldsmith's witty *She Stoops to Conquer*, whose Young Marlow, tongue-tied before ladies, can only woo girls of low social class.
[49] Duckworth, 239; *Adelphoe*, ed. Martin, 146–7.

The King perceives immediately that Bertram's reluctance springs from delusions about human worth, phrased as delusions about the nature of honour. He responds generously to Bertram's indignant refusal: "'Tis only title thou disdain'st in her, the which / I can build up' (II. iii. 117–18). Helena's virtues, the King goes on to argue, 'breed' the very honour that Bertram thinks she lacks. This king's response completes the deconstruction of the inscribed New Comedic paradigm, wherein fathers frequently oppose the marriage of their sons to lower-class women. We recall as well the *senex amans* variations—with the father blocking because he wants the girl for himself—in *Casina* and *Mercator*; the complex handlings of Terence in *Heauton Timorumenos* and *Adelphoe*. Here the blocking humour, a headstrong and prideful concern with title and social status, originates in the son.

Faced with such compunctions, the *senex*, ironically, becomes *iratus*. Wed Helena, the king threatens, or feel ever after his 'revenge and hate' (II. iii. 164). This anger recovers the wrathful energies of the stereotype while inverting the standard motivation. It forecasts that of the Countess later in the play who, upon learning of Bertram's desertion, declares: 'He was my son, / But I do wash his name out of my blood, / And thou art all my child' (III. ii. 66–8). Employing the 'vi et via pervolgata patrum' (*HT* 101, 'the forceful method that is usual with fathers'), the King and Countess echo the sentiments of other angry parents in comedy who threaten disassociation (e.g. Menedemus, *HT* 106–8). Shakespeare's parent figures, however, make the threat of disassociation for precisely the opposite reason: not because the son loves a lower-class woman, but because he fails to.

Shakespeare carefully articulates his inversion of the New Comedic paradigm, emphasizing centrally Helena, an adapted *virgo* who embodies other traditions as well. Helena resembles the energetic heroines of the *capa y espada* comedies in Spain. She also, Clubb observes, resembles the Italian 'woman as wonder', the spiritualized *innamorata* who, like Giletta in Boccaccio's tale, manifests the workings of divine providence.[50] Part untitled *virgo*, part comic heroine, part wondrous woman, part simple serving maid, part religious sermonizer (II. i. 134 ff.), part incantatory folk-tale sorceress (161 ff.), Helena persuades the King and audience of her

[50] Clubb, *Italian Drama*, 65–89.

good intentions and power. Undertaking the cure, she names the punishments that may befall her for failure:

> Tax of impudence,
> A strumpet's boldness, a divulged shame,
> Traduc'd by odious ballads; my maiden's name
> Sear'd otherwise; ne worst of worst, extended
> With vildest torture, let my life be ended.   (170–4)

Even though Helena has an ulterior motive, the willingness to risk all is an impressive act of faith. And it is no accident that Helena's alter ego, Diana, will suffer the tax of impudence while Helena herself is counted dead—these two ordeals recalling this pledge and linking Helena's curing of the King with her curing of Bertram. Helena's willingness to risk differentiates her from the classical *virgo*, often mute, passive, and off-stage, sometimes pathetic (Palaestra in *Rudens*) rarely spirited (Saturio's daughter in *Persa*), but never a complex woman capable of self-sacrifice. Unlike them, Helena is equally unlike the devious *meretrix* many critics make her out to be, the passionate schemer relentlessly serving selfish desires.[51] (One need only contrast the portrayal of female lust in Fracastoro's *La venexiana* to appreciate Shakespeare's genial romanticism.) Helena trusts in her dead father's art and depends on circumstances and on providence throughout the play, her actions, as she says, 'sanctified / By th' luckiest stars in heaven' (I. iii. 245–6). 'Heaven hath through me restor'd the King to health' (II. iii. 64), she declares, and the play repeatedly insists on the formulation (II. i. 149 ff.; II. iii. 23–4, 31; III. iv. 27). (Cf. the echoing word 'grace,' I. iii. 220, II. i. 160, IV. v. 17.) When Bertram rejects her, Helena retreats and abandons the whole plan (II. iii. 147–8). And when she receives the cruel conditions for marriage with Bertram, she undertakes a pilgrimage; she does not, as does Giletta, immediately purpose 'to finde meanes to attaine the two thinges, that thereby she might recover her husbande' (Bullough, ii. 392). Neither overly ingenuous (as portrayed in many sentimental adaptations, beginning with that of John Philip Kemble, 1793) or overly ingenious, Helena makes one with Shakespeare's other Plautine heroines—Bianca, Hero, Anne Page, and, especially

---

[51] For a survey of reactions to Helena see Champion, 217–18. Denigrators read purposeful intrigue in the pilgrimage and lust in her desire; they tend to ignore the theatrical power of the magical cure and of her modest devotion, viz. Bertram's arrogant rudenesses.

Viola—those adapted *virgines* who make their own occasions mellow, who show passivity as well as a capacity for independent action and intrigue that any *callidus servus* might admire.

Shakespeare creates the *processus turbarum* of *All's Well* by declining and refiguring the *alazoneia* of the *miles gloriosus*, whom both Greek and Latin New Comic dramatists portrayed with dual aspect—that of braggart warrior and boasting lover. An Italian descendant, Della Porta's Martebellonio in *Gli duoi fratelli rivali*, neatly illustrates both aspects of the traditional figure:

> Credo che non sia minor virtute e grandezza ferir un corpo con la spada, che un'anima con i sguardi; ben posso tenermi io fra tutti gli uomini glorioso, ché posso non men con l'una che con l'altra; ché non può starmi uomo, per gagliardo che sia, con la spada in mano innanzi, né men donna, per onesta e rigida, a i colpi de' sguardi miei: e se con la spada fo ferite, che giungono insin al cuore, con gli occhi fo piaghe profondissime, che giungono insin all' anima.

> I believe it's no less a sign of power and greatness to wound a body with one's sword than a soul with one's glances: well may I deem myself glorious among men, for I'm as powerful in the one way as in the other; for no man, no matter how hardy, can stand up to me when I have my sword in hand, nor any woman, no matter how chaste and unbending, can resist the onslaught of my glances; and if with the sword I can pierce to the heart, with my eyes I make the deepest wounds, which penetrate to the very soul.   (tr. Clubb, 198–201)

Parolles embodies the military aspect of the stereotype, Bertram the amorous. The lover's *alazoneia* does not express itself in the usual rumbustious rhetoric and swagger, but, more seriously, in his values and actions. Grossly overvaluing the self and undervaluing others, both Parolles and Bertram endure parallel ordeals and exposures.[52] Parolles' expedition for the lost drum parallels Bertram's affair with Diana Capilet; the mock-capture corresponds to the bed-trick; Parolles' unmasking anticipates Bertram's exposure. In the manner of classical comedy, Shakespeare creates comic action that exposes errors of mind, ἁμαρτήματα τῆς ψυχῆς (*Tractatus Coislinianus* viii).

As Nicholas Rowe recognized in 1709, Parolles combines two New Comedic types: 'The Parasite and the Vain-glorious in

---

[52] Shakespeare's invention of Parolles as ironic counterpart, Cole (*The 'All's Well' Story*, 129–30) observes, has precedent in Accolti's early reworking of the Giletta story, *Verginia*; there, similarly, Ruffo's humiliation prefigures his master's.

Parolles, in *All's Well that ends Well*, is as good as any thing of that Kind in *Plautus* or *Terence*.'[53] On one level, at least, Bertram and Parolles reformulate the archetypal soldier-parasite pairing originating in Middle Comedy. The soldier is a 'braggart . . . found an ass' (IV. iii. 336), one whom audiences have delighted in at least since the time of Theophilus Cibber's performance (1742). Kin to Armado, Pistol, and Falstaff, Parolles speaks the *magnifica verba* (*Eun.* 741) of Thraso or Pyrgopolynices, boasting of past exploits like the wounding of one Captain Spurio (appropriately named) (II. i. 42–3), patronizing the younger nobles, 'Mars dote on you for his novices!' (II. i. 47), carrying on preposterously about his lost drum. Shakespeare prepares for the grand humiliation by using two popular stage routines that characterized and exposed the braggart. The first is the rationalized retreat, the invention of some absurd excuse to avoid confrontation.[54] When Helena mocks him for his cowardice, Parolles lamely responds, 'I am so full of businesses, I cannot answer thee acutely' (I. i. 206–7); he hastily changes the subject and exits. The second is the entrance of the adversary immediately after the braggart makes empty threats.[55] After Parolles declares 'I'll beat him, and if I could but meet him again' (II. iii. 240–1), Lafew re-enters and continues his abuse, 'if I were but two hours younger, I'd beat thee' (253–4). The strutting Hercules becomes the quivering Aguecheek. Like his classical forebears, Parolles fools very few. Helena taunts him for retreating from battle (I. i. 195 ff.), Lafew mocks him mercilessly, calling him a 'window of lettice' (II. iii. 213), thus recalling Pistol's 'red-lattice phrases' in *Wives* (II. ii. 27); the Clown knows him for a 'knave' (II. iv. 28); Diana calls him 'That jack-an-apes with scarfs' (III. v. 85), the French lords think him a 'hilding' and a 'bubble' (III. vi. 3, 5). Only Bertram considers Parolles 'very great in knowledge, and accordingly valiant' (II. v. 8–9). So thinking, he contrasts with the others in the play, not to mention Palaestrio and Gnatho, the slave

[53] Vickers (ed.), ii. 195. See also the praise of Parolles by Charles Gildon (1710) and Arthur Murphy (1757) (ii. 244; iv. 295). On this point Rowe is right against Hunter, Arden edn. (1959, xlvii), who says that Parolles is 'not essentially a *miles gloriosus* (in many ways he is nearer to the classical parasite)'. The combination of the two types was common, as evidenced by Falstaff, Pistol, Quintiliano (*May Day*), and Bessus (*A King and No King*).

[54] Amply documented by Boughner, 84 ff.

[55] Miles enters to bash and abash the blustering Thersites in an early Tudor play (*Thersites*); in a later one Giuliano arrives to beat Bobadilla, who has just vowed to 'bastinado' him (*Every Man in his Humour*, Quarto IV. ii. 93 ff.).

and parasite who serve their boastful masters only to serve their turns upon them.

Bertram's misperceptions are precisely at issue throughout the play and they stand for stringent correction as Parolles reveals his true nature. In the company of the lords Bertram goes from gull to intriguer, inveigling Parolles to fetch his drum, participating fully in the false capture. First there is the eavesdropping, then the capture and imprisonment in which Parolles, like Malvolio, is kept 'dark and safely lock'd' (IV. i. 94–5), and finally, the elaborate masquerade. Like Falstaff at Gadshill, the blindfolded Parolles shows his mendacity and cowardice spectacularly. The letter to Diana betrays Bertram's friendship, a betrayal that appears even worse in light of Parolles' function as ring-carrier and the hint of his own amorous intentions (IV. iii. 228, 231–2), 'Men are to mell with, boys are not to kiss', 'Thine, as he vow'd to thee in thine ear, Parolles' (228, 231–2). Parolles' ordeal is thoroughly Plautine. Like Pyrgopolynices, Parolles stands amidst a group of hostile, jeering persecutors and begs for mercy. The Roman boaster loses permanently his tunic, military cloak, and sword (1423); Parolles will lose his scarves and bannerets, symbols of his vanity. 'The soul of this man', Lafew well observes, 'is his clothes' (II. v. 43–4). Such stripping harks back to the archetypal comic perception of Livius Andronicus, Rome's first playwright, 'ornamento incedunt gnobilid ignobiles' ('in noble trappings march ignoble men', Warmington (tr.), ii. 23). Italian comedy, Boughner notes, reappropriates and refines the stripping, sometimes depicting the humiliated soldier in the rag-clad poverty of the *bravo*.[56] Shakespeare here adopts this alternative, portraying Parolles finally as a wretched beggar (v. ii). Thus he reveals the parasite in the *miles gloriosus*, that core of predatory self-interest also displayed in the ignoble and impecunious ends of Pistol, Nym, and Falstaff. Both ancient and Renaissance braggart are thankful to escape with their lives: *Pyrgopolynices*: 'gratiam habeo tibi' (1425); *Parolles*: 'Yet am I thankful' (IV. iii. 330).

How carefully Shakespeare interweaves the deceptions of Parolles and Bertram in Italy is clear even from cursory examination. The night of Parolles' imprisonment coincides with that of Bertram's rendezvous. Shakespeare presents the two comic actions

---

[56] *Braggart*, 80–1.

in alternating scenes, beginning with III. v, Helena's arrival and the procession, followed by III. vi, the hatching of the plot against Parolles, III. vii, the hatching of the plot against Bertram, IV. i, the springing of the first trap, IV. ii, the springing of the second, iv. iii, the exposure of Parolles, IV. iv, preparation for the exposure of Bertram. What is more, Shakespeare unites the two actions by use of military imagery such that Parolles' solitary expedition in quest of the lost drum, the 'instrument of honour' (III. vi. 66), parallels Bertram's expedition to Diana, questing after 'the spoil of her honour' (IV. iii. 16–17). Bertram uses 'engines of lust' (III. v. 19), to lay down a 'wanton siege' (III. vii. 18); Diana, however, prizing her 'tender honor', 'is arm'd for him, and keeps her guard / In honestest defence' (III. v. 72–4). The word 'honour' and its variants echo throughout the play, notably in the language of the king (sixteen times in eighty-seven speeches). Bertram's prowess on the field is 'most honorable service' (III. v. 3–4), but 'his sword can never win / The honor that he loses' (III. ii. 93–4) in love, as the Countess observes. The word 'honour' suggests the military standard Bertram upholds and the amorous one he violates, unmarking and marking him as a comic butt like Parolles.

The double comic action reveals the falseness of swaggering language, be it military bluster or romantic blarney. The lords show Parolles to be 'an infinite and endless liar, an hourly promise-breaker' (III. vi. 9–10); the ladies prove that Bertram's extravagant protestations and 'oaths / Are words and poor conditions, but unseal'd' (IV. ii. 29–30). Parolles and Bertram are moral identical twins, frauds infatuate with self-love who seek to deceive others. Consequently, they suffer similar punishments. Parolles' ordeal, Dessen has shown, foretells Bertram's, the two linked together by many suggestive parallels.[57] Parolles' lost drum becomes Bertram's lost ring. Parolles, blindfolded, stands trial under the judgement of three figures, just as Bertram, with velvet patch, will stand in front of the King, the Countess, and Lafew. Both are taken off guard, both slander present witnesses, both get into deeper trouble.

To set up Bertram's exposure Shakespeare again draws from the capacious repertory of New Comedy, reworking a situation, familiar from *Mostellaria* or *Cistellaria* (cf. Lucian's adaptation, *Dialogues of the Courtesans* vii). The passionate *adulescens* ardently

---

[57] *Late Moral Plays*, 124 ff.

woos with money and gifts a *meretrix*, who keeps company with an older and more wordly woman. In Florence Bertram takes on precisely the role he refused to play earlier with Helena—that of importunate *adulescens*. Like Philolaches or Alcesimarchus, he courts the lady, earnestly imploring mercy, willing to disappoint family and friends, eager to pay any price for sexual favours. The Widow acts the role of the older woman, Scapha (*Most.*) or Syra (*Hecyra*), for example, attentive to her charge and to harsh economic realities, experienced in the sinister ways of men ('My mother told me just how he would woo, / As if she sate in 's heart. She says all men / Have the like oaths,' IV. ii. 69–71). Diana plays the New Comedic courtesan who has her price, Bertram's ring. Never in fact the 'common gamester' (V. iii. 188) whom he reviles, she turns out to be a chaste and resourceful *virgo* who uses her sexual attractiveness to her own and Helena's ends. Diana makes the youthful lover a dupe very like the *miles gloriosus*, Pyrgopolynices, who also thinks himself beloved only to find himself befooled.

Like the mock-capture of Parolles, the bed-trick dupes Bertram by substituting a false impression for the occurring reality. The darkness of the blindfold and of the night prevents the victim from recognizing familiar faces and enables the impostures. The bed-trick presents an ingenious variation on the wooing by means of the disguise, proxy, and impersonation characteristic of New Comedic intrigue. Not deriving from Plautus or Terence, however, but from Boccaccio and novella traditions, the bed-trick strikingly reconstitutes the sexual action of the deep source, *Hecyra*, i.e. Pamphilus' casual rape of Philumena before the action of the play, and that of many New Comedies.[58] This reconstitution inverts the gender dynamics of New Comedic rape, reversing the poles of dominance and subservience. The helpless and passive *virgo* off-stage becomes now the resourceful and active intriguer. Boccaccio's Giletta displays 'perseveranza' (IV. 331); Accolti's Verginia, 'tanta arte' and 'estremo ingegno' (sig. F3). Shakespeare too emphasizes the woman's ingenuity in meeting the impossible conditions set by

---

[58] On this sexual action see W. S. Anderson (126): 'It seems to be a safe general rule, then, that in Menander, when a girl is raped, she will sooner or later be married to the man who raped her and, because he has changed for the better afterwards, the marriage will have good prospects'; see also Gossett, ' "Best Men are Molded out of Faults".'

the husband. Helena, in fact, reprises the role of the clever slave who uses a purse of gold (cf. III. vii. 14) and masterminds the intrigue; like Tranio (both Plautus' and Shakespeare's), she writes the script, casts the characters, directs (and stars in) the play.

The exposure of Parolles begins literally with his unbinding and ends in the short scene with Lafew, who finally says to him, now a chastened beggar, 'though you are a fool and a knave, you shall eat' (v. ii. 53–4). The curve of action in Parolles' story, from *alazoneia* through humiliation and loss of honour to present forgiveness and new life, establishes the pattern for Bertram. Parolles makes a brief but telling admission that should guide response later, 'O my good lord, you were the first that found me!' (v. ii. 42–3). This 'finding' is crucial to the play, where 'find' and its variants occur some forty times. The aim of the intrigue against Parolles is 'finding', i.e. exposure, not the forced acquisition of self-knowledge or internal reformation. This finding discovers for all the true identity of a person. It is, in Aristotle's terms, anagnorisis, ἐξ ἀγνοίας εἰς γνῶσιν μεταβολή (*Poet.* 1452a30–1, 'a change from ignorance to knowledge'), accompanied by peripeteia, a reversal of fortune, in this case, from good to bad. Just as in *Twelfth Night*, *Ado*, and other comedies the discovery reveals moral character not merely social status.

The finding of Bertram is likewise the result of his ordeal, but Shakespeare creates a complex exposure that radically revises antecedent sources and traditions. He features Diana, who, unlike the gentlewoman's daughter of the novella, travels to Rossillion, publicly accuses Bertram, and climactically presents his ring. Not the strumpet Bertram makes her out to be, Diana, nevertheless, reprises the functions of the courtesan Bacchis in *Hecyra*. Bacchis likewise arrives to present Pamphilus with his ring, to reveal that a previous sexual encounter occurred between him and his present wife, to provide for recognition and resolution. Though some precedent appears in Habrotonon of Menander's *Epitrepontes*, commentators like Donatus thought the 'bona meretrix' one of Terence's 'res nouae', notable innovations.[59] Shakespeare varies the original innovation by casting in the *meretrix* role the chaste

---

[59] *Terentius* (1560), 616. On Terence's innovations see McGarrity, 'Reputation vs. Reality in Terence's *Hecyra*'; Konstan, *Roman Comedy*, 130–41. George Bernard Shaw, of course, thoughtfully re-examines the 'bona meretrix' in *Mrs Warren's Profession*, which excuses the prostitute and indicts societal hypocrisy.

Diana, significantly named. Whereas the gentlewoman's daughter in the novella hopes to attract a husband, Shakespeare's refigured *meretrix*, disillusioned by the perfidy of men, vows to 'live and die a maid' (IV. ii. 74).

The resolution, of course, proceeds much more smoothly in both *Hecyra* and the tale of Giletta than it does in *All's Well*. Upon hearing that he is the father of his wife's child, Pamphilus joyfully accepts her, 'quis me est fortunatior venustati'que adeo plenior' (848, 'Who is more fortunate or luckier in love than I?'). The astonished Beltramo, likewise glad, promises henceforth to love and honour Giletta. Bertram, however, false, cold, and arrogant, denies the revelation, lies about his past, and slanders the witness. Rejecting Diana, huffing about the absurdity of sinking his honour so low, displaying fully his arrogance, Bertram replays con brio the earlier rejection of Helena. 'It is worth remembering', writes Kenneth Muir, 'that all Bertram's worst traits were added by Shakespeare—his friendship with Parolles, his rejoicing at the death of his wife, his promise of marriage to the girl in Florence, the parting with the ancestral heirloom, his smirching of the girl's character.'[60] Bertram's actions render untenable the earlier prattle about freedom of choice (we have seen him, after all, choose Diana) and show him a liar and a snob in need of exposure.

To expose Bertram's *alazoneia* Shakespeare draws on his past experience with Plautus. As in *Menaechmi*, *Errors*, and *Twelfth Night*, the playwright winds up the *epitasis* to its height before the resolution. In Shakespeare's errors plays an authority figure tries to resolve the confusion, but is baffled by the escalating din of claims and counterclaims. The Duke hears Antipholus of Ephesus, falsely arrested, and his accusers in the 'intricate impeach' (V. i. 270). Orsino hears Antonio, also arrested, as well as Olivia, who, like Diana, claims a husband on stage. So the King in *All's Well* hears and arrests Bertram and Diana in angry confusion. The resolution in *Errors* and *Twelfth Night*, as well as in the Plautine archetype, *Menaechmi*, comes at a single stroke in the form of a dramatic entrance.[61] The appearance of Menaechmus of Ephesus, Antipholus

---

[60] *Comic Sequence*, 132.

[61] Salingar (*Traditions*, 321) discusses other parallels—the disclosing of 'successive identities in a judicial hearing', the mending of broken marriages, 'the emotional theme of the judge and the nun'. Riemer (117 ff.) points out, in addition, similarities between Helena and the Abbess of *Errors*, who both project an aura of magic and miracle and appear at the end to mend broken family bonds.

and Dromio of Syracuse, Sebastian, and here of Helena cuts the knots and resolves the difficulties in each play. It also substitutes life for death, which looms for Egeus and Antonio and has, in yet other variations, reportedly claimed Hero and Helena. The reported death followed by miraculous reappearance, not present in the tale of Giletta, Shakespeare borrows from Italian traditions, particularly those of the *commedia grave*. Like Borghini's Elfenice, Della Porta's Carizia, Bargagli's Drusilla, Oddi's Erminia and Alessandra, Clubb notes, Helena returns from death to clarify the confusions and create new life, instilling in all a sense of humility and wonder.[62] Shakespeare combines classical and contemporary traditions in a stunning *coup de théâtre*.

To complete this complex resolution, Shakespeare transforms two ubiquitous motifs from New Comedy, a recovered ring and pregnancy. Recognition by artificial tokens like rings or necklaces was an old stage device by Aristotle's time, one that drew his censure as least artistic, ἡ ἀτεχνοτάτη, used largely through helplessness, δι' ἀπορίαν (*Poet.* 1454b20–1). This judgement notwithstanding, Menander, Plautus and Terence made good use of artificial tokens as did many later playwrights. In *All's Well*, Shakespeare doubles the device as found in Boccaccio, providing two rings and introducing Helena's as a surprise which begins the process of exposure. Bertram's ring symbolizes the family honour he stands so haughtily on but, in the heat of passion, proves unworthy of. As David Bevington aptly observes, 'The ring of the husband suggests a journey of self-betrayal leading to repentance, while that of his wife tells a story of maligned virtue forced to disguise itself until at last truth is revealed'.[63] Bertram's ring also suggests the marital love and fidelity he owes to Helena, who appropriately, returns it to him in a new wedding ceremony. These rings are not mere proofs from the past, but symbols of selves lost and found, of identities formerly created, now claimed, and always to be honoured. Helena's pregnancy not only fulfils the other impossible condition, but, as often in comedy, summons the husband to the real world of work, responsibility, and marriage.[64] In *All's Well* there are rich symbolic associations, implicit perhaps in Giletta's earlier hope that

---

[62] Clubb, *Italian Drama*, 84–5.   [63] *Action is Eloquence*, 58.

[64] Compare the couple of the deep source, *Hecyra*; Giletta's less delicate presentation of bouncing twin boys; Armado and the pregnant Jaquenetta in *LLL*; and the grimly oviparous pair of Ionesco's aptly titled parodic fantasy, *The Future is in Eggs*.

she might become pregnant, 'Idio grazia' (iv. 329), by grace of God. The pregnant Helena carries in her the miraculous promise of new life, not only for herself, but for her child and husband, who promptly asks forgiveness: *Helena*. ''Tis but the shadow of a wife you see; / The name and not the thing.' *Bertram*. 'Both, both. O, pardon!' (v. iii. 307–8).

Bertram's plea for forgiveness marks the complex moment of *cognitio* towards which the entire play tends. This moment includes two recognitions, actually, the recognition of Bertram as liar, cheat, and husband and the recognition of Helena as wife. The first recalls other New Comedic recognitions, often coinciding with exposures of *alazoneia*, but often effecting a change in fortune for the better. Menander's boasting soldiers, for example, though exposed, often wind up with the girl—Thrasonides (*Misoumenos*), Stratophanes (*Sikyonios*), and (probably) Polemon (*Perikeiromene*). Terence's Thraso, at the end of *Eunuchus*, is permitted to enter Phaedria's house as a mock-rival for Thais.[65] Furthermore, the ending of *All's Well* recalls other New Comedic conclusions, wherein virtuous woman often becomes citizen wife. Here vicious man becomes citizen husband.

Attempting a mix of moral satire and romantic comedy in *All's Well*, Shakespeare shows himself a perfectly orthodox neo-classicist.[66] The daring strategy that casts a comic butt as romantic lead is not without risks, as the history of dissatisfaction with Bertram for failing to be Romeo or even Demetrius, Posthumus, or Claudio shows. Johnson's evaluation rings throughout the ages: 'I cannot reconcile my heart to *Bertram*; a man noble without generosity, and young without truth; who marries *Helen* as a coward, and leaves her as a profligate: when she is dead by his unkindness, sneaks home to a second marriage, is accused by a woman whom he has wronged, defends himself by falshood, and is dismissed to happiness.'[67] Shakespeare's care to endow Bertram with some

---

[65] Baïf (*L'Evnvqve*, ed. Marty-Laveaux, 3) read the arrangement less cynically than many later, observing that Thraso and Phaedria 'sont faicts amis, & jouissent en commun de leurs amours'. Della Porta's Martebellonio finally gets more than he bargained for, winding up with the insatiable serving maid Chiaretta, instead of the expected and beautiful Callidora.

[66] Smith (*Ancient Scripts*, 134–98) well demonstrates that the blending of moral satire and romantic comedy characterizes Renaissance (and later) productions of Plautus and Terence in England, whether academic, courtly, or popular.

[67] Ed. Vickers, v. 114.

admirable qualities, his attractiveness and courage in battle, has not much influenced critical disaffection. Part of the problem here is the perceived ineloquence of Bertram's brief contrition. Our sense of poetic justice demands more breastbeating, perhaps in the manner of Charisios (*Epitrepontes* 909 ff.), who recognizes painful truths about himself and his treatment of his wife.[68]

Another part of the problem here is the unfair expectation that Bertram display psychological verisimilitude, that he travel a well-marked path to self-knowledge; the play is not a *Bildungsroman*. Recollecting the sources and antecedents as well as later examples of the repentant *adulescens* in drama can adjust our expectations. In the deep source, Terence's *Hecyra*, Pamphilus has no accountability for the earlier rape and robbery of his future wife. In fact, Donatus describes him as 'lenissimus in vxorem maritus, & item deditus matri suae' ('a husband very gentle to his wife and at the same time devoted to his mother'). Willichius, likewise, thinks him 'exemplum egregium humanitatis & pietatis', as does Melanchthon, who praises especially in the play 'humanitas, & fides Pamphili'. In his view the *catastrophe* does not in any sense provide a moral comeuppance; instead it illustrates how often by errors and false suspicions it happens that spouses fall out, 'quae monet saepe errore & falsis suspicionibus fieri, vt dissentiant coniuges'.[69] Creating a story of the Impossible Tasks, Boccaccio too passes over the issue of personal morality, specifically the Count's cruelty and lust, hinting only at the unfairness of the tasks in his use of 'durissimo' (rendered as 'churlishly' by Painter) and 'la dura condizione' (iv. 325, 'the hard condition'). Accolti's version of the story likewise imputes to the Prince no wrongdoing, even going so far as to present the lady, Verginia, as begging his forgiveness in the last scene, a boon he magnanimously grants.

Unlike these precedents, Shakespeare's play depicts quite pointedly the immorality of the *adulescens* who is the romantic lead, thus creating difficult moral and emotional problems for the audience. Facing similar problems with such a character, various playwrights tried various solutions. Shadwell ignores the problem altogether in his adaptation of Terence, *The Squire of Alsatia*,

---

[68] Yet the scene can be moving in the theatre, as the success of Tyrone Guthrie's major production (1959) attests; see St Clare Byrne, 'The Shakespeare Season', 557–8.

[69] *Terentius* (1560), 616 (Donatus), 674 (Willichius); *Comoediae* (1552), 5 (Melanchthon).

wherein the *adulescens* blithely dismisses two former lovers (one with a child and driven mad by the desertion) to marry happily the chaste Isabella. Other dramatists were not so cavalier. Molina's guilty *adulescens* in *El Burlador de Sevilla* suffers fantastic punishment; Cibber's rakish young man in *Love's Last Shift* repents climactically and sentimentally, thus attracting the scornful incredulity of Vanbrugh's witty, aptly entitled sequel, *The Relapse*. Neither ignoring the moral issues, nor devising cruel retribution, nor contriving an unbelievable change of heart, Shakespeare depicts a guilty *adulescens* but articulates his folly as a kind of *alazoneia* curable by public ridicule and some repentance. Pamphilus can conceal the final revelation from his father: 'placet non fieri hoc itidem ut in comoediis / omnia omnes ubi resciscunt' (*Hecyra* 866–7, 'It pleases me that this not happen as things do in comedies, where everyone gets to know everything'). Bertram must endure a public humiliation in full view of the older generation, 'ut in comoediis'. His arrogant imposture receives condign comeuppance as Shakespeare lightly sketches in the familiar contours of Terence *moralisé*. To some degree, Bertram embodies the sin-repentance-forgiveness paradigm of contemporary drama, especially that of the Prodigal Son plays, which typically include an affair with a *meretrix*.[70] According to this paradigm the repentant sinner need not win our approval to receive forgiveness, any more than a young man in a comedy need win our affections to receive a young woman's love. And Helena both loves and forgives Bertram: she is comic heroine and an agent of grace—a grace that is, as often, unexpected and undeserved. This marriage, human and imperfect, is both a festive conclusion and also a 'precarious beginning'.[71]

The final scene complements the discovery of Bertram with the discovery of Helena, alive, faithful, forgiving, and loving. Returned from the ranks of the dead, Helena again seems a miraculous restorative figure, one who, like Hero, redeems past wrongs with present love. And this love—a complex mixture of sexual desire and selfless devotion—ripens from lyrical adoration to knowing acceptance, from youthful infatuation to marital affection. Helena

---

[70] See Turner, 'Dramatic Conventions'; Beck; Barton (*Ben Jonson*, 242 ff.) interestingly notes other variations on the Prodigal Son story in Jonson, Middleton, Cooke, Fletcher, and Rowley.

[71] Good on the mixed quality of the play and resolution is Neely, *Broken Nuptials*, 58–104, from whom I quote (65). On grace in the play and the age see Lewis, ' "Derived Honesty and Achieved Goodness" '.

exposes Bertram's vanity and routs the forces that would demean or undervalue her, as do the merry wives with Falstaff;[72] but unlike them, she rewards the offender with her devotion. Bertram's discovery of this Helena constitutes an Aristotelian anagnorisis, a change from ignorance to knowledge; and, as Aristotle prescribed, it conduces to friendship or hatred, ἢ εἰς φιλίαν ἢ εἰς ἔχθραν (*Poet.* 1452a31). Aristotle's illustrations of this change, Else explains, show in such changes the crucial ingredient of φιλία, a bond between two people such that one finds a) in an enemy the loved one (Oedipus and father); or b) in a loved one the enemy (Clytemnestra and son).[73] Bertram, having found in Parolles a traitor, now experiences a comic variation of Aristotle's first type, discovering in the detested clog his loving wife.

All's Well shows a sophisticated mastery of New Comedic conventions, themes, and characters, one that raises and upsets audience expectations, fluently creates and dissolves New Comedic fictions. Shakespeare's pervasive appropriation of New Comedy here contrasts with other attempts: Heywood's *The English Traveller* and Jonson's *The Case is Altered*, for example, present New Comedic action in diverting subplots that bear only tentative relations with the rest of the plays. *All's Well* integrates New Comedy thoroughly and purposefully into its design, thus resembling *Twelfth Night* and *The Alchemist*. *All's Well* incorporates elements from Shakespeare's other comedies, notably from Shakespeare's earlier *miles gloriosus* play, *The Merry Wives of Windsor*. There, as here, two tricky women conspire to lead on the amorous captain, bedazzled by the prospect of sexual pleasure. The wives merely tease Falstaff, while Helena and Diana, through the bedtrick, actually satisfy Bertram's desires. In both plays, however, the women control the male libido, transforming attempts at illicit sex into ratification of existing marriages. Both actions expose the vanity of the principals and then provide for forgiveness and reintegration—slightly in Page's invitation of Falstaff to dinner, and hugely in Bertram's reconstituted marriage. The intrigue plays also figure importantly here. As in *Shrew*, a broken nuptial soon mends by the

---

[72] Such initiative and purposefulness, according to G. B. Shaw (*Collected Plays*, ii. 506) illustrate the reality of relations between the sexes in Shakespeare and in life; Shakespearean heroines like Rosalind, Mariana, and 'the lady doctor' in *All's Well* ('an early Ibsenite heroine') become Ann Whitefield in *Man and Superman*, the irresistible life force personified.

[73] Else, *Aristotle's Poetics*, 350.

taming of one partner through the other's use of disguise, proxy, and impersonation. As in *Much Ado*, the *adulescens* comes repentant to a new marriage only to find his former wife resurrected. In Claudio and Bertram Shakespeare struggles with the moral and theatrical limitations of the *adulescens*, whose youthful impetuousity, both times contracted into a cold regard for honour, seems inadequate to the demands of love. Hero and Helena, to varying degrees, supply such deficiencies. And their wondrous reappearances—filled with love and forgiveness—anticipate the restorations in Shakespeare's New Comedic romances, especially *Pericles* and *The Tempest*.

5

New Comedic Romance

THE influence of New Comedy on Shakespeare's romances—
Pericles and *The Tempest*, especially—has been perceived but
fitfully.[1] Yet, New Comedy contributed significant structural elements to romance and remained an important presence in the
genre, early and late. Romance may have originated with Homer
but it took shape from Euripides, who, as Satyrus observed, '"per-
fected" plots containing quarrels within a family, rape or abduc-
tion, "sudden changes of fortune" and recognitions by means of
tokens'. Such action became the 'mainstay' of New Comedy.[2]
Witness Scaliger's description of New Comedic plot:

> In noua igitur Nuptiae, & Amores maxima ex parte: Riualitates multae:
> Virgines emptae à lenonibus, quae sint liberae, quaeq; liberae inueniantur,
> aut annulo, aut crepundiis, aut nutricibus, à patre, à matre, ab amatore, à
> fratre, semper cum lenonum infortunio.   (*Poetices* 148)

In New Comedy then, marriages and love affairs are the chief subjects.
There are many jealous rivalries. Virgins are brought from bawds so that
they may be free; some may be discovered to be free by a ring, by rattles
or amulets, by nurses, recognized by a father, mother, lover, or brother,
always to the great discomfort of the bawds.

Menander, Plautus, and Terence variously refined these basic elements, all of which would be repeatedly rearticulated in romance:
there separations arise from sea storm, shipwreck, and pirates; the
hero or heroine endures consequent travels and trials, including
threats to the chastity of the vulnerable *virgo*; the action ends in
miraculous recognitions and recoveries. Directly and indirectly,
New Comedy supplied models for many later expressions of
romance: the enormously influential Hellenistic fictions—Achilles

---

[1] Among the percipient are Doran, 172 ff.; Riehle, 31–5, 249 ff. For a helpful discussion of the problematic term 'romance' see Wells, 'Shakespeare and Romance',
Later Shakespeare, ed. Brown and Harris, 48–79.

[2] Salingar, *Traditions*, 147 (cf. 125, 148); see also Knox, *Word and Action*,
250–74; *Cambridge History of Classical Literature*, i. 335–7.

Tatius' *Leucippe and Cleitophon*, Chariton's *Chaereas and Callirhoe*, Longus' *Daphnis and Chloe*, Xenophon of Ephesus' *Ephesiaca*, and Heliodorus' *Aethiopica*, the Roman prose fiction of Apuleius, Elizabethan prose narratives like those of Sidney and Greene, pious tales like *Apollonius of Tyre*, and Renaissance tragicomedy.[3] The standard elements received endless refiguration in later ages, none wittier than the arrangement in Wilde's incomparable parody, *The Importance of Being Earnest*: playing the conventional role, the orphaned Jack Worthing explains to Lady Bracknell that he has lost both his parents. 'Both?', she retorts, 'To lose one parent may be regarded as a misfortune—to lose *both* seems like carelessness.'[4] Instead of the standard pirate or shipwreck, the dotty Miss Prism caused the initial separation by mistakenly leaving the infant in a handbag at Victoria Station, Brighton Line.

Wilde was not the only playwright to effect sea changes on New Comedic models. Plautus' *Rudens*, for example, an important romance play adduced as independent source for both *Pericles* and *The Tempest*, appears 'redrizzato alla forma moderna' in Dolce's interesting adaptation, *Il ruffiano*.[5] In the original the pimp Labrax storms the temple of Venus to recover two girls seeking refuge there. In *Il ruffiano*, as in its predecessor Beolco's *La piovana*, the temple becomes a Catholic church, where 'sono istracciate le touaglie, rouinati gli Altari, i Crocifissi gettati in terra . . . I poueri Santi sono tutti guasti et fracassati, gli Apostoli, gli Angioli, i confessori, le lampade, & ogni cosa tutto è ito a rouina' (fol. 24, 'the linens are torn, the altars ruined, the crucifixes thrown on the ground . . . All the poor saints are broken and smashed, the Apostles, the angels, the confessors, the lamps, and every thing has gone to ruins'). The pimp and his accomplice are Lutherans: 'sono Lutherani: due ghiotti della scola de Martin Luthero' (p. 25). New Comedic action furnishes Counter-Reformation satire.

Though rarely pointed so specifically, Renaissance transformations of classical romance usually exhibit the same Christianizing tendency, incorporating classical configurations and motifs into the wider, more familiar moral patterns of loss and recovery, sin and

[3] Perry, *Ancient Romances*, 72–3; on Longus, R. L. Hunter, *Study*, 67–70; Schmeling, *Chariton*, 50, 158; on Heliodorus, Anderson, *Ancient Fiction*, 48; Schmeling, *Xenophon of Ephesus*, 101–4; on Apuleius, Winkler, *Auctor and Actor*, 200–3, Tatum, *Apuleius*, 24–6, 96, 147.

[4] p. 494.

[5] *Comedie* (1560), fol. 3.

forgiveness, death and rebirth. Instructive paradigms appear in the explicit and didactic accommodations of the *sacra rappresentazione*, the Italian culmination of the miracle play. In one group of these plays, the Christianizing arranges itself into a recurrent pattern that features miraculous preservation of virginity. Inflected further, the pattern results in *tragedia sacra*, those popular stories of virgin martyrs that eventually issue in Dekker's play about Dorothea, *The Virgin Martyr*.[6] The passive classical *virgo* becomes the sanctified Christian hero. The traditions of Christianized Terence further illustrate the hermeneutic transforming the recovery of classical texts. Beginning with Hrosvit and extending through the works of Schonaeus, Reuchlin, Frischlin, Macropedius, Gnaphaeus, Grimald, Gascoigne, and others, this large and influential corpus blended classical and biblical elements to promote virtue and confirm faith. According to Marvin Herrick, these plays 'in working out a reformed kind of Terentian drama, actually arrived in most instances at tragicomedy'.[7] Here the classical *deus ex machina* often becomes the Christian God who personally intervenes to avert tragedy and bring about comedic resolution. Indeed, this is the entire action of Grimald's *Christus Redivivus* (pr. 1543), a play that dramatizes the Resurrection of Jesus, advertising itself as 'Comoedia Tragica, sacra & noua'.[8] Less apocalyptically, Heywood's *The Captives*, an adaptation of *Rudens* closely analogous to *Pericles*, emphasizes the virtue of the *virgo* and moves the final scene from the temple of Venus to a monastery.

While demonstrating the pervasiveness and flexibility of New Comedy, these plays illustrate the various ways in which Christian ethos and classical form cohere in the Renaissance. They constitute a tradition of New Comedic adaptation that blossoms finally in Shakespeare's romances, which also feature triumphantly chaste *virgines* and providential action. And yet, Shakespeare's plays radically revise their constituent elements. For one thing, these elements are many and varied, including Hellenistic romances,

[6] On these dramatic developments see Clubb, *Italian Drama*, 205–29. Such plays ought to be viewed against the background of scriptural and patristic teaching on chastity and virginity, outlined conveniently, for example, in *The New Catholic Encyclopedia*; see also Brown, *The Body and Society*.

[7] *Tragicomedy*, 16–62 (27); see also Herford, 70–164; Doran, 162 ff.

[8] This play features a prototype in Christ for the various resurrections that figure so largely in later tragicomedy; consequently, the victory over death here is universal, 'mortem morte deleuit sua / Nostram, ac vitam nobis rediuiuus attulit' (1582–3).

medieval works, travel books, contemporary fiction and drama; the subtexts contribute distinctive and competing energies to the whole. For another, the worlds of Marina and Miranda reflect the intersecting political and moral concerns of their age, when female chastity was a marketable commodity, the legal guarantor of property exchange, and a sign of male honour.[9] Accordingly, chastity in these plays earns substantial material as well as immaterial rewards: Marina marries the governor of Myteline, Miranda, the Prince of Naples. Both *Pericles* and *The Tempest* exhibit subtly, suggestively, fitfully, and problematically the workings of chaste virtue and those of grace, forgiveness, and providence.

Pericles

It may seem tendentious to claim New Comedic influence on *Pericles*, a play that so obtrusively insists on its origins in John Gower. And some of the best studies of the play have analysed its medieval character, comparing the peculiar design and effect to those in miracle plays (especially the Digby *Mary Magdalene*), saints' plays, or moralities.[10] But Shakespeare here, as ever, ranges freely within the zodiac of his and others' wits. Composing or revising *Pericles*, he harks back to old-fashioned romance dramas like *Clyomon and Clamydes*, *Mucedorus*, *The Rare Triumphs of Love and Fortune*. He also recalls New Comedy, including an early experiment with Plautus, *The Comedy of Errors*—particularly its felicitous combination of Gower's Apollonius story and *Menaechmi*. New Comedy provides the principles and motifs which Shakespeare uses to adapt Greek romance: specifically it contributes the *senex–virgo–adulescens* pattern, symbolic localities—the sea, brothel, temple, the motif of the casket, the paradigm of familial (especially father-daughter) reunion. New Comedic elements, conjoined to elements of romance narrative and early religious drama, appear in unfamiliar shapes and forms here; but their presence, whether transmitted directly or indirectly, shapes the play and our response to it.[11]

---

[9] See Stone, *The Family, Sex and Marriage*, 501 ff., 636–7.

[10] See Hoeniger, Arden edn. (1963), lxxxviii–xci; R. G. Hunter, 132–41; Felperin, *Shakespearean Romance*, 143–76.

[11] On *Rudens* here see Holt White, ed. Vickers, vi. 598–9; Simpson, 17 ff. Studies

Modifying his sources, Gower's *Confessio Amantis* and Twine's *The Pattern of Painful Adventures*, Shakespeare casts the action of his play into various New Comedic configurations. The most striking of these is the *senex–virgo–adulescens* pattern, familiar from *Shrew*, *Ado*, and *Wives*. The opening scene in Antioch reveals the perverse possibilities in the triangulation: the *senex* is not only *iratus* and *durus*, a blocking figure who deals harshly with suitors, but he is also *amans*, in this case, the incestuous lover of his own daughter. Shakespeare suppresses the pathos of Gower's and Twine's accounts, which narrate the father's cruel rape and the daughter's sorrowful complaints to the nurse. He focuses instead on Antiochus, infatuate, devious, and forbidding; and he gives the daughter two revealing lines addressed to Pericles: 'Of all, 'say'd yet, may'st thou prove prosperous! / Of all, 'say'd yet, I wish thee happiness!' (I. i. 59–60). These lines subtly tilt the characterization from innocent female victim to New Comedic daughter, whose father harshly and unreasonably blocks the importunate suitor. Upon solving the riddle, Pericles pointedly casts off the role of *adulescens*, 'Good sooth, I care not for you' (I. i. 86). Moral corruption shatters Plautine fiction, as the *senex* plots to murder the *adulescens*. We witness a hideous perversion of the expected comic sequence: boy meets, gets, and loses girl.

The familiar configuration reappears later in Pentapolis where the New Comedic triangle consists of Simonides, Thaisa, and Pericles again. Simonides admires Pericles, champion of the tournament, excellent in the civil arts of dancing and music. Discovering his daughter's intention to wed the stranger knight, he approves, then expresses resentment and annoyance at her independence:

> 'Tis well, mistress, your choice agrees with mine;
> I like that well: Nay, how absolute she's in't,
> Not minding whether I dislike or no!
> Well, I do commend her choice,
> And will no longer have it be delayed.
> Soft, here he comes, I must dissemble it.   (II. v. 18–23)

Simonides' counterparts in Gower and Twine simply rejoice at the match; he, however, proceeds to stage a version of the New

of other influences include Gesner, *Shakespeare and the Greek Romance*, 84–90; Welsh, 'Heritage in *Pericles*', in Tobias and Zolbrod (1974), 89–113; Dunbar, ' "To the Judgement of Your Eye" ', in Muir (1983), 86–97; Hillman, 'Shakespeare's Gower and Gower's Shakespeare'.

Comedic scenario encountered in Antioch. Playing the *senex iratus*
and *durus*, he sharply accuses Pericles: 'Thou hast bewitch'd my
daughter, and thou art / A villain' (II. v. 49–50), while repeatedly
confessing his approval in asides. Critics have loudly condemned
this sequence, thinking it poorly devised, possibly the work of an
amateur dramatist.[12] But the classical fiction both expresses and
exorcises the fatherly possessiveness which, perverted, can lead to
disaster; Antiochus' foul passion becomes merely Simonides' petty
crankiness. The charade serves also to test both Pericles and
Thaisa. When Pericles responds spiritedly to the charge of treason,
Simonides murmurs an approving aside, 'Now by the gods, I do
applaud his courage' (II. v. 58). When Thaisa publicly reveals her
love for Pericles (II. v. 71–2), the king terminates the charade:
'Either be rul'd by me, or I'll make you—/ Man and wife' (II. v.
83–4). The compressed and fictionalized New Comedic triangle
satisfies expectations raised and frustrated in Antioch, substituting
comedic fulfilment for tragic action.

The familiar configuration appears one more time, when Pericles
must play *senex* to his own daughter and her suitor, Lysimachus.
In the miraculous moment of recovering Marina, Lysimachus says
to the amazed father, 'when you come ashore, / I have another
suit' (v. i. 260–1). Pericles responds magnanimously, 'You shall pre-
vail, / Were it to woo my daughter, for it seems / You have been
noble towards her' (261–3). When next we hear of the suit it is a
fait accompli: Pericles introduces Lysimachus as Marina's betrothed
(v. iii. 71). The entire action, sketched in the lightest of strokes,
takes place off-stage. Through repeated use of the New Comedic
configuration, Shakespeare thus invests Gower's rather colourless
ablative absolute, 'patre consenciente' (Bullough, vi. 415) with new
meaning: Pericles' love for his daughter is not unnaturally possessive, nor even normally cranky and testy, but free, generous, and
noble. And even at the high moment of New Comedic *catastrophe*,
time proves to be continuous, and life, here as in the intrigue play
marriages, goes beyond convention and the satisfying closures of
fiction. Even in the recovery of Marina is the beginning of loss.

As before, New Comedic topography provides Shakespeare with
resonant symbolism. From Menander onwards, the sea is the setting for various journeys, for personal and professional disasters,

---

[12] See, for example, Evans, 228.

for storms and shipwrecks, for *praedones* and *piscatores* ('pirates' and 'fishermen'). As we have already noted, trouble at sea often causes the initial separation that the play action mends; New Comedy often features the conventionalized return from a sea voyage; and Roman dramaturgy sometimes associates stage left with the harbour and the great open world beyond. Doran (174 ff.) well observes that the woodcuts illustrating Renaissance editions of Terence, particularly the seascapes, show how easily classical comedy conforms to the fashions of narrative romance. This observation finds splendid confirmation in *Terentius Comico Carmine* (Argentia, 1503), a beautiful early edition whose coloured illustrations of *Andria* and *Eunuchus* feature backgrounds composed of a ship and the sea. Italian neo-classicists, ingeniously creating a third genre of pastoral tragicomedy or romance, had already coined the term 'boschereccia' or 'marittima' ('for piscatory variations substituting seaside for woodland settings').[13]

The storm and shipwreck near Pentapolis, II. i, recapitulate more specific Plautine moments.[14] Palaestra's appearance in *Rudens*, drenched and exhausted, soliloquizing about the 'hominum fortunae . . . miserae' (185), may inspire that of Pericles, '*wet*', and his reflections on mortal miseries, 'Wind, rain, and thunder, remember, earthly man / Is but a substance that must yield to you' (2–3). Like Plautus in *Rudens*, Shakespeare presents several fishermen, not the single one of his sources. Their conversation recounts the storm and shipwreck from the perspective of sympathetic onshore observers:

3. FISH. Faith, master, I am thinking of the poor men that were cast away before us even now.
1. FISH. Alas, poor souls, it griev'd my heart to hear what pitiful cries they made to us to help them.   (18–21)

This perspective, which Heywood also adopted in his revision of *Rudens* (*The Captives*, I. iii), and which Shakespeare again employs in *The Tempest*, may well descend from Sceparnio's sympathetic onshore observations earlier (162 ff.).

In *Rudens* Plautus' fishermen speak about their hard lot in life,

[13] Clubb, *Italian Drama*, 181.
[14] In the eighteenth century Holt White (ed. Vickers, vi. 599) first compared the fishermen of *Rudens* II. i to those whom stranded Pericles meets, and other editors (Bellinger, Yale edn., 1925; Hoeniger) have accepted the suggestion.

about dying, 'ut piscatorem aequomst, fama sitique speque falsa' (312, 'a true fisherman's fate—by hunger, thirst, and false hope'). This cynicism turns satirical in Shakespeare, whose fishermen complain about the rich misers who, like 'whales', feed on smaller fish and 'never leave gaping till they swallow'd the / whole parish, church, steeple, / bells, and all' (cf. the 'belching whale', III. i. 62). This text teasingly echoes a passage in Day's *Law-Tricks*; it also echoes another passage from *Rudens*. Charmides reproaches Labrax: 'Iam postulabas te, inpurata belua, / totam Siciliam deuoraturum insulam?' (543–4, 'So you expected yourself, you dirty beast, to devour the whole island of Sicily?'). Labrax responds: 'quaenam ballaena meum uorauit uidulum, / aurum atque argentum ubi omne compactum fuit?' (544–5, 'What whale has devoured my trunk, all packed with gold and silver?').[15] The trunk in *Rudens*, which Gripus the fisherman hauls in from the sea, becomes the object of a tug-of-war with Trachalio in the comic scene that gives the play its name.[16] The Plautine *vidula* becomes Pericles' rotten armour, an innovation from Gower and Twine, likewise hauled on to the stage but freely and generously given away. Not merely a fleeting comic counterpoint like their Plautine doubles, nor an occasion for some slapstick merriment like Gripus, Shakespeare's humorous and ordinary fishermen show the compassion of Twine's *piscator* and provide Pericles with the means of restoration; in their homely way, they help undo the harm of a Fortuna that seems malevolent.

The all important New Comedic trunk or casket that contains the tokens necessary for concluding *Rudens*, *Cistellaria*, or *Vidularia* Shakespeare refigures again, this time as Thaisa's coffin. In the midst of another sea storm, Pericles calls on Lucina to assist his wife's delivery (III. i. 10 ff.). The invocation echoes the familiar New Comedic invocation to Lucina, usually voiced by the mother-to-be (e.g. *Andria* 473). Like the *vidula* in *Rudens*, the coffin is thrown overboard and then recovered; but this time, containing Thaisa, it becomes the occasion for the magical art of Cerimon

[15] On the connections with Day see Hoeniger, 172–8; Wood, 'Shakespeare and the Belching Whale'. The whale in *Rudens*, not noted by critics, also appears in Dolce's *Il ruffiano*, wherein someone hopes that the pimp has made a good meal for the whales, 'che egli era apunto pasto per le Balene' (fol. 13v.).

[16] There is a parallel recovery in the fragmentary *Vidularia*: *Cacistus*: 'ibi ut piscabar, fuscina ici uidulum' (frag. vii, 'There as I was fishing, I struck the bag with my fishing spear').

and for rebirth. New Comedic deep structure furnishes the wondrous imaginings of romance.

This structure defines also the experience of Marina, separated
from home, abducted by pirates, trapped in a brothel. Her story
resembles that of Selenium in *Cistellaria*, abandoned as an infant,
given to a *lena*, Melaenis; of Glycerium in *Andria*, separated from
her guardian by shipwreck, given eventually to the *meretrix*
Chrysis; of Pamphila in *Eunuchus*, seized by pirates, sold as a
slave, bought by a soldier; of Palaestra in *Rudens*, stolen by a
pirate, sold to a greedy pimp ('eam de praedone uir mercatur pes-
sumus', 40). Shakespeare provides Marina with a worldly-wise and
experienced New Comedic *lena*, who, without any precedent in
Gower or Twine, resembles Scapha (*Mostellaria*) or Syra
(*Cistellaria*). Like her predecessors the Bawd lectures the neophyte
on harsh economic realities and on the world of men. Expanding
the accounts of Gower and Twine in New Comedic fashion,
Shakespeare also focuses on the mercenary *leno* (pimp or
slavedealer), cut from the same cloth as the greedy Labrax of
Rudens, or any others of the type—Ballio in *Pseudolus*, Sannio in
Adelphoe, Dorio in *Phormio*.[17] Jealous of their investments, concerned about their business, the *leno* blusters and threatens force.
Pandar, Bawd, and Boult, likewise harried traders in flesh, worry
about their financial futures, and also threaten force. Fearing that
'she'll disfurnish us of all our cavalleria' (IV. vi. 11–12), Boult tries to
crack 'the glass' of Marina's virginity (IV. vi. 142). This confrontation between *virgo* and *leno* does not end, as one might expect, in
his discomfiture by intrigue or conversion; instead, Marina gives
Boult gold and promises to get more by teaching. The solution is
Terentian in style: portrayed with some sympathy and humour,
Sannio and Dorio are neither 'cheated of money nor taken to
court; on the contrary, they are each paid in full for their girls'.[18]

In Marina Shakespeare transforms again the classical *virgo*.
Predecessors like Planesium (*Curculio*) and Palaestra (*Rudens*) are
saved from prostitution by the discovery of true identity or by
external intervention. Marina, however, saves herself. No friend or

[17] Wilkins's novel, *The Painfull Adventures of Pericles Prince of Tyre* (1608), deriving from Twine, lists the Boult figure simply as 'A *Leno*', Bullough, vi. 494.
Shakespeare replicates the figure by adding Pandar.

[18] Duckworth, 263. More moralistically, Heywood (*The Captives*, v. iii. 183 ff.)
has Mildew convert from evil ways and furnish information for the recognition.

lover intercedes for her; the recognition and reunion with her father come later. Like St Agnes who remained miraculously chaste in the brothel, or like other Christian saints—Theodora, Serapia, or Denise—Marina actively resists the surrounding evil, converting sinners to repentance.[19] In this she bears notable resemblance to the heroines of Hrosvit, pioneer in the tradition of Christianized Terence, to Constantia (*Gallicanus*), the holy virgins (*Dulcitius*), and Drusiana (*Callimachus*), and to Dekker's Dorothea. These virtuous women, confident in God, struggle to preserve their chastity; Hirena, in fact, resists enforced prostitution. By virtue of purity, faith, and courage, Marina too escapes the snares of world, flesh, and devil. Shakespeare, well within traditional bounds, transforms the New Comedic situation into a minature Christian miracle play, one that blends moral message and classical form into zestful comedy.

Or at least tries to. Marina's ordeal finds problematic resolution in the marriage to Lysimachus, whose conversion, perhaps unfaithfully represented in the surviving text, is hardly eloquent or inspiring. Shakespeare, in fact, diminishes the love interest here, departing from the example of *Rudens*, from that of contemporary adaptors like Dolce and Heywood, and from his own past experiments. Again, as in *All's Well*, the *adulescens*, a would-be debaucher, seems unworthy of the *virgo*; but this time the problem is complicated not resolved by the peculiar virtue of the heroine. For Marina's chastity expresses divine purity even as it asserts very human resistance against male aggression and domination. The stage here mirrors the contemporary situation wherein, as Jordan observes, chastity could lead 'to a woman's escape from patriarchal proprietorship' into celibate communities, or to the more conventional end of marriage.[20] The vigour of Marina's chastity, its hagiographic resonances, seem to fit her for the first option, while the play recuperates her, like Isabella of *Measure for Measure*, into the second. Fitting his unconventional *virgo* to a conventional ending, Shakespeare leaves the tensions unresolved, de-emphasizes the match, and concentrates, instead, on the reunions with Pericles and Thaisa.

[19] See Denomy, ed., *The Old French Lives of Saint Agnes*; Bullough, vi. 352; Schulenburg, 'The Heroics of Virginity', in Rose (1986), 29–72. Helms ('The Saint in the Brothel') identifies another *locus classicus* in Seneca the Elder's *controversia* of the Prostitute Priestess.

[20] *Renaissance Feminism*, 30.

The entire play works to create an exquisite version of an archetypal New Comedic scene, the reunion of father and long-lost daughter. In this reunion Shakespeare significantly departs from the powerful conventions of Greek Hellenistic fiction. As Gesner observes:

The traditional blow which Apollonius gives his as yet unidentified daughter is modified to a vague request of Marina that Pericles do no 'violence' on her. . . . Shakespeare has excised at last the ugly tradition reaching all the way back to Chariton that a Greek romance hero should strike the heroine, having failed to recognize her.[21]

This change suggests Shakespeare's movement from the conventions of Greek romance to those of New Comedy, where such reunions typically proceed by the revelation of the girl's woeful story and culminate in the father's happy recognition. As Simpson first suggested, the reunion of Palaestra and Daemones in *Rudens*, in fact, exhibits specific parallels to the scene in *Pericles*.[22] The father, looking at the strange girl, thinks of his lost daughter: *Daemones*: 'trima quae periit mi iam tanta esset, si uiuit, scio' (744, 'at three years old she died to me; now she would be as big as this one, I'm sure, if she lives'). *Pericles*: 'such a one / My daughter might have been' (v. i. 107–8). In both plays the mother's name provides the conventional confirmation of identity: *Daemones*: 'Loquere matris nomen hic quid in securicula siet' (1163, 'Tell me the name of the mother which is on this little axe'). *Pericles*: 'What was thy mother's name?' (v. i. 200). Here, as elsewhere, the reunion restores losses and begins new life.[23]

With the possible exception of the reunion in *Captivi* (which rejoins a father and long-lost son), the reunions in New Comedy do not evoke much emotion in the participants or the audience; nor are they meant to. Light in tone, set amidst busy intrigues, they resolve in a stroke complications of plot and typically reveal that the girl is, after all, an Athenian citizen and, therefore, free to marry the fortunate *adulescens*. The news discomfits some and delights others. Shakespeare varies the archetypal scene in *Pericles*,

[21] p. 87.   [22] pp. 19–21.
[23] Overturning this matrix of conventions all at once, Middleton very knowingly declined to present the expected father–daughter reunion in *Michaelmas Term*; there the Country Wench, corrupted rather than saved from the brothel, asks her disguised father to become her bawd. He does not recognize her and eventually drops out of the play, unrecognized and unreconciled.

where he focuses on the father's emotional and spiritual state, on the man 'who for this three months hath not spoken / To any one, nor taken sustenance / But to prorogue his grief' (v. i. 24–6). Like a typical romance hero—Sir Clyomon or Mucedorus—Pericles wandered the world purposefully and actively, solving Antiochus' riddle, feeding the hungry at Tharsus, showing valour and courtliness at Pentapolis. Now, however, he shrouds himself in isolation and sorrow, benighted by errors. Gower's and Twine's accounts provide clues to Shakespeare's conception:

> For he lith in so derke a place,
> That there maie no wight sen his face.

I [Athanagoras] am come downe unto thee to bring thee, if I may, out of darknesse into light.   (Bullough, vi. 413, 463)

The staging, whereby Pericles must be isolated from the others, behind a locked door, covered in grey garments, wrapped in a shroud, conveys spiritual isolation.[24] As such, the scene recalls Shakespeare's previous experiences with New Comedic errors: Pericles resembles Antipholus of Ephesus and Dromio, imprisoned for madness 'in a dark and dankish vault' (v. i. 248). His prison, however, is of his own making. The scene also reformulates the enclosures and occlusions of *Twelfth Night*: Pericles is a more serious version of Orsino, melancholy, yearning, self-absorbed, aloof; of Olivia, grieving (or trying to grieve) excessively behind her veil; and of Malvolio, reputed mad and suffering imprisonment, darkness, and isolation. The *epitasis* of *Pericles* features confusion in character as well as complication in plot—a knot of entangled incident and spiritual despair.

Summoned from shore, Marina is the virginal *maga*/healer, more like Helena than the relatively helpless Palaestra or her New Comedic sisters. She undertakes the curing of the king, at which task others, including Lysimachus and good Helicanus, have failed. Marina's singing recalls Cerimon's recourse to music at Thaisa's resurrection; her riddling response to Pericles' question about her origins from these shores, 'No, nor of any shores, / Yet I was mortally brought forth, and am / No other than I appear' (v. i. 103–5), recalls the daughter's riddle at Antiochus. Throughout the scene

---

[24] These are the respective choices of the BBC version, the 1979 production at The Other Place, and the 1984 production by The Cheek by Jowl Theatre Company. See Mulryne, 'To glad your ear', 40; Lomax, *Stage Images*, 93.

Marina is fully present and alive, vacillating between doubt and confidence, injured maiden and magical healer, victimized orphan and recovered daughter. Far from merely untying the knots in the action, she is yet another version of the holy virgin healer—of St Agnes, who raises the Provost's boy from death, of Dekker's Dorothea, who brings Sapritius back to consciousness. She is also the woman as wonder, that Italianate *donna* evident in *All's Well*, virtuous in misfortune, surrounded by foils, possessed of healing power, graceful and mysterious.[25]

The power and beauty of the recognition scene struck even early detractors of the play like Charles Gildon and Edmond Malone and still strikes modern audiences.[26] Pericles cries out:

> PER. O Helicanus, strike me, honored sir,
> Give me a gash, put me to present pain,
> Lest this great sea of joys rushing upon me
> O'erbear the shores of my mortality,
> And drown me with their sweetness. O, come hither,
> Thou that beget'st him that did thee beget.   (v. i. 190–5)

Unlike any of the classical reunions, this one signals a second birth for the dead king. And unlike those many classical *virgines*, discovered but not discovering, this one heals and restores her father. The terms of his resonant polyptoton, 'Thou that beget'st him that did thee beget', portray Pericles as a child newly begotten by Marina, the mother. The paradoxes again evoke the earlier riddling in Antioch, but now betoken creative natural love, not foul unnatural incest. Shakespeare, it has been well noted, replays here some elements from the reunion scene of Lear and Cordelia and the restoration (though fleeting) of the aged king to health; there is the kneeling, the music, the call for fresh garments, the moving tenderness. It has not been observed, however, that the scene reverses the usual New Comedic practice, where the discovery of

---

[25] On such healers see Hoy, *Introductions, Notes, and Commentaries*, iii. 179–98; on Marina, Ewbank, '"My name is Marina"', in Edwards (1980), 111–30. Cf. Shakespeare's achievement in this scene with the uninspired reunion between father (Bomelio) and son (Hermione) in *The Rare Triumphs of Love and Fortune*, 952 ff.

[26] Gildon (1710) found the discovery, 'tho' built on the highest Improbability', 'very moving'; Malone (1780), noting the absurdities and irregularities of the whole, nevertheless thought the reunion 'eminently beautiful', ed. Vickers, ii. 261; vi. 297. T. S. Eliot recreated the moment in a moving lyric, 'Marina'. On the staging see Warren, *Staging Shakespeare's Late Plays*, 228–34.

identity usually frees the daughter. Here, both daughter and father find freedom and new life.

This new life comes to full deliverance in the final scene at Ephesus. The sea voyage from the stews of Myteline to the Ephesian temple of Diana, facilitated as ever by Gower's choral intervention, provides a fittingly New Comedic close to the play. Here Shakespeare completes his transformation of New Comedic topography into a landscape of the soul and the world. The sea, as we have noted, wrecks ships and divides families, but casts up the rusty armour, bears the encoffined Thaisa to Cerimon, and carries Pericles to his daughter and wife. Neptune is a god who tries poor mortals but ultimately provides for reunion and redemption, here as in *Errors*, where there is also a movement from the Courtesan's house to the Ephesian priory. In *Pericles* the brothel is a dark house of sin that tests Marina's pluck and virtue, enabling both to shine forth all the brighter. The temple is again a place of restoration and divinely-ordained fulfilment. Obedient to Diana's command, Pericles changes course from Tharsus, where he intends revenge upon Cleon and Dionyza, to Ephesus, where he offers sacrifice. In this change of purpose, a deliberate suppression of the subsequent revenge action of the sources, Pericles anticipates Prospero. The New Comedic localities—sea, brothel, temple—express spiritual meanings, functioning in an intermittent but resonant morality, wherein virtue is rewarded and evil punished.

The final scene at the temple evokes in other ways Shakespeare's earlier blending of Gower and Plautus, *The Comedy of Errors*.[27] As in that play, the *catastrophe* occurs in two stages: first there is the recovery of a long-lost family member and the finding of self; then there is the reunion with wife and mother. The Abbess, drawn from Gower's prototype, has a second incarnation in Thaisa, who is more gracious and wondering than the earlier versions. Recalling New Comedic practice and, perhaps, the business with the Courtesan's ring in *Errors*, Shakespeare adds to his sources' accounts the conventional token, 'The King my father gave you such a ring' (v. iii. 39). But no such reunion in Plautus or Terence could inspire Pericles' emotional response:

[27] Marina's remarkable account of her father 'clasping to the mast' in a sea storm (IV. i. 55) probably derives from *Errors* I. i. 78 ff. Kahn (*Man's Estate*, 213–14) explicates in psychological terms 'the shift from twin to daughter as the figure through whom the hero gains his final identity'.

> You [gods] shall do well,
> That on the touching of her lips I may
> Melt and no more be seen. O come, be buried
> A second time within these arms.   (v. iii. 41–4)

Here, as in Thaisa's eloquent half-line greeting of Marina, 'Blest, and mine own!' (v. iii. 48), Shakespeare departs from precedent, adding depth and genuine emotion.[28]

On its simplest level *Pericles* shows the triumph of comedy, a victory that another 'mouldy tale', *Mucedorus*, depicted allegorically in its Prologue and Epilogue. *Pericles* emphasizes the importance of human patience and divine providence in this triumph, but it does not present consistent, whole, or well-articulated allegory.[29] Unlike Venus in *Rudens*, Diana hardly qualifies as the tutelary deity, despite several references to her and despite her late appearance.[30] We may contrast, for example, the thematics and theophany of *Clyomon and Clamydes*, wherein Providence descends just in time to prevent Neronis from killing herself, ordering, 'Stay, Stay thy stroke' (1550). Shakespeare's *comoedia sacra*, descending directly from his errors plays, is more comedy than sacred. Again there is trust in time and happy accident and distrust of intrigue as an instrument of resolution. In *Pericles* the intriguers do not merely suffer comic comeuppance, however, as do Malvolio and Sir Toby, but, as befits their malevolence, serious punishment. 'A fire from heaven' (II. iv. 9) shrivels up wicked Antiochus and his daughter; the enraged people of Tharsus burn Dionyza and Cleon in the palace (v. iii. 98). This is a deliberate and proleptic departure from the sources: Pericles travels to Tharsus to expose the crime of the king and queen, who are hung, drawn, and burnt in Gower's version, bound, driven out of the city, and stoned to death in Twine's (Bullough, vi. 421, 476). Shakespeare's Pericles and Marina participate finally not in revenge but in joyful reconciliation. This resolu-

---

[28] Ionesco (*The Bald Soprano*) wittily parodies such moments in his version of the conventional spousal reunion. Mr and Mrs Martin arrive at a party to discover that they live on the same street in the same house with the same daughter and ('How curious!' 'How bizzare!') are husband and wife. The devastation of the conventional scene is complete when the maid tells the audience that the Martins, being not really the Martins, are sadly mistaken.

[29] On patience as an active virtue especially helpful against the spiritual paralysis of *melancholia–tristitia–acedia*, see Heckscher, 35 ff. See also Hoeniger, lxxxvi–lxxxviii.

[30] On Venus see Leach, 'Plautus' *Rudens*: Venus Born from a Shell'; for another view of Diana, Knowles, '"The More Delay'd, Delighted"'.

tion clearly anticipates the more complex and ambivalent harmonies of Shakespeare's final Plautine romance, *The Tempest*.

The Tempest

The Tempest, included with the Comedies in the First Folio, is an extraordinarily eclectic play which owes not to a single source but to various texts and traditions. Commentators have traced its elusive harmonies to dramatic romances like *Mucedorus* and *The Rare Triumphs of Love and Fortune*, to the scenari of the *commedia dell'arte*, to contemporary prose fiction, to travel books and journals (especially works by Richard Eden, William Strachey, and Silvester Jourdain), to a host of other antecedents, including Montaigne, Isaiah, Jonson's masques, Vergil's *Aeneid*, Ovid's *Metamorphoses*, and, sporadically, New Comedy.[31] The play observes the classical unities of time, place, and action and embodies the classical structure (prologue, *protasis*, *epitasis*, *catastrophe*) derived from Terence's *Andria*.[32] Building his play around the conflict between opposed brothers, Shakespeare applies to new ends the New Comedic principle of binary construction that developed naturally from the limited repertory of classical masks and character types. Accordingly, Shakespeare's enchanted isle features two fathers, Prospero and Alonso; two children, Miranda and Ferdinand; two pairs of brothers, Alonso and Sebastian, Prospero and Antonio; two servants, Ariel and Caliban; two conspiracies, one against Prospero, the other against Alonso; two kinds of magic, one black, one white, and so on. We have already noted that Renaissance educators like Erasmus and translators like Maurice Kyffin often discerned in such pairings instructive moral antinomies. Prospero and Antonio—one a good, the other a wicked intriguer—recall the temperamentally contrastive brothers of *Adelphoe*, as well as the fraternal pairs of *Much Ado* and *King Lear*.

The Tempest recapitulates fitfully all of Shakespeare's New

---

[31] Some interesting studies include Knox, '*The Tempest* and the Ancient Comic Tradition'; Gesner, '*The Tempest* as Pastoral Romance'; Lea, 201 ff., 443–53, 610 ff.; Schmidgall, *Shakespeare and the Courtly Aesthetic*.

[32] See Boughner, 'Jonsonian Structure in *The Tempest*'; Kermode, Arden edn. (1954), lxxiv ff.

Comedic modes—errors, intrigue, and *alazoneia*. New Comedic errors will finally succeed intrigue, as a climactic entrance dissolves misunderstanding, restores identity, and transfigures anagnorisis. *Alazoneia* here manifests itself in Caliban, Stephano, and Trinculo and again leads to exposure. Shakespeare's sophisticated recension of New Comedy in *The Tempest* rings changes on standard configurations—the *senex–virgo–adulescens*, master–servant, parent–child relations—all located in the resonant seascapes of Plautine romance. Familiar devices—eavesdropping and disguise—appear in new forms.

Moreover, there are specific points of contact between New Comedy and *The Tempest*. Scaliger opined prophetically that *Rudens* would have been better named 'Tempestas'; perhaps Shakespeare thought so too. He 'took strong hints, if not his shaping ideas, from Plautus' *Rudens*' for *The Tempest*, 'with its incidental fantasies of empire and its dominant motif of the just man in exile requited by Providence through a storm'.[33] Both *Rudens* and *The Tempest* open with a storm that causes a shipwreck; the action in both plays transpires on shore, where various groups of shipwrecked travellers meet Daemones, 'senex, qui huc Athenis exul uenit' (35, 'an old man who came here as an exile from Athens'), and aged Prospero, exile from Milan. Both Daemones and Prospero defend helpless daughters against sexual assault and make possible good marriages for them while exercising firm control over rebellious servants. The plays conclude in discovery, reconciliation, and liberation. Again, these suggestive signs need not be construed according to the limited lexicon of traditional *Quellenstudien*; *Rudens* may function instead as a seminal subtext, frequently mediated and reconstituted, which offered dramatists a generic set of romance possibilities.

Shakespeare's New Comedic romance works three important variations on classical predecessors. New Comedic eros again gives way to romantic love, characterized by self-sacrifice and chastity. The traditional opposition between masters and servants becomes here refigured into a complicated discourse on mastery and service, on personal, social, and political power. The intrigues and external *machina* by which ancient comedies come to resolution yield to

---

[33] Scaliger, *Poetices*, 296. Salingar, *Traditions*, 173. See also Simpson, 21–2; Duckworth, 414–5, 416–17; Torrão, 'Reflexos da *Rudens*'; Svendsen, 'The Fusion of Comedy and Romance', in Hartigan (1983), 121–34.

internal remedy—resignation and forgiveness. While liberally
deploying familiar conventions and configurations, *The Tempest*
thus challenges its New Comedic origins.

The reformation of eros into romantic love begins with the tempest itself, the device that brings the lovers together and reveals
their characters. Contemporary accounts of the 'wracke and
redemption' of Sir Thomas Gates provided raw material for this
opening, which Shakespeare put into New Comedic shape, reprising also the shipwreck and familial splitting in *Errors*. Other
aspects of the storm presentation in *The Tempest* recall *Rudens*.
Both plays, like the various adaptations by Beolco (*La piovana*),
Dolce (*Il ruffiano*), and Heywood (*The Captives*), feature the commentary of sympathetic onshore observers. Sceparnio's happy relief
at the girls' survival, 'cum admiratione pronuntiandum' ('to be
expressed with wonder'), Lambinus comments, may have provided
inspiration for the fishermen's compassion in *Pericles*;[34] here the
wonder and the pity echo again to suggest Miranda's innocence
and compassion:

> O! I have suffered
> With those that I saw suffer! A brave vessel,
> (Who had, no doubt, some noble creature in her)
> Dash'd all to pieces! O, the cry did knock
> Against my very heart!   (I. ii. 5–9)

Both plays depict survivors washed up on shore. Palaestra, like
Pericles later, laments her wretched fortune (*Rud.* 185 ff.). The
other lover, Ferdinand, cools 'the air with sighs / In an odd angle
of the isle, and sitting, / His arms in this sad knot' (I. ii. 222–4).
Ariel's humorous description of Ferdinand's distress provides a
supernatural perspective, thus lightening potentially tragic experience. Ampelisca's voice stirs Palaestra out of her melancholy and
she follows the sound to the discovery of her friend; similarly,
Ariel's music allays both the fury of the waters and Ferdinand's
'passion' (I. ii. 393), and he follows the sound to Miranda.

The storms in *Rudens* and *The Tempest* are actually supernatural, punitive occurrences, not simply natural phenomena. Serving
as the Plautine prologue, Arcturus provides background, identifies
the villains, takes credit for raising the storm, explains its purpose.
In a delayed New Comedic prologue, I. ii, Prospero likewise

[34] *Opera* (1577), 933.

reviews the past and reveals to Miranda his controlling hand in the tempest that has wrecked their enemies. The adapted Plautine prologue, however, does not simply forecast an anagnorisis, it actually achieves one. Instructing Miranda, 'ignorant of what thou art, nought knowing / Of whence I am' (I. ii. 18–19), Prospero reveals her true identity, daughter of a Duke. The standard New Comedic recognition of the girl's citizenship here includes notice of her royal blood. Beginning the action instead of ending it, this recognition will lead to loss as well as gain, to the marriage of Ferdinand and Miranda and the establishment of new order.

The love affair at the centre of *The Tempest* draws on the topography of New Comedic romance and on the errors plays. Ferdinand emerges from a sea that is powerful, mysterious, and ultimately benevolent.[35] Evoked briefly in *Menaechmi*, this sea also carries Egeon to Ephesus, Viola and Sebastian to Illyria. Often, it takes travellers away from the corrupt city, from Athens of *Rudens*, where the good Daemones earns banishment, from Shakespeare's Milan, where brother usurps brother. Mysteriously, it brings them to undreamt shores, to Cyrene and Prospero's isle, where the good flourish and the evil founder, where the fullness of time brings restoration and harmony. Prospero imagines the *cognitio* of the play in marine terms: 'Their understanding / Begins to swell, and the approaching tide / Will shortly fill the reasonable shores / That now lie foul and muddy' (v. i. 79–82). Prospero's isle also bears some striking similarities to Ephesus, Shakespeare's Pauline adaptation of the Plautine other place. In this city of magic and imagination, dazed travellers wander 'twixt sleeping and waking, sometimes falling in love. We remember Antipholus of Syracuse: 'Sleeping or waking, mad or well-advis'd?' (II. ii. 213).[36] Making literal these metaphors, Prospero and Ariel purposefully create a twilight realm between sleeping and waking. Prospero puts Miranda to sleep (I. ii. 185) then wakes her (305); Ariel similarly charms the mariners (I. ii. 231–2). Prospero casts Ferdinand into a

---

[35] This sea may also have been suggested by travel accounts, as Brockbank observes, 'The Tempest: Conventions of Art and Empire', in Brown and Harris (1967), 182–201; Frye (*Natural Perspective*, 149 ff.) comments on the mythic and biblical associations of the sea here.

[36] Cf. Cumber in Munday's historical romance, *John a Kent and John a Cumber*: 'Sleep I? or wake I? dreame I? or doo I dote?' (1311). On possible relations between this play and *The Tempest*, see Reed, 'The Probable Origin of Ariel'; Bradbrook, 'Romance, Farewell! *The Tempest*'.

trance, 'as in a dream' (I. ii. 487); Ariel puts to sleep all of the Court party (save Sebastian and Antonio) (II. i), only to rouse them in time to prevent the murders (300 ff.); Caliban talks of his sleep and dreams (III. ii. 135 ff.). The traveller's comic *aporia* becomes a mode of being on the tragicomic isle. Shakespeare largely foregoes the obvious opportunity for slapstick comedy which the transformation presents and which he takes fully in previous plays (III. ii, the scene of Ariel's ventriloquism and Trinculo's beating, is a digression in an earlier mode). Instead, the setting here tests and transports character and audience, all the while suggesting the haunting truth of Prospero's declaration, 'We are such stuff / As dreams are made on; and our little life / Is rounded with a sleep' (IV. i. 156–8). This isle hosts a transubstantiated errors play, wherein the finding of true identity requires confrontation with unpleasant truths about oneself, with a reality that includes human passion, old age, selfishness, sinfulness, bestiality, and even unregeneracy.

Shakespeare casts the love affair on the isle into familiar New Comedic configurations, again returning to the *virgo–senex–adulescens* pattern. Miranda is another adapted *virgo*, the 'woman as wonder', whose very name proclaims kinship with the Italian type and with Shakespeare's other adaptations—Helena, Hero, Isabella. Acting the role of the *senex iratus*, Prospero likewise recalls multiple predecessors, most recently Antigonus and Simonides of *Pericles*. Like those angry fathers before him, Prospero stands firmly between his nubile daughter and her lovers. First he blocks the advances of Caliban, who returns Miranda's kindness by attempted rape. Yearning and inept, Caliban represents a demonized version of the libidinous classical *adulescens*; like the typical lover in New Comedy, he shows appreciation for the lady's beauty (e.g. III. ii. 98–103) as well as violent desire for satisfaction. Prospero's first performance as *senex iratus* protects his daughter from brutish violation; his second performance, however, occurs for different reasons. Like Simonides in *Pericles*, Prospero self-consciously plays the role of *senex iratus*, 'lest too light winning / Make the prize light' (I. ii. 452–3). Ferdinand is Caliban's opposite, a sanitized version of the *adulescens*—noble, unselfish, chaste. He is no Chaerea, disguised as a eunuch to commit rape; nor is he a Mucedorus, disguised as a shepherd to observe the lady and to prove his innate virtue. Astonished by Miranda's beauty, Ferdinand immediately reveals his identity and proposes marriage, thus departing from both classical and romance conventions.

Subsequent action expands the contrasts between the two *adulescentes*. Caliban complains bitterly about his confinement to the rock (I. ii. 341 ff.); Ferdinand, in the prison of Prospero's power, finds 'space enough' (493) so long as he can gaze on Miranda. Caliban resents his 'burthen of wood', resolving, 'I'll bear him no more sticks' (II. ii. 163); Ferdinand, refusing help, is a 'patient logman' (III. i. 67). The lover's performance of physical labour as proof of his worth has important precedent in New Comedy. Sostratos of *Dyskolos*, for example, humorously and ineffectively takes up the mattock in the hot sun. Smitten with Ampelisca, Sceparnio of *Rudens* enters blithely with the jug of water she requested:

> Pro di inmortales! in aqua numquam credidi
> uoluptatem inesse tantam. ut hanc traxi lubens!
> nimio minus altus puteus uisust quam prius.
> ut sine labore hanc extraxi!   (458–61)

O immortal gods! I never believed there could be so much pleasure in water. How gladly I drew this up! The well seemed much less deep than before. In fact, I drew this up with no sweat at all.

Similarly smitten with Miranda, Ferdinand enters joyfully with a log:

> This my mean task
> Would be as heavy to me as odious, but
> The mistress which I serve quickens what's dead,
> And makes my labors pleasures.   (III. i. 4–7)

The superficial similarities in situation and sentiment, however, only serve to point up the differences. Sceparnio, a randy servant who delights in the opportunity to play *adulescens* with an attractive girl, carries the water as payment for anticipated sexual pleasure. Ferdinand carries the wood as a gift of self-sacrifice; his work is prelude to the scene in which both he and Miranda pledge their love and faith, a scene all the more moving because of Miranda's energy and complexity.[37] This heightening of the love interest, characteristic of Renaissance neo-classicism, continues on in later

---

[37] These qualities are well observed by Orgel (Oxford edn., 1987, 16–17).

adaptations of the play, notably those by Sir William D'Avenant, John Dryden, and David Garrick.[38]

Pointedly revising classical precedents, the *virgo–senex–adulescens* pattern in *The Tempest* works to affirm a virtue central to *Pericles*—chastity. After granting the lovers his blessing, Prospero sternly adominishes Ferdinand:

> If thou dost break her virgin-knot before
> All sanctimonious ceremonies may
> With full and holy rite be minist'red,
> No sweet aspersion shall the heavens let fall
> To make this contract grow; but barren hate,
> Sour-ey'd disdain and discord shall bestrew
> The union of your bed with weeds so loathly
> That you shall hate it both.   (IV. i. 15–22)

Here the *senex iratus* threatens not his own disfavour but proposes a grim allegory in which evil consequences naturally and inevitably follow lapses in order, decorum, and ceremony. Ferdinand responds to the charge by swearing that nothing can melt his 'honor into lust' (IV. i. 28). Later Prospero repeats the warning (IV. i. 53) and Ferdinand again promises to be chaste. The following wedding masque celebrates love and fruition but pointedly excludes Venus and Cupid, patrons of intemperate and earthly love, pagan divinities of wanton charms and illicit passions.

In recent criticism such moments are often said to reveal Prospero's own repressed incestuous desires. According to the current psychoanalytic reading, Prospero suffers from 'paternal narcissism'; from a 'possessive father's hostility to his usurper rival'; from displacing his own 'phallic potency'.[39] Such judgements fit the character to a pseudo-Freudian template, universally applicable to all fathers (even fictional ones) of all times and places. As is usual in modern critical parlance 'desire'—always painful and destructive—

---

[38] D'Avenant and Dryden's adaptation, *The Tempest, or The Enchanted Island. A Comedy* (1667), doubles the lovers, introducing Dorinda, Miranda's innocent sister, who falls for one Hippolito, who never saw woman. Even Ariel finally pairs off with his love, Milcha, ed. Vickers, i. 76 ff. Garrick's operatic adaptation (1756) also focuses on the lovers and ends with a duet between Ferdinand and Miranda and a choral blessing, ibid., iv. 228.

[39] Sundelson, 'So Rare a Wonder'd Father', in Schwartz and Kahn (1980), 34; Nevo, *Shakespeare's Other Language*, 135; Stockholder, *Dream Works*, 205. On the fundamental problems with this kind of criticism see Vickers, *Appropriating Shakespeare*, 272–324.

replaces all talk of 'love'—never joyful, generous, or creative. Like other psychoanalytic readings, moreover, this one discovers essential aspects of human experience in a text without much regard for literary or cultural context. Put simply, Prospero becomes a case study in human pathology. Also reviled by feminists as a patriarch, Prospero now seems to embody every evil associated with sexual and civil domination.

Recollection of Shakespeare's New Comedic heritage and his literary/historical moment provides grounds for a different understanding. Like Spenser in *The Faerie Queene*, Jonson in his contemporary masques, and Shakespeare in *Pericles*, Prospero celebrates allegorically the virtue of chastity. Rescripting classical comedy thus, Shakespeare aggressively controls the energies of eros that regularly motivate New Comedic action. This containment is entirely orthodox and comprehensible. As we have seen, Renaissance apologists worked long and hard to rehabilitate the sexual immorality of New Comedy—deleting or moralizing objectionable parts, refashioning the characters and action. Shakespeare's habit of converting libidinous youths into romantic lovers, elsewhere evident in his work, culminates quite naturally in Ferdinand and Miranda. In this play, of course, such containment has a political dimension as well as a moral one; in the age of Elizabeth and James, virginity is a 'crucial attribute of royal power' which holds 'not only civilization but the promise of infinite bounty within a hegemonic order'.[40] Accordingly, Ferdinand and Miranda's purity is the guarantor of their future inheritance and power.

Shakespeare's moralized and romanticized New Comedy retains the deep structures of its origins, particularly the traditional opposition between masters and servants. Illuminating *The Tempest*'s general indebtedness to New Comedy, Bernard Knox discerns throughout the play variations of the familiar master-slave paradigm.[41] Ferdinand gets Shakespeare's version of the chains-and-prison diet of the Plautine slave. Ariel, like many ancient predecessors, seeks freedom. Prospero's reference to the mill-wheels

---

[40] Orgel, 49. Shakespeare's treatment of chastity, often denounced as heavy-handed, seems adept in comparison with John Fletcher's artificial *The Faithful Shepherdess* (1608–9), which arranges its characters down from Clorin, chastely mourning her dead paramour, to the lustful Cloe and the Sullen Shepherd.

[41] See n. 1 above. The quotations below appear on 64, 65–6.

(I. ii. 281), place of punishment for slaves, evokes the classical world, and Ariel's promise of speedy performance for the masque, 'sounds remarkably like the half-ironical servile exaggeration of the Plautine slave promising miracles of speed'. And, of course, it is. Ariel plays a transformed *callidus servus*, working through disguises and deceptions that are magical metamorphoses. On the ship Ariel first takes the form of fire, dividing and burning in many places; on the isle he sounds enchanting and deceptive music for Ferdinand as later for Caliban and company. At Prospero's bidding Ariel makes himself like a 'nymph o' th' sea' (I. ii. 301), though no one else, except the audience, can see him. Ariel hums a warning in Gonzalo's ear (II. i), impersonates Trinculo (III. ii), appears and performs as a harpy (III. iii), and probably plays Ceres in the masque. Such changes raise to a new level the classical slave's ability to deceive and perform theatrically. At the end of the play Ariel's intercession for the defeated enemies evokes Prospero's climactic reflection on his humanity and his forgiveness. According to Knox, the scene presents 'a magnificently imaginative version of the scenes in which the comedy slave surpasses the master in qualities which are traditionally those of the free man—in intelligence, courage, self-sacrifice'.

This inversion of the master-slave paradigm accompanies other unsettling articulations in the play. Stephano, Knox observes, recalls the standard figure of the slave who drinks all of his master's wine. He aspires to fabulous wealth and power, in this resembling other fantasizing slaves—Gripus of *Rudens*, for example, who wants to be a king of kings ('apud reges rex,' 931), to build a city in his own name, to found an empire ('regnum magnum,' 935a). Stephano imperiously orders Caliban and Tinculo around, dreams of his kingdom on the isle, imagines life with his beautiful queen.

To anatomize such *alazoneia* and its punishment Shakespeare recalls earlier experiences with New Comedy. Stephano re-enacts Thraso's famous and ill-fated expedition in *Eunuchus*, a play important to *Wives*. Superior intrigue as well as brute force again rout ignorant presumption. Ariel leads Stephano and company into 'th' filthy-mantled pool' (IV. i. 182), a punishment that strikingly recalls that of Falstaff, unceremoniously dumped in the dirty ditch by Datchet Mead. Stage traditions and imagery concerning the clothing of the braggart soldier may also lie behind the puzzling

episode of the 'glistering apparel'. Impostors on stage usually pro-
claimed their importance by wearing regal and gorgeous dress. We
recall the climactic stripping of Pyrgopolynices, exposed and humiliated by the loss of his cloak, and that of Parolles with his scarves
and bannerets. Stephano preens absurdly, draping himself in a
royal gown, just before the final rout, the attack of the spirits as
hunting dogs. Here Shakespeare presents a particularly raucous
version of the ignominious defeat/retreat, a standard comeuppance
for the *alazon* in antiquity and in the Renaissance.

These variations on the master-slave relationship contribute surprising perspectives on mastery and service as well as various interpretive possibilities. Stephano adds to the play some rambunctious
humour as well as a measure of ambivalence and complexity. The
butler's *alazoneia* furnishes a comic counterpoint to the other wills
to power, to the other examples of vicious and virtuous sover-
eignty, rightful and wrongful domination; it blurs comfortable dis-
tinctions, striking off odd angles of sight and insight. Stephano's
attempted coup reflects parodically on the more serious political
actions of the play—on Antonio's usurpation of Prospero, on the
attempted assassination of Alonso, and, most important, on
Prospero's dominance over Caliban.

The relationship between Prospero and Caliban, of course, has
become central to modern reproductions (both critical and theatrical) of the play.[42] Caliban replays several New Comedic characters
simultaneously—an *adulescens*, as we have seen, 'a sullen slave (a
Sceparnio), a cursing slave (a Toxilus), and . . . a lecherous one'.
In his role of redrawn New Comedic slave, according to the now
dominant political interpretation, Caliban represents the victim of
Prospero's political and cultural imperialism. The play thus presents the discourse of colonialism, the rhetorical strategies and
tropes by which European cultures demonized and dominated
native ones.[43] To the extent that this interpretation resonates in
modern readings and productions, the play represents a final sub-

[42] See Vaughan and Vaughan, *Shakespeare's Caliban*. The quotation below is
from Knox, 69.

[43] See, for example, Greenblatt, 'Learning to Curse', in Chiappelli (1976), 561–80;
Brown, ' "This thing of darkness" ', in Dollimore and Sinfield (1985), 48–71;
Cartelli, 'Prospero in Africa', in Howard and O'Connor (1987), 99–115; Greenblatt,
Shakespearean Negotiations, 129–63; Skura, 'Discourse and the Individual'; Willis,
'Shakespeare's *Tempest*'. With others, I believe that this play provides grounds for
criticism of the colonial enterprise, rather than simple complicity.

version of the classical master-slave paradigm. This slave does not merely challenge the conventional order by reversing roles with the master or by outwitting him, both activities safely circumscribed by the confines and conventions of comedic plot. Instead he may undermine the underlying principles of societal ordering, subverting the bedrock assumptions upon which such hierarchies depend. Like Caliban's richly poetic descriptions of the isle, his final vow to 'seek for grace' (v. i. 296) may show him to be as far beyond Prospero's judgement ('this thing of darkness I / Acknowledge mine', 275–6) as he is, finally, beyond his power.

As is evident from Ariel's many shifts and tricks, the action and counteraction of *The Tempest* extend Shakespeare's use of New Comedic intrigue, wherein characters eavesdrop, don disguises, devise complicated plans to gain private ends. Standing apart from the action through most of the play, Prospero and Ariel overhear the plots of the various groups. Shakespeare elevates New Comedic eavesdropping from an occasional comic device to a central dramatic principle, orchestrating a consistent discrepancy in awareness between the master intriguers—Prospero and Ariel—and everyone else in the play. Such actions appropriately and effectively respond to the other intrigues of the play. They frustrate the plans of Caliban, who, for all his appeal and broad humour, threatens rape and murder. More important, they answer to the original sin of Antonio's fraternal usurpation, almost re-enacted a second time by him and Sebastian against Alonso.

In this play, however, Shakespeare demonstrates finally the limitations of New Comedic intrigue, even when it succeeds. After Prospero has successfully manipulated his enemies, he renounces his instruments of deception and intrigue—mantle, staff, and book—in order to come to final resolution. As in *Ado*, there is the awareness of intrigue's darker potential. In his renunciation of magic, Prospero echoes Ovid's Medea to declare himself, by contrast, intransigently mortal, limited, subject to time and change. Abjuring a magic that is in some sense also reminiscent of Sycorax, Prospero renounces 'that untransmuted residue of self-dramatization and self-aggrandizement inherent in any effort to recreate the world after one's desires and in one's own image'.[44] Forsaking intrigue, reliant no longer on external resources, espousing virtue

[44] Felperin, 277.

not vengeance, the *magus* becomes man, unaccommodated, compassionate, and, at last, himself. Appropriately, Prospero orders a costume change:

> Fetch me the hat and rapier in my cell.
> I will discase me, and myself present
> As I was sometime Milan.   (v. i. 84–6)

He then steps out to confront the others, relinquishing his position of higher awareness, coming down to the level and levelling plain of the ordinary. The shock of this descent drives mad another *magus*, Bomelio of *The Rare Triumphs of Love and Fortune*, a play Shakespeare probably used in *Cymbeline*.[45] Here it brings Prospero to exhausted sanity and hard-won humanity. As in other intrigue plays, notably *Mostellaria* and *Shrew*, the return of the absent master abashes some as it unties knots and restores order. Shakespeare transfigures the reappearances of Theoproprides and Vincentio, however, depicting Prospero's return not merely as a mechanism of plot, but as an end to all plotting and a complex spiritual achievement.

Prospero's renunciation of magic is then, metaphorically, a renunciation of New Comedic intrigue. The external mechanisms of eavesdropping, disguise, plotting, and the like cannot alone effect conversion, create harmony, bring about new life. In so far as these ends are met here, Shakespeare achieves them by recourse to the errors plays. In *Menaechmi*, *Errors*, and *Twelfth Night* the action culminates in a dramatic entrance that leads to the restoration of self and the reintegration of society. A twin enters to confront his long-lost double; the mists of Epidamnus, Ephesus, and Illyria lift to reveal separate and autonomous beings. The ensuing process of revelation clarifies exactly who and what each individual is. So the entrance of Prospero as Milan begins the process of clarification:

---

[45] Compare Bomelio upon discovering that his books are gone: 'What canst thou tel me? Tel me of a turd. What and a come? I coniure thee, foule spirit, down to hell! Ho, ho, ho! The deuil, the deuill! A coms, a coms, a coms vpon me, and I lack my books' (1506–9). Such renunciation would also be unthinkable for Munday's John a Kent, another intriguing *magus*, who achieves his ends in the second act and designs new plots 'to sporte my selfe awhyle' (535). Munday responds to the problem of maintaining dramatic suspense in a *magus* play by simply piling up complications; Shakespeare, however, substitutes the internal theatre for the external one.

> The charm dissolves apace,
> And as the morning steals upon the night,
> Melting the darkness, so their rising senses
> Begin to chase the ignorant fumes that mantle
> Their clearer reason.   (v. i. 64–8)

Like Egeon, Prospero appears as the *pater familias*, released from bondage, restored to his rightful place in society. Almost ritualistically, he speaks to those in the charmed circle, naming and identifying them, explaining who and what each is. Finally, he introduces himself: 'Behold, sir King, / The wronged Duke of Milan, Prospero' (106–7). With a new note of melancholy, Prospero can say with Kichesias, γέρων ὅς εἰμι γέγονα (*Sicyonios* 354, 'I am become the old man I am').

Providing classical comedic closure, Shakespeare simultaneously subverts the resolution. He here denies Prospero the comforts of comedic anagnorisis, ἐξ ἀγνοίας εἰς γνῶσιν μεταβολή, ἢ εἰς φιλίαν ἢ εἰς ἔχθραν (*Poet.* 1452a30–1, 'a change from ignorance to knowledge that conduces to friendship or hatred'). In this transfigured errors play Prospero makes no new discoveries about the character or identity of his companions, nor does he find new friendship or enmity; he simply forgives, anyway. Indeed, the final action confirms what he has known all along: Gonzalo remains the loyal counsellor of old, Antonio, 'most wicked' (v. i. 130) and unnatural. Evoking the errors pattern of reconciliation and restoration, the playwright inverts the Aristotelian recognition in yet another way: he transfers the discovery from the main character to the others. They discover Prospero alive not dead, while he, with sad knowledge, accepts them as they are and always have been, confused, sinful, unredeemed. The untying of knots here depends on no casket or ring, but upon the motions of the spirit within, on Prospero's rejection of tragic action and his clear-eyed choice of comic fulfilment, howsoever imperfect.

This fulfilment is costly. Like many fathers in New Comedy who lose their offspring, Alonso undergoes separation as prelude to final joyful reunion. His loss, however, unlike theirs, initiates a painful process of grief, repentance, and purgation, a penance for his original crimes against Prospero. Disconsolate, Alonso hears Ariel's reminder of guilt and promise of salvation, but threatens suicide (III. iii. 95–102). Saved from his rashness, brimful of sorrow and dismay, Alonso finally faces Prospero. As the charm dissolves, so does his furious despair: 'since I saw thee, / Th' affliction of my mind amends, with which / I fear a madness held me' (v. i. 114–16). Immediately he resigns Prospero's dukedom and begs pardon, after which he recovers Ferdinand. Like Apollinius, Hegio in *Captivi*, Daemones in *Rudens*, Egeon, and Pericles, Alonso experiences a peripateia that reunites him with a lost child. The New Comedic pattern of loss and recovery here again sketches the internal progress of the sinner through repentance to grace.

Not everyone, of course, experiences Alonso's joy. Prospero, himself, shows a world-weary melancholy in place of the conventional comedic wonder and delight. True to several New Comedic formulas at once, Alonso marries off his daughter, recovers his lost son, and approves a wedding. 'I say amen, Gonzalo!' (v. i. 204). In some ways, Prospero reverses Alonso's progress from losing a child to joyful recovery; he establishes his daughter's identity in I. ii and then in v. i loses her 'In this last tempest' (v. i. 153). The onward movement of the new generation, he sadly perceives, must necessarily leave the old behind. His gain leads inevitably to his loss. Wearily Prospero deflects Alonso's excited enquiries, frustrating the natural comedic impulse for full revelation. The end of *The Tempest* will not be 'itidem ut in comoediis / omnia omnes ubi resciscunt' (*Hecyra* 867–8, 'the same as in comedies, where everyone gets to know everything'). Retired in Milan, Prospero speculates, every third thought will be his grave. Shakespeare modifies the New Comedic and romance paradigms to create a moving coda, replete with poignant minor chords.[46]

The complex music that closes *The Tempest* contrasts with the simpler harmonies closing *The Comedy of Errors*. There the final action recapitulates and resolves all confusions and the simple joy of recovery predominates. Here, however, the entanglements of plot recede before the rarer action of virtue than vengeance. And, despite the occasional upward glance towards providence, Prospero's victory over his anger and passion, over the tempest that beats within, is essentially his own. Unlike other romance heroes, Prospero receives no joy or inspiration from a wife, an

---

[46] Since the days of Frye's comedic reading, published piecemeal but gathered together in his introduction to the Pelican edn., (1959, rev. 1970, 14–24), we have been attuned to the darker strains and complexities of the play by critics like Berger, jun., 'Miraculous Harp'; Siskin, 'Freedom and Loss in "The Tempest" '; Miko, 'Tempest'; Orgel.

Emilia, Thaisa, Imogen, or Hermione, lost and then found. And unlike Shakespeare's other romances, this one features no divine intervention, no oracle to guide human action, no theophany to point the way to resolution. The thunder is not Jove's but Prospero's own. On the contrary, *The Rare Triumphs of Love and Fortune* requires for closure a host of divinities—Mercury, Venus, and Fortune. The wedding masque of Ceres, Iris, and Juno, however, is a vanity of Prospero's art, a vision of ideal harmony, order, and beauty which must vanish before the ugly realities lurking in the brush and the need for human response. The intrigues of art yield to the power of resignation and forgiveness. Originating in a flawed human, this forgiveness is itself flawed: it seems to require prompting; it leaves unreported present corruption; it cannot transform everyone. But Prospero's forgiveness is miracle enough, perhaps more precious for its imperfection. Though brother manifestly does not exit hand-in-hand with brother, as in *Comedy of Errors*, they do return to Milan, chastened and restored to their proper places. Shakespeare's New Comedic romance does not conclude with the ringing certainties of its predecessors, nor with the satisfying schematics of the courtly aesthetic (*pace* Schmidgall). It does, however, unite young lovers in hope and present a *senex iratus* who can, finally, grow beyond anger.

6

Heavy Plautus

PLAYWRIGHTS did not confine a source so rich, potent, and flexible
as New Comedy to strict generic boundaries. Plautus and Terence
inspire Renaissance romance or tragicomedy and also tragedy
itself. This last manifestation is not so much an *excursus* as a
return home, a coming full circle. For as noted from antiquity
onwards, tragedy contributed significantly to the formation of New
Comedy.[1] In the Renaissance New Comedy reciprocated appropriately, contributing variously to tragedy. Sometimes the gift is a
simple donation: Garnier, for example, transfers passages from
Amphitruo and *Cistellaria* into his *Hippolyte*.[2] Sometimes it takes
the form of a subordinate character or line in a larger action, e.g.
Basilisco in *Soliman and Perseda*, Pistol and Falstaff in
Shakespeare's histories, the sub-plot of Heywood's *The English
Traveller*. At times, New Comedy integrates itself into the fabric
and structure of tragedy itself, as in Middleton's *The Changeling*
and *Women Beware Women*. Surveying a wide variety of plays,
Harbage long ago identified Plautus and Terence as sources for the
intrigue so dominant in Elizabethan tragedy.[3] And among
Shakespeare's plays critics have well discerned New Comedic elements in *Romeo and Juliet* and *Othello*.[4]

This contamination of traditional genres should not surprise.
Such blending and reconstruction is everywhere characteristic of
the cinquecento, whose dramatists created new pastoral and tragicomic plays, and of the English Renaissance. Shakespeare, Sidney,
and Scaliger, Orgel observes, considered genre as a set of expectations and possibilities, not as a prescriptive set of rules.[5] And

---

[1] See Satyrus, above, 140; Quintilian, *IO* x. i. 69; Webster, *Studies in Menander*,
153–94; Webster, *Introduction*, 56–67; Katsouris, *Tragic Patterns in Menander*; Bain,
148–9; below, n. 18.

[2] Mouflard, *Les Sources*, 295–6.

[3] 'Intrigue in Elizabethan Tragedy', in Hosley (1963), 37–44.

[4] See Snyder, *Comic Matrix*, 56–90. J. H. Smith's *Othello* bibliography lists about
a dozen pertinent references (esp. 2615, 2917, 3102).

[5] 'Shakespeare and the Kinds of Drama'.

always more or less implicit in comedy resided energies destabilizing and subversive. From the beginning, of course, Aristotle recognized this darker potential, carefully stipulating that the ἁμάρτημά
τι καὶ αἶσχος, ('fault, error, or deformity'), of comedy be ἀνώδυνον
καὶ οὐ φθαρτικόν ('not painful and not destructive', *Poet.*
1449a34–5). The pre-emptive strike here, phrased in a double negative, reveals precisely what in comedy can never be wholly ignored,
denied, or excluded. Playwrights after Aristotle continually trans-
gress the boundaries that define genre, creating plays that exploit
in new ways conventions and expectations.

Ironically enough, such transgression receives impetus from the
very sources that would contain it—namely, the traditions of
humanistic commentary on classical texts. Renaissance editions of
Terence frequently begin with an influential preface, 'De tragoedia
et comoedia', consisting actually of two essays, one by Evanthius,
the other by Donatus. Here the grammarians clearly outline and
schematize the genres, carefully balancing the differences in persons, subjects, endings, and origins; witness Evanthius:

inter tragoediam autem et comoediam cum multa tum inprimis hoc distat,
quod in comoedia mediocres fortunae hominum, parui impetus periculo-
rum laetique sunt exitus actionum, at in tragoedia omnia contra, ingentes
personae, magni timores, exitus funesti habentur; et illic prima turbulenta,
tranquilla ultima, in tragoedia contrario ordine res aguntur; tum quod in
tragoedia fugienda uita, in comoedia capessenda exprimitur; postremo
quod omnis comoedia de fictis est argumentis, tragoedia saepe de historia
fide petitur.[6]

Now between tragedy and comedy then, these differences are important: in
comedy the fortunes of men are ordinary, the forces of danger, slight, and
the outcomes of action, joyful. But in tragedy everything is opposite: the
characters are grand, the terrors great, the outcomes deadly. And in comedy the beginning is turbulent, the end tranquil, while in tragedy the opposite holds true. Tragedy depicts life as something to be fled, comedy, as
something to be seized. Finally, all the plots of comedy are fictitious,
whereas those of tragedy are often truly historical.

Comedy is useful, so the argument ran, because it offers positive
and negative examples to its audience. And yet, in practice the
moral imperative operative in humanistic commentary and
Renaissance adaptation collapses these oppositions between the

---

[6] Donatus, ed. Wessner, i. 21.

genres. The overriding urge to polemicize comedy, to find in every scene morally instructive 'theses', for example, confers upon the action a consequence and seriousness appropriate to tragedy. The duping of Chremes by Davos and the partially complicitous Mysis, an analogue from *Andria* (740 ff.) for Edmund's and Edgar's deceits in *Lear*, elicits the following commentary from Petrus Marsus:

Versutos homines, & callidos viros, miros modis & multiplici vaframento moliri deceptionem, nec esse cuiuis facile dolos interpretari ac uerum dispicere, docet haec scena. Multos enim recessus habet vita hominis & varias latebras vt in Epistolis scribit Plinius. Et boni viri prudentia, quae virtuti semper adhaeret, malitiosorum versutiis ac simulationibus ideo decipitur, quoniam ex se alios iudicat, nec simulationem putat id esse quo capitur, sed officium.[7]

This scene teaches that wily men and clever fellows, by many means and schemes, engineer deceptions, and that it is not easy for someone to see through their tricks and to discover the truth. For the life of a man has many recesses and various hidden places, as Pliny writes in his letters. And the prudence of the good man, which always attaches itself to virtue, is for that reason deceived by the tricks and simulations of the wicked; for the good man judges others by himself, and doesn't think it is a trick by which he is taken in, but a well-intentioned act.

A bright and lively comic scene inspires reflection on the prevalence of deception, the illusory nature of truth, the dark recesses of human life, the disadvantages of prudence, the deceit of the wicked, the myopia and victimization of the good. For an audience trained on such commentary the adaptation of comedic devices to tragedy must have seemed an entirely natural, indeed inevitable, development.

Shakespeare's most complex adaptations of New Comedy, though largely unremarked, appear in *Hamlet* and *King Lear*. In these plays New Comedy consists of inherited traditions and conventions, not specific source texts. Shakespeare's long experience with Plautus and Terence colours and modifies his appropriation of the other sources. New Comedy shapes the secondary characters and subordinate plot lines—Polonius, Ophelia, Laertes, Gloucester, Edmund, and Edgar. Moreover, both Ophelia and Cordelia appear as Italianate versions of the New Comedic *virgo*, problematized. And even the main characters themselves, reprising a dazzling vari-

---

[7] *Terentivs* (1560), 156.

ety of generic and theatrical possibilities, at times wear New Comedic masks and enact New Comedic roles: Hamlet plays *eiron*, Lear, the *misanthropus*. Deploying familiar characters and configurations, these plays finally subvert comedic design, i.e. the inner dynamic and its agencies—be they natural or supernatural—by which comedy comes to happy conclusions. The comedies and these tragedies variously use the same agencies—human effort, providence, sheer luck—to precisely opposite ends. The protagonists of the tragedies, portrayed in a chiaroscuro that reveals virtues and vices, exist in a world that is ultimately beyond human power to order; often it seems that an inscrutable power, not benevolent as in the comedies, but hostile or indifferent, rules all. From its inception New Comedy has always registered anxieties about *tyche*; consider the following fragments:

ἄλλος κατ, ἄλλην δαιμονίζεται τύχην. (Kassel-Austin, vii. 306)

Each is possessed by the god his chance decrees.

ἐπιστατεῖ τις τοῦ βίου νυνὶ τύχη
ἄγροικος ἡμῶν οὔτε παιδείαν ὅλως
εἰδυῖα᾽ τί τὸ κακόν ποτ᾽ ἢ τί τἀγαθὸν
ἔστ᾽ ἀγνοοῦσα παντελῶς, εἰκῇ τέ πως
ἡμᾶς κυλίνδουσ᾽ ὄντιν᾽ ἂν τύχῃ τρόπον·
οἶμαί γε. (Edmonds, iiiA. 186)

Is our life now ruled by some chance, rude and wholly uneducated, completely unable to tell bad from good, rolling us without plan or purpose any which way it pleases? I think it so.

τοῦτ᾽ ἔστι τὸ κυβερνῶν ἄπαντα καὶ στρέφον
καὶ σῶιζον, ἡ πρόνοια δ᾽ἡ θνητὴ καπνὸς
καὶ φλήναφος. (frag. 417)

[Chance] governs all, both overturning and preserving; human forethought is mere smoke and nonsense.[8]

These lines gloss fittingly the bleakest moments of *Hamlet* and *King Lear*; that they come from Philemon, Apollodorus of Carystus, and Menander, not Aesychylus, Sophocles, or Euripides, indicates the essential nexus between comedy and tragedy. The *tyche* that arranges the closing harmonies of comedy, in darker manifestation, composes the disastrous endings of tragedy. The

---

[8] On *tyche* in new comedy, see LeGrand, 312–15; Hunter, *New Comedy*, 141–4.

New Comedic configurations inscribed in *Hamlet* and *Lear* enable the playwright to probe the excruciating truth of this paradox.

Hamlet

Not surprisingly, commentators have perceived comedic elements in *Hamlet*, that compendious gathering of dramatic convention and generic possibility. Susan Snyder well discusses the most frequently observed instances: the gravediggers' jokes, the characters of Polonius, Osric, Rosencrantz and Guildenstern, Hamlet himself— 'role-player, manipulator, crafty madman, wit, and eiron'. Anthony Dawson and Jean MacIntyre discuss *Hamlet*'s relations with the early comedies; Peter Davison notes the humour of the play in performance. Maurice Charney analyses the comic elements under six headings: irrelevance, satire, madness, aggression, exuberance, and mastery of anxiety.[9] Such studies encourage discussion of New Comedic presence in the play.

The stage direction for II. i begins '*Enter old* Polonius', thus providing a curiously obtrusive clue to a character who is largely Shakespeare's invention. Addressing Polonius, Hamlet fills out the description in mockingly precise detail:

the satirical rogue says here that old men have grey beards, that their faces are wrinkled, their eyes purging thick amber and plum-tree gum, and that they have a plentiful lack of wit, together with most weak hams.

(II. ii. 196–200)

Louise Clubb observes that Polonius' 'genesis was a fusion of the expected *consigliere* of tragedy with the unexpected *vecchio* of *commedia erudita* or Pantalone of *commedia dell'arte*'.[10] Behind the latter two of course, and behind Hamlet's stereotype, stoops the familiar classical old man, the *senex*. Polonius is a New Comedic *pater* relocated into the murky world of Elsinore. Like a Terentian father, he gives self-consciously sage advice and speaks in *sententiae*; he recalls his heyday gone by; he acts an uncomprehending target for jokes and repartee. He is as pompously certain in his dealings with offspring as Simo, Chremes, Micio, and

---

[9] Snyder, 91–136 (91); Dawson, *Indirections*, 44–51; MacIntyre, 'Hamlet and the Comic Heroine'; Davison, *Hamlet*, 27–33; Charney, *Hamlet's Fictions*, 131–51.
[10] *Italian Drama*, 202.

Demea, and just as wrong and foolish.[11] Creizenach, in fact, noted a parallel between old Micio (*Adel.*) and Polonius, both reflecting on the caution that is characteristic of old age:[12]

> By heaven, it is as proper to our age
> To cast beyond ourselves in our opinions,
> As it is common for the younger sort
> To lack discretion.   (II. i. 111–14)

> ad omnia alia aetate sapimus rectius;
> solum unum hoc vitium adfert senectus hominibus:
> adtentiores sumus ad rem omnes quam sat est.   (832–4)

In all other matters we grow wiser as we get older; only this one flaw old age brings: we are all too concerned with wealth.

The parallel is not in itself persuasive and a misplaced emphasis on verbal iteration as proof of influence can obscure its real importance. Shakespeare does not imitate a specific passage here but employs a Terentian trick of characterization: the *senex* explains and often excuses behaviour by reference to age: certain follies are appropriate to old age, others to youth.[13] Like many Terentian *senes*, Polonius is an orthodox literary critic, insisting on decorum as the first rule of characterization.

Sure in his conceit, the *senex* initiates a counterplot designed to expose the truth. Like Demea in Menander's *Samia*, Polonius eavesdrops ineptly, misinterpreting what he hears, drawing precisely the wrong conclusions. Moreover, the confrontations between Polonius, Claudius, and Hamlet recall various scenes from New Comedy, with Hamlet alternating between *adulescens* and *callidus servus*. Hamlet's sarcastic treatment of Polonius in the 'fishmonger' sequence recalls Tranio's needling of the obtuse *senes*, with his teasing references to a crow pecking at two vultures (*Most.* 832 ff.) The mocking aside to Rosencrantz and Guildenstern ('that great baby you see there is not yet out of his swaddling-clouts', II. ii. 382–3) is a more common New Comedic device of exposure, as is the manipulative improvisation displayed in the

---

[11] Renaissance commentators like Pino (*Consideratione*, sig. b2) thought the right relations between fathers and their families Terence's principal subject: 'in quelli di Terentio chiaramente dimostrata la uirtù de Patroni in ben gouernare le famiglie & le case loro.' And like Terentian fathers, Polonius can be quite complex on stage; for discussion of some possibilities, see Tony Church, *Players of Shakespeare*, ed. Brockbank, 103–14.

[12] *English Drama*, 74 n.

[13] For discussion see LeGrand, 131–5; Hunter, *New Comedy*, 97 ff.

conversation about the shapes of clouds (III. ii. 376 ff.). Hamlet's
barbed ridicule of the *senex* expresses a familiar aggression.
Epidicus, for example, gleefully watches old Periphanes, the bird
on his left, 'aui sinistera' (182–4):

> acutum cultrum habeo, senis qui exenterem marsuppium.   (185)
> I have a sharp knife to eviscerate the old man's purse with.

Epidicus wants to suck the blood ('exsugebo sanguinem', 188) out
of the old; and the soldier later informs Periphanes that his servant
'te articulatim concidit' (488, 'has cut you up limb by limb').
Hamlet acts out the New Comedic impulse to violence, cruelly
stabbing Polonius behind the arras. The stock dehumanization of
the *senex* for comic purpose takes on a disturbing urgency when
performed post-mortem: 'Thou wretched, rash, intruding fool,
farewell!', 'I'll lug the guts into the neighbor room'; 'if indeed you
find him not within this month, you shall nose him as you go up
the stairs into the lobby' (III. iv. 31, 212; IV. iii. 35–7). No mere *jeu
d'esprit*, the macabre comedy here indicates what, at least momentarily, Hamlet has become.

   Not merely a recognizable character, Polonius has also several
New Comedic roles to play. We have observed in many of the
works here discussed Shakespeare's fondness for New Comedic,
usually amatory, sub-plots. The Polonius-Hamlet-Ophelia story follows suit, featuring the blocking father, amorous *adulescens*, and
pursued *virgo*. (Laertes, the brother concerned about his sister's
welfare, acts out a distinct and well-attested New Comedic variation, evident, for example, in Menander's *Dyskolos* and Plautus'
Trinummus.) This particularly rich and malleable configuration, of
course, drives the main plots of *A Midsummer Night's Dream*,
Romeo and Juliet, and *Othello*, and provides secondary action in
Merchant, *Wives*, *Pericles*, and the *Tempest*. Shakespeare imports
the pattern in defiance of Saxo and Belleforest, who feature an
unnamed woman in an unsuccessful sexual test of Hamlet's sanity.
Polonius portrays Hamlet as the passionate *adulescens*, in 'the very
ecstasy of love, / Whose violent property fordoes itself / And leads
the will to desperate undertakings' (II. i. 99–101) Like the prototypal Euclio of *Aulularia*, perhaps recalled in Shylock, the father
tries to blight his daughter's budding romance, commanding her to
'lock herself from' Hamlet's 'resort' (II. ii. 143); so doing, he would
make Hamlet *amator exclusus*.

The passionate *adulescens*, however, pointedly refuses to play his role. Hamlet does not discuss his amatory troubles with his sympathetic friend Horatio; nor does he try to circumvent the *senex* by intrigue. Instead, he rejects Ophelia on his own, against the precedent of Saxo, wherein Amleth is forewarned, and against that of Belleforest, wherein the girl favours and assists him. This rejection (III. i. 120 ff.), voiced in bitterness, cynicism, and loathing, fractures the comedic structure irreparably. Bertram's rejection of Helena is mere pique, a blocking humour in a foolish boy, destined to be overcome by wit; Hamlet's rejection of Ophelia is the symbol of his ruined life, the consequence and expression of his spiritual anguish.

Ruin, in more specific and spectacular form, also attends the story of Ophelia. At first Ophelia plays to perfection the largely passive classical *virgo* and, unlike the many witty and resourceful variations in Shakespeare and later comedy, obeys her father. This passivity, however, is short-lived, and so is Ophelia's conformity with the inscribed classical role. Ophelia's celebrated mad scenes shatter familiar stereotypes, overturn gendered expectations, and, as recent criticism has shown, reveal hidden sensuality, pathos, and rage.[14] The discovery of this Ophelia inverts the traditional revelation of identity that leads to marriage and integration into society. This anagnorisis leads to death; and the Ophelia who emerges only in madness dies not as she lived—wholly integrated into social order, tightly constricted by brother, father, and lover—but alone. The thwarted energies of the inscribed comedy, so clearly engaged and so systematically subverted, augment the tragic sense of frustration and loss.

Polonius and Laertes play out another New Comedic configuration that Shakespeare adds to the source story, that of sententious, meddlesome father and son. The relations between father and son receive constant attention in comedy, from Aristophanes' *Clouds* and *Wasps* and Menander's *Samia* to many works of Plautus and Terence, to their descendants in the Renaissance (e.g. the Prodigal Son plays) and after, especially Shadwell's *The Squire of Alsatia*

---

[14] See Leverenz, 'The Woman in Hamlet', in Schwartz and Kahn (1980), 110–28; Showalter, 'Representing Ophelia', in Parker and Hartman (1985), 77–94; Neely, *Broken Nuptials*, 102–4. From another perspective, Guilfoyle (*Play within Play*, 7–19) well argues that images and motifs from medieval Mary Magdalene legends compose Ophelia's story and enrich the tragedy.

and Sheridan's *The Rivals*. Terence featured this relationship in three plays—*Andria*, *Heauton Timorumenos*, and *Adelphoe*—all of which explore the ironies and intricacies of growing old and raising the young. Paraphrasing *Adelphoe*, Jonson's *Every Man in his Humour* (Folio, I. ii. 129–34) provided inspiration closer to home in the meddlesome, gullible Kno'well and his son Edward. Polonius' concern with the proper behaviour of his children, his habit of didactic moralizing, his unwarranted self-assurance recall several Terentian *senes*, particularly the confident and platitudinous Chremes, who lectures his son in similarly pompous fashion (*HT* 200 ff.). Both Chremes and Polonius, apparently, believe that such counsel will insure good behaviour. Polonius' 'fetch of wit' (II. i. 38), whereby he enjoins Reynaldo to use the 'bait of falsehood' to take the 'carp of truth' (II. i. 60), also has Terentian precedent. Simo of *Andria* lies about his son's forthcoming wedding in order to discover his real feelings, 'ut per falsas nuptias / vera obiurgandi causa sit' (157, 'that through the false wedding, [we may see] true cause for censure').

As before, the whirling progress of the play shatters the inscribed comedic structure; Hamlet kills Polonius, and Laertes changes from comic *adulescens* to tragic revenger. Though ephemeral, this inset fiction illuminates by parallel and counterpoint the Claudius–Hamlet relationship. Claudius insistently refers to himself as 'father' and Hamlet as 'son'. Soon after Polonius reluctantly permits Laertes to return to France (I. ii. 58–61), Claudius bars Hamlet's return to Wittenburg (I. ii. 112–17). He outdoes Polonius' moralizing in the hypocritical, neo-Stoic sermon on the death of fathers and the necessity for moderate grief. Directly after Polonius commissions Reynaldo to spy on Laertes (II. i), Claudius commissions Rosencrantz and Guildenstern to spy on Hamlet (II. ii). Like Polonius, Claudius believes in a decorum based on age: 'youth no less becomes / The light and careless livery that it wears / Than settled age his sables and his weeds' (IV. vii. 78–80). And both fathers practise eavesdropping. Of course, the differences here loom large and important. Claudius slips into the role of New Comedic *senex* to hide murderous intention, transposing the conflict between youth and age into a tragic key; and once again Hamlet does not rest content with his prescribed role, the *adulescens*, choosing instead other masks from New Comedy's capacious tiring-house.

The *senex-adulescens* configuration defines and finally fails to
define the complex relationships between fathers and sons in the
play. Like a New Comedic *senex*, Norway checks the rash
impulses of Fortinbras, who in turn seeks to play avenger for his
dead father. The Elder Hamlet *qua* Senecan ghost, Frye observes,
plays the tragic counterpart to Polonius' retreating paternal *eiron*
and, it may be added, to Claudius, the false patriarch.[15] The ghost
also recapitulates, in tragic fashion, the comedic return of the
absent father. Elder Hamlet and Claudius present anew the device
of opposed brothers; that New Comedic contrast well deployed in
Ado, *Tempest*, and *Lear*, here supplies the moral axis of the play.
Gertrude complicates matters further: hypocritically playing the
role of the virtuous New Comedic *matrona*, she in fact reconstitutes the mythical Clytemnestra as well as the Adulterous Wife of
Italian comedy.[16] Energies from conflicting genres and traditions
oscillate wildly throughout the play, pulling Hamlet this way and
that, simultaneously casting and uncasting him. Bedazzled and
bewildered, Hamlet wanders in theatrical uncertainty, trying on
various parts in rapid succession, masking and unmasking, acting
and refusing to act.

Long recognizing the centrality of theatrical imagery to the play,
critics have well observed the prince's sophisticated and self-
conscious struggle with tragic drama, particularly with revenge-
play conventions.[17] This preoccupation with tragic drama appears
also in classical comedy, though there the prevalent purpose is parody. Aristophanes repeatedly sends up Euripides, quickly switching
into and out of tragic idiom and metre.[18] Menander uses tragic
idiom frequently and variously; in *Aspis*, for example, Daos begins
the action with a tragic lament for his supposedly dead master, and
then later (399 ff.) repays the rhetoric, *con brio*, replete with tragic
quotations, as part of a scheme. Like Aristophanes, Plautus echoes
Euripides parodically at the end of *Mercator*; and like Menander,

[15] 'Characterization', 275.
[16] On the *matrona*, see Duckworth, 255–8; on the Italian comic type, Hosley,
'Formal Influence', 140.
[17] Gottschalk, 'Hamlet and the Scanning of Revenge'; Bulman, *Heroic Idiom*,
75–82; Kastan, ' "His semblable is his mirror" '; Miola, *Classical Tragedy*, 32–67.
[18] Individual editions of Aristophanes' plays are best consulted on this topic. On
tragedy in later plays and fragments see Leo, *Plautinische Forschungen*, 132 ff;
Webster, *Studies in Later Greek Comedy*, 61, 69, 73, 81–97, 168–9; Duckworth, 11,
103 n., 335 n., 370 n.; Hunter, *New Comedy*, 114–36.

he puts tragic idiom to other uses, weaving into his mythological travesty, *Amphitruo*, for example, moments of serious thought and feeling. The shuttling into and out of tragic idiom also character-izes Hamlet, who adopts the ancient comic technique as his own. He wrings himself up to a climactic burst of rodomontade, 'Bloody, bawdy villain! / Remorseless, treacherous, lecherous, kind-less villain!' (II. ii. 580–1), then punctures the rhetorical balloon:

> Why, what an ass am I! This is most brave,
> That I, the son of a dear father murthered,
> Prompted to my revenge by heaven and hell,
> Must like a whore unpack my heart with words.   (582–5)

Acting as a chorus for the mousetrap, Hamlet misquotes two lines from an old revenge play, *The True Tragedy of Richard the Third* (1594), 'The screeking Rauen sits croking for reuenge. / Whole heads of beasts come bellowing for reuenge' (1892–3). He then pro-saically explains the tale and its origins in 'very choice Italian' (III. ii. 263). Confronting Laertes at Ophelia's grave he offers to drink eisel, eat the crocodile, and be buried under millions of acres till 'our ground, / Singeing his pate against the burning zone, / Make Ossa like a wart' (V. i. 281–3); he closes the Senecan hyperbole with the ironically deflating resolve to 'rant' (284) as well as Laertes. Part parody, part earnest attempt at self-creation, these switches into and out of tragic idiom limn Hamlet's great struggle to create his part in the evolving and confusing drama at Elsinore.

Such rapid switching, marked by sharp contrasts in tone and mood, recalls comedic rather than tragic practice. These moments resonate with the many references to theatre and playing, begin-ning with Hamlet's opening remark about the forms, moods, and shapes of his grief as 'actions that a man might play' (I. ii. 84), continuing on in his encounters with the actors, his various meta-morphoses into spectator and player, and ending with Fortinbras' command to bear him dead 'like a soldier to the stage' (V. ii. 396). In various ways, *Hamlet* insistently calls attention to itself as play simultaneously to affirm and threaten the dramatic illusion, to encourage and discourage belief. This insistence, Empson observes, causes *Hamlet* to break dramatic illusion more boldly than any other Shakespearean play.[19] Such breaking also characterizes New Comedy, where references to playing and acting coexist with direct

---

[19] *Essays on Shakespeare*, 85 ff.

references to present performance.[20] Pseudolus directs attention to the 'tibicen' (573a) that performed between acts (perhaps an analogue to Hamlet's rather direct reference to 'cellarage', I. v. 151, a technical term for the space under the stage); Acanthio, to the slumbering spectators (*Mer.* 160); Toxilus, to the stage-supplier and aediles (*Persa* 159–60). Chrysalus mentions another Plautine play and insults an actor, one Pellio (*Bacc.* 214–16); Euclio begs the audience to help him (*Aul.* 713 ff.); Gripus compares Daemones' preaching to a typical speech by comic actors ('comicos', *Rudens*, 1249). Hamlet's play at the borders of illusion, like Stoppard's *Rosencrantz and Guildenstern Are Dead*, is subtler and more complex, designed not simply to raise a laugh but to probe the problematic nature of art and of reality itself.

The Prince himself, no less than the larger configurations and motifs of the play, embodies comedic stereotypes and patterns. Hamlet acts the *eiron*, discussed as a primary comic character type in *Tractatus Coislinianus* xii. Aristotle's *Nicomachean Ethics* (1127b) defines the *eiron* as a self-deprecator who may be contemptible or praiseworthy. In Old and New Comedy the *eiron* victimizes impostors by masking his cleverness under a show of foolishness.[21] New Comedy, rather than the source chronicles, gives Hamlet's *eironeia* specific shape and form. Imitating the style of the *callidus servus* and possessing a familiar bag of tricks, Hamlet plays the intriguer. Like his ancient, less-privileged predecessors, he has a remarkable talent for improvisation, performing wittily and spontaneously with Rosencrantz and Guildenstern, Polonius, and Osric. And like Epidicus and Pseudolus, he alternates impromptu performances with soliloquy, wherein he urges himself to action (*Epidicus* 194 ff.; *Pseud.* 401 ff.). Hamlet's soliloquies, of course, echo Seneca rather than Plautus, but their alternation with skilful public performance articulates a distinctly comedic rhythm, one wholly absent in Saxo and Belleforest. Moreover, Hamlet deceives by letter, a stock comic device. Whatever we make of the note to Ophelia—a sample of juvenilia or a ruse—the forged letter to England is a 'sport' (III. iv. 206) that hoists enginers with their own petard. It recalls

---

[20] See Duckworth, 132–6; Bain, 185–222; Hunter, *New Comedy*, 77–82; Slater, *Plautus in Performance*, passim. Slater ('Transformations', in Redmond (1987), 1–10) suggests that the physical set-up of Roman theatre encouraged Plautus' anti-illusionism.

[21] General discussions of the *eiron* include Cornford, 119–22; Frye, *Anatomy*, 172–5; Janko, 216–18.

well-attested Plautine antecedents: the ghost-writing of a letter to a
father from his son by Chrysalus (*Bacchides*); the hiding of letters
in clothing and the subsequent teasing in *Persa*; Pseudolus' inter-
ception of a letter to carry out an imposture, theft, and multiple
dupings; the Swindler's forged letters in *Trinummus*. No wonder
Figaro, many years later, listed tampering with seals and intercept-
ing letters among the stock tricks of politics and intrigues—an
interesting doubling for *Hamlet*.[22]

Moreover, Hamlet's antic madness draws on the wide traditions
of comedy as well as those of tragedy. Anaxandrides, Diodorus,
Diphilus, and Naevius wrote comedies entitled 'The Mad One(s)';
Terence rejects the mad scene as a stock comic routine (*Phormio*
6–8); Plautus parodies the madnesses of Orestes and Hercules
(*Men.* 830 ff.; *Mer.* 931 ff.; *Casina* 621 ff.).[23] *Menaechmi*, in fact,
provides a source for the antic madness very close to home. In one
of the few actual deceits in that errors play, the travelling
Menaechmus pretends he is mad to frighten away his brother's
wife and her father. In Shakespeare's first adaptation, the angry
Antipholus of Ephesus only appears mad to his mistaken wife and
Pinch; in *Twelfth Night*, Feste and his accomplices pretend that
Malvolio is mad. Hamlet, feigning madness and insulting Ophelia
and Polonius, recovers the deceit and the approximate circumstances of the Plautine prototype. Furthermore, the menace in
Hamlet's madness recalls the threatening Menaechmus rather than
the mud-wallowing, cock-crowing Amleth. When Hamlet drops the
antic madness it is hard to convince Gertrude he is sane. As Levin
observes, 'Both positions could easily be reduced to a comic level:
the plight of the man who is generally misunderstood and the pose
of the man who deliberately invites misunderstanding.'[24] Hamlet's
antic disposition radically blurs the distinction between the two,
thus calling into question human judgement and reason.

Hamlet *qua* comedic intriguer stages one climactic deceit—the
mousetrap play. Like Chrysalus, Tranio, Palestrio, or Pseudolus, or
the Shakespearean counterparts—Maria, Tranio, Don Pedro, and

---

[22] Beaumarchais, *Marriage of Figaro*, 162. On other Renaissance tricksters see
Beecher, 'Intriguers and Trickster', in Beecher and Ciavolella (1986), 53–72.

[23] See Webster, *Studies in Later Greek Comedy*, 69–73; Hunter, *New Comedy*,
128–9; for Naevius, tr. Warmington, ii. 88–9.

[24] Levin, *The Question of Hamlet*, 120. Valentine will have a similar problem
with Angelica, who pretends to disbelieve him in a later variation, Congreve's *Love
for Love*.

Prospero—Hamlet plans the production, edits the script, casts the parts, directs, and acts a role. He appropriates *The Murder of Gonzago*, a neo-Senecan revenge tragedy, to comedic ends: the play aims to 'catch the conscience of the King' (II. ii. 605), i.e. to expose a victim who, like Parolles or Malvolio, will become an unwilling participant. Pointed references to comedy and comedic festivity set the context for the mousetrap. In the advice to the player Hamlet 'exploits the genre of "critical" Terentian prologue fashionable in Italy', recasting the Ciceronian formula, 'imitatio vitae, speculum consuetudinis, imago veritatis' ('to hold as 'twere the mirror up to nature: to show virtue her feature, scorn her own image, and the very age and body of the time his form and pressure', III. ii. 21–4).[25] The well-known strictures against the overplaying clown accompany in Quarto 1 ridicule of the 'warme' clown, who keeps a stock of well-worn jokes, who cannot improvise, who 'cannot make a iest / Vnlesse by chance, as the blinde man catcheth a hare'. Right before the play-within-the-play Hamlet calls God the only creator of theatrical song-and-entertainment, 'your only jig-maker' (III. ii. 125), and sarcastically laments the forgotten 'hobby-horse' of May festivities. During the play he intrudes with jokes and asides; after the abrupt end, he sings, calls for music and recorders, provides a parodic remembrance of *The Spanish Tragedy* as epilogue: 'For if the King like not the comedy, / Why then belike he likes it not, perdy' (III. ii. 293–4). Significantly, Hamlet here substitutes the word 'comedy' for the original 'tragedy'.

Moreover, the mousetrap play functions as do New Comedic fictions in *Twelfth Night*, *Shrew*, and *Ado*: it is or becomes true in surprising ways. In revenge tragedies like *The Spanish Tragedy* or *Titus Andronicus* the play-within-the-play provides a climactic theatrical and metatheatrical occasion for spectacular revenge. No such occasion here. Instead, as in New Comedy, this supposed fiction, the improbable story of poison and betrayal, truly represents the facts of life and death in Elsinore. *The Murder of Gonzago* replays 'The Murder of Hamlet'; and, in its portrayal of Lucianus, the hesitant assassin, nephew to the King, *The Murder of Gonzago* forecasts 'The Murder of Claudius', that dramatic fiction Hamlet dreams and finally realizes. To his own horror and dismay, Hamlet here plays New Comedic fabricator of multiple fictions and multiple truths.

---

[25] Clubb, *Italian Drama*, 202; see also Frye, *The Renaissance Hamlet*, 286–7. For the quotation below see *Shakespeare's Plays in Quarto*, 598.

The mousetrap play functions also as New Comedic *pistis*, or proof. According to the *Tractatus Coislinianus* and to later commentators, the *dianoia* or thought of comedy consists largely in rhetorical proofs and disproofs of its various questions and propositions.[26] Here the proof that resolves the question at issue, namely the ghost's veracity and the king's guilt, is one of those Aristotle called ἔντεχνοι (*Rhet.* 1355b35, 'artistic', i.e. proofs requiring the skill or art of a speaker). Altman credits Kyd with the innovative use of the play-in-the-play as Terentian *pistis*; Cave notes that this device leads to anagnorisis, viewing it as so well attested in Shakespeare that it might well qualify as an addition to *Poetics* 16, 'recognition by dramatic representation'.[27] Though Hamlet's *pistis* leads to anagnorisis, the expected peripateia or reversal does not follow. Hamlet refuses to act as Aristotle might have prescribed, to kill the king at prayer, in order to unite anagnorisis and peripateia; instead, he consents to his own removal to England. The comedic intrigue ends successfully but the tragedy continues.

This deferral is entirely consistent with Shakespeare's usual practice. Comedies like *Twelfth Night* and *Ado* show clearly the inadequacy of intrigue to effect resolution and Shakespeare elsewhere shows a clear preference for errors. At its most profound levels *Hamlet* is an errors play. As Levin remarks, it abounds in '*errors* or *supposes*, misconceptions contrived and coincidental. Even the Ghost raises the question of a possible disguise, and Polonius dies a martyr to mistaken identity'.[28] The play raises to a higher power the standard questions about identity, the nature of illusion and reality. The tutelary goddess again, as in Menander's *Perikeiromene*, is Agnoia, 'misapprehension', though she appears here in subtler, more disturbing form. Despite his attempts to play the intriguer, Hamlet, like Menaechmus and Antipholus, wanders in the mists of error. He suffers a tragic version of the errors-play *aporia*, a deep confusion about his own identity and the strange world in which he finds himself. Finally, the large impersonal workings of plot, not his own design or that of Claudius and Laertes, clarifies this confusion. Climactically, Hamlet abandons purposeful intrigue for passive 'readiness' (v. ii. 222);[29] so doing, he becomes, like Viola, a schemer without a scheme, one who trusts

[26] On *pistis* see Janko, 219; Herrick, *Comic Theory*, 29–30, 179–89.
[27] pp. 277–9; Cave, 234 n.   [28] *Question*, 120.
[29] See Calderwood, 'Hamlet's Readiness'.

in time to untangle difficulties. Shakespeare pointedly chooses this comedic pattern to end his play, rather than the familiar revenge model that crowns the revenger's intrigue with bloody destruction. The ready Hamlet differs strikingly from the scheming avengers of Kyd, Marston, and Chapman, as well as Shakespeare's own Titus Andronicus; he also differs from Amleth, who plans and executes an elaborate and bloody ruse in both Saxo and Belleforest. On the contrary, *Hamlet*, especially the last two acts, 'gives eloquent testimony to the failure of deep-searching wit to extricate itself from the limitations of its own condition'.[30]

Such testimony, of course, characterizes New Comedic romance, a subgenre also evident in Hamlet. The sea, vast and mysterious, again works its magic here, providing an escape from Denmark and a means of personal transformation for the Prince. Since the chronicles supply small precedent for the pirates in *Hamlet*, critics have traced them to contemporary events and Sidney's *Arcadia*.[31] They may as well derive from New Comedy and its descendant Greek romances, where *praedones* appear frequently to kidnap children and to initiate the confusions (see, for example, *MG* 118, *Bacc.* 282, *Poen.* 897, *Rud.* 40, *Eun.* 114).[32] Later Italian playwrights like Cecchi, in a culture that did not practise infant exposure and that experienced the raids of Turkish corsairs, also used pirates as a plot-device to set up recognition.[33] In *Hamlet* the pirates play their conventional New Comedic role, intruding unexpectedly on the narrative and taking a main character prisoner. They prove to be, however, 'thieves of mercy', who exchange Hamlet's freedom for an unnamed 'good turn' (IV. vi. 21–2). They do not rob Hamlet's identity but restore it; they do not separate him from his family but return him home.

This homecoming, of course, inverts the touching homecomings and reunions of New Comedic romance. The father-figure Claudius pretends to feel joy but lays lethal traps; there is no reunion on-stage and the mighty opposites communicate through intermediaries until the final confrontation. Ophelia shatters conventional

---

[30] Altman, 10–11.
[31] See Bullough, vii. 41–8; Wentersdorf, 'Hamlet's Encounter with the Pirates'; Quarto 1 omits the pirates.
[32] *Praedor* means predator but is often used for seafaring robbers or pirates; see LeGrand, 204.
[33] Radcliff-Umstead, 'Cecchi and the Reconciliation of Theatrical Traditions', in Davidson (1986), 134–5.

expectations one last time. The discovery of her dead cruelly parodies the conventional romance reunion and nuptial, as Gertrude
dimly witnesses: 'I hop'd thou shouldst have been my Hamlet's
wife. / I thought thy bride-bed to have deck'd, sweet maid, / And
not have strew'd thy grave' (v. i. 244–6). Unlike the romance heroines, for whom the sea functions as mysterious means of deliverance, Ophelia drowns in a brook, suffering 'muddy death'. This
water is not miraculous, but a 'sore decayer of your whoreson
dead body' (v. i. 172). And unlike Elfenice, Drusilla, Hero, Helena,
Thaisa, and the rest, Ophelia will not enjoy any miraculous
rebirth, will not reappear at the end to bestow grace and love on
the errant, often erring, hero. The *pistis* that finally resolves the
multiple confusions takes the form of the duel with Laertes. Like
the βάσανοι or ordeals of Shakespeare's other romance heroes—
Marina, Ferdinand, and, as we shall see, Cordelia—this one,
devised by others, tests Hamlet's virtue—his generosity, courage,
and strength of character. He passes the test but loses his life. The
final *cognitio* does not take the form of a simple discovery of identity. Instead, the revelation will be continuous and ongoing as
Horatio draws his breath in this harsh world to tell Hamlet's
story, inscribing him not in the rolls of comedy but in those of history and tragedy.

As in the errors plays and romances, intrigue here is finally
unsuccessful or irrelevant, the resolution depending on some unexpected chance or chances. Significantly, Horatio will describe the
action in terms of 'accidental judgments, casual slaughters' and
'purposes mistook' (v. ii. 382–4). Hamlet, of course, like most in
the Renaissance, saw (or tried to see) divine providence in such
chance:

> Our indiscretion sometime serves us well
> When our deep plots do pall, and that should learn us
> There's a divinity that shapes our ends,
> Rough-hew them how we will.   (v. ii. 8–11)[34]

The glance here, as at the end of errors plays and romances, is
upward, to the providence which orders 'the fall of a sparow' (v.
ii. 220), and which, replacing New Comedic *tyche*, takes a leading

---

[34] These lines do not appear in Quarto 1. Lull argues that Quarto 1 emphasizes
heroic individualism rather than Folio's submission to providence, 'Forgetting
Hamlet', in Clayton (1992), 137–50.

role in Renaissance translations and adaptations of Plautus and Terence. At the end of Ariosto's *I suppositi*, for example, Cleandro concludes that all was ordered in heaven ('in Cielo, o Philogono / Era cosi ordinato'); Philogono responds, 'Credo che sia cosi ne che una minima / Foglia qua giu si muoua, senza lordine / Di Dio'[35] ('I know this is true, because not even the smallest leaf falls without the command of God'). Hamlet's providence, attending the fall of a sparrow, evokes the same beneficent power that reunites parted families, recovers what is lost, proves tempests kind and salt waves fresh in love. No such reunion, recovery, or proof occurs here, however. Whether Hamlet feels towards providence weary acquiescence, cynical disillusion, or quiet joy, the ending of the play leaves the audience purged, exhausted, saddened, little disposed to extol the wonders of providential care. Hamlet's own critical hermeneutic, endlessly employed in Italian and English adaptation of Plautus and Terence, is simply the last mode of understanding shown to be inadequate. And this cancellation, along with that of the other New Comedic configurations, heightens immeasurably our perplexity and our sense of loss.

King Lear

Commentators have seen in *King Lear* traces of general comedic conception and structure. In an early essay, '*King Lear* and the Comedy of the Grotesque', G. Wilson Knight discerns in the King 'a tremendous soul . . . incongruously geared to a puerile intellect'. Snyder notes general comedic structures, motifs, and devices in the play—the double plot, Fool, concern with the passing of power from old to young, the use of disguise, the movement to and from a natural setting, the multiple disorders, the manifest improbabilities. Jones perceives structural and thematic echoes of earlier comedies—*As You Like It*, *All's Well*, and *Twelfth Night*. Frye observes that the play presents 'the ironic parody of the tragic situation, most elaborately developed'; he also characterizes the sub-plot as essentially comedic, 'Gloucester's story being the regular comedy theme of the gullible *senex* swindled by a clever and unprincipled son'.[36]

---

[35] *I suppositi* (1551), 42.
[36] Knight, *The Wheel of Fire*, 160–76 (162); Snyder, 137–79; Jones, *Scenic Form*,

Frye's insight into the Gloucester-Edgar-Edmund configuration, *en passant*, has gone largely unnoticed, while other contexts—pastoral romance, medieval literature, and Machiavellian intrigue—have dominated attention. These contexts, however, invite rather than preclude further discussion of New Comedy. Sidney's *Arcadia*, the direct source for the sub-plot, is itself 'based on a Terentian structure of exposition, action, complication, reversal, and catastrophe (with an unexpected anagnorisis and peripeteia at the end)'.[37] And Renaissance playwrights, especially Shakespeare, mix diverse sources and traditions liberally and eclectically. Edmund traces his genealogy to Sidney's Plexirtus, the medieval Vice, the stage Machiavel; he is also, by his own admission, a New Comedic intriguer, the *architectus doli*. Plotting against his brother and father, he comments on the comedic neatness of Edgar's entrance, thus exhibiting the literary self-consciousness of a Pseudolus, Tranio, or Chrysalus: 'Pat! he comes like the catastrophe of the old comedy. My cue is villainous melancholy with a sigh like Tom o' Bedlam' (I. ii. 134–6). Here he evokes in manner and in matter 'old comedy', not Aristophanes, but in our terms New Comedy, the plays of Plautus and Terence as understood and analysed by humanistic commentary.[38] And he identifies the victim's entrance with the advent of *catastrophe*, the turn that resolves the plot, cheekily confident that the intrigue will work, in fact, has already worked.

Edmund's evocation of New Comedy illuminates subsequent events and the curious opening scene where Gloucester nonchalantly introduces him as his 'whoreson' (24), a stock term of abuse that, nevertheless, briefly conjures a distant *meretrix*. That scene presents scraps and traces of New Comedic motifs—the past indiscretion of the father, the present casual, even nostalgic, acknowledgement, the illegitimate child now returned. The subsequent scheming of a son against a father for money (or in this case land) is archetypal, though here Edmund will play both *adulescens* and *callidus servus*. Like Plautine intriguers, and unlike the alleged

171 ff.; Frye, *Anatomy*, 175; see also Miller, 'King Lear and the Comic Form'; Thompson, *King Lear*, 19–21. Leggatt (*King Lear*, 23) notes that Granville Barker 'allowed, even insisted on, the comedy of the play'. Here I use Evans's edn. but remain aware of the separate Quarto and Folio texts there conflated by check against Michael Warren's *The Parallel King Lear 1608–1623*.

[37] *Arcadia*, ed. Robertson, xx.   [38] See Baldwin, *Five-Act*, 316.

source figures, Sidney's Plexirtus and the Iberian stepmother, Edmund speaks in soliloquy and aside, relies on 'wit', on his ability to 'fashion fit' (I. ii. 183–4), congratulates himself on the easy riding of his 'practices' (182), improvises to take advantage of occasions like Cornwall's arrival (II. i). The use of a forged letter for deception, as we noted in *Hamlet*, is a well-attested Plautine device. Shakespeare used this device, wholly absent from the source accounts of *Lear*, in earlier comedies, notably *The Two Gentlemen of Verona*, an early experiment in New Comedic and other conventions. In *Lear* the device will turn deadly when Edmund uses a stolen letter to betray his father.

The intrigue proceeds in II. i by familiar means, a scene staged to mislead concealed or off-stage auditors. The duel with Edgar, complete with phony outcries—'Yield! Come before my father. Light, ho, here! . . . Torches, torches!' (31–2)—and the self-wounding creates a version of the disinformative eavesdropping we have observed elsewhere, especially in *Ado*.[39] An important *locus classicus* for such deception, one that bears interesting similarities to Edmund's practice, is the scene (732 ff.) Davos stages in *Andria*, a standard grammar school text. In order to deceive the eavesdropping *senex*, the clever servant invents a quarrel with Mysis, who co-operates in the deceit but does not understand it. As here, the deceit in *Lear* displays the imaginative and theatrical abilities of the intriguer: Edmund creates the script, casts the performers, plays the leading role, uses props, and tricks the unwary audience. Edmund also plays critic, explaining the meaning of the play, narrating the fictitious tale of Edgar's betrayal with a flair for superfluous supernaturalism that any Plautine intriguer would admire: 'Here stood he in the dark, his sharp sword out, / Mumbling of wicked charms, conjuring the moon / To stand's auspicious mistress' (II. i. 38–40). In classical comedy the scam often turns on the intriguer's ability to persuade the *senex* that he is in danger, be it financial, personal, or, as here, both.

Edmund's inset intrigue concludes in II. i with Gloucester's false *cognitio*—the discovery of Edgar's perfidy and Edmund's loyalty:

> the villain shall not scape;
> The Duke must grant me that. Besides, his picture

---

[39] There is a similar practice in Sidney's *Arcadia*, but the Edgar figure is the eavesdropper, Bullough, vii. 410 ff.

> I will send far and near, that all the kingdom
> May have due note of him, and of my land,
> Loyal and natural boy, I'll work the means
> To make thee capable.   (II. i. 80–5)

This recognition parodies the New Comedic discovery of offspring, as this *senex* entirely confuses his legitimate and illegitimate sons, his 'loyal and natural boy' and his 'villain'. Edmund early on achieves the comedic goals of land and legitimized identity, but he does not rest with these achievements. Instead, he enacts literally the stock jokes of sons against fathers, attempting to realize in fact the comedic wish for paternal death.[40] Later, speaking for a long line of such sons, Molière's Cléante will protest the stinginess of his own father and of fathers in general: 'et on s'étonne après cela que les fils souhaitent qu'ils meurent' ('And, after this, people are surprised that their sons wish them dead').[41] Later still, Christy Mahon's supposed killing of his 'da' in J. M. Synge's *The Playboy of the Western World* will present a richly tragicomic reworking of the motif. Betraying Gloucester to Cornwall and then abandoning him to unspeakable punishment, Edmund, to be sure, travels well beyond comedic conventions and traditions into the darker regions of tragedy and human betrayal. Yet, he stands as Shakespeare's developed study in the evil potentialities of comedic intrigue, heir and successor to Don John. And here as there, the illegitimate evil intriguer is half-brother to a legitimate good intriguer. The fraternal contrasting of Edmund and Edgar, echoed in the sororal opposition between Cordelia and her sisters, varies again that arrangement evident in *Ado*, *Hamlet*, and the traditions of Terence *moralisé*, especially the good and bad brothers of the classicized Prodigal Son plays. The rest of the play will feature Edgar's counter-intrigue—complex, purposeful, and in salient aspects, New Comedic.

Edgar protects himself from the dangers threatening him by use of three comedic devices that are absent from the source tale in Sidney's *Arcadia*—disguise, feigned madness, the gulling of his father. The first is a ubiquitous feature of classical plays and their descendants, managed with baroque inventiveness here as Edgar changes from Poor Tom, to the incognito stranger, to the Somerset

---

[40] See Naevius, tr. Warmington, ii. 108–9; *Most.* 233–4; *Truculentus* 660–2; Segal, *Roman Laughter*, 17 ff.

[41] *L'Avare*, ed. Jouanny, ii. 263.

man, to armed champion. Feigned madness, as we have noted in connection with Hamlet, has a specific precedent in Plautus' *Menaechmi* (830 ff.), where Menaechmus of Syracuse pretends to be mad in order to frighten off persecutors. Deceiving his father at Dover Cliff, Edgar replays inventively the familiar gulling of the *senex* by fast talk and disguise. The routine was so familiar to Elizabethan audiences that Angelo of Chapman's *May Day* could mock it as the 'stale refuge of miserable Poets, by change of a hat or a cloake, to alter the whole state of a Comedie, so as the father must not know his owne child forsooth' (II. iv. 150–2). The scene springs more specifically from Launcelot's practice against his father, Old Gobbo, in *The Merchant of Venice*. Struggling with the fiend at his elbow (II. ii. 1 ff.), Launcelot runs away from his master, Shylock, and, encountering his nearly blind father, tries 'confusions with him' (37–8). Pretending to be someone else, he informs the old man that his son is dead. 'It is a wise father that knows his own child' (76–7) Launcelot teases, a maxim with peculiar resonance for *King Lear*. The deceit ends in a *cognitio* and restoration of identity and family bonds.

The parallels between Edgar's and Edmund's practices point up their similarities as comedic intriguers and their differences. Edgar intercepts a letter (IV. vi) and uses another to initiate the process of retribution (V. i). Like Edmund in the mock-duel, Edgar writes, plays in, and produces the play at Dover Cliff, likewise deceiving the target audience, his father. Like Edmund, he plays post-performance critic, explaining the meaning of the action to his confused father, even outdoing his brother in superfluous and supernatural fantasy. He describes the 'beggar' above:

> As I stood here below, methought his eyes
> Were two full moons; he had a thousand noses,
> Horns welk'd, and waved like the enridged sea.   (IV. vi. 69–71)

Unlike Edmund's performance, however, this one is played for Gloucester's good. Edgar pretends here to enact the New Comedic wish for paternal death in order to give Gloucester life, to cure his despair and bring him free and patient thoughts. Edgar's intrigues, like Edmund's, proceed through the rest of the play, enfolding and incorporating medieval and romance traditions. The duel between the two brothers, however, concludes in a discovery that publicly rectifies Gloucester's false *cognitio*:

I am no less in blood than thou art, Edmund;
If more, the more th' hast wrong'd me.
My name is Edgar, and thy father's son.   (v. iii. 168–70)

The New Comedic restoration of family bonds, begun off-stage in
the reunion with Gloucester, is here complete, as Edgar triumphantly reclaims his lost identity.

Few today would agree with Tolstoy, who dismissed as merely
distracting 'the utterly superfluous characters of the villain
Edmund, and unlifelike Gloucester and Edgar'.[42] The sub-plot resonates with the main one in many well-remarked ways. Moreover,
both Gloucester and Lear generally resemble *senes* in New
Comedy—often credulous, wrongly judgemental of their offspring,
deceived.[43] Withholding Cordelia's dowry in I. i, Lear plays in a
more specific New Comedy configuration—the familiar *senex iratus*
blocking a marriage—though those ancient fathers generally inter-
fere with the amours of their sons, not daughters. Still, the disposal
of a nubile girl and her dowry are centrally at issue in many plays,
in Menander's *Aspis*, for example, which turns on Athenian laws
governing marriage, dowries, and inheritance; in Plautus'
Trinummus, where the wealthy father returns to supply his daughter's missing dowry and to enrich her fiancé, Lysiteles, who had
planned to marry her anyway. The variation closest to Lear occurs
in *Aulularia*: here the miser Euclio refuses to offer any dowry for
his daughter; the suitor, Megadorus, responds in accents reminiscent of France: 'ne duas. / dum modo morata recte ueniat, dotata
est satis' (238–9, 'Don't. As long as the girl has good manners, she
has dowry enough');[44] FRANCE: 'She is herself a dowry' (I. i. 241).
Aulularia ends, we surmise from the fragments, with Euclio's reformation and his gift of a pot of gold to his daughter and her lover,
Lyconides.

In the opening scene Lear recalls these fathers, as, variously,

---

[42] As quoted in *The King Lear Perplex*, ed. Bonheim, 56; cf. Bradley
(*Shakespearean Tragedy*, 254) who thought the 'principal structural weakness' of the
play to arise 'chiefly from the double action'; Thompson, 15–17. Yet, appreciative
recognition of the double plot would qualify strict gender readings such as that of
McLuskie, 'The patriarchal Bard', in Dollimore and Sinfield (1985), 88–108.

[43] As earlier with Old Gobbo and Gloucester, comic precedents for Lear also lie
closer to home. Jones (*Scenic Form*, 176 ff.) sees models for the duped and isolated
king in Parolles and Malvolio.

[44] Plautine commentators identified the response as gnomic, citing parallels from
Plautus, Horace, Menander, and Antipater, *Opera* (1577), 161.

Silvia's father, Baptista, Egeus, Page, Capulet, Leonato, Polonius, Brabantio, even as he looks ahead to Pericles, Cymbeline, and Prospero. Shakespeare makes several subtle changes from the earlier chronicle play, *King Leir*, to portray Lear as a capricious, blocking figure: in that play the love test is a previously revealed scheme to apportion dowries and arrange political marriages; in *Lear* the test is entirely whimsical, motivated solely by the old man's vanity. In the old play there is no precedent for Burgundy and France arrives later; in *Lear* these two are present as suitors, one effectively removed by the King's anger and subsequent disinheritance of Cordelia, the other thereby tested and validated. These changes depict Lear as an angry and childish father, while focusing attention on his relationship with Cordelia *qua* nubile *virgo*. Shakespeare then exploits the tragic potential of the comedic configuration, transforming Lear's authority into patriarchal tyranny, Cordelia's innocence into proof of her purity and virtue. Disclaiming all paternal care, Lear inverts the comedic example of the King in *All's Well*, who offers to enrich the poor Helena, and also that of Timon, who gives a fortune to his servant to enable him to marry.

As the play progresses Shakespeare departs from the chronicles and *Leir* to recast the action into a familiar comedic configuration—the lock-out. In Geoffrey of Monmouth's *Historia Anglicana* Leir leaves the first sister and finds at the home of the second 'an honourable Reception' (Bullough, vii. 313); after a later quarrel, he betakes himself to Cordeilla's home in Gaul. Similarly, Holinshed says that the daughters showed 'unkindnesse', and so Leir, 'constreined of necessitie', fled into Gallia, where he 'was no lesse honored, than if he had beene king of the whole countrie himselfe' (Bullough, vii. 318). In *Leir* Ragan hypocritically welcomes her father, then receives the letter from Gonorill and begins to plot his murder. He later flies to Gaul. In none of the sources is there any denial of admittance; and in all the King, upon discovering the true nature of his daughters, goes freely to Cordelia in France. How different the action in *King Lear*. Arriving at Gloucester's house, Lear finds that she and Cornwall 'deny to speak' with him (II. iv. 88); the Fool points the appropriate moral and prophesizes the shape of things to come: 'Fortune, that arrant whore, / Ne'er turns the key to th' poor' (Folio only, II. iv. 52–3). Regan refuses to accommodate him: 'I am now from home, and out of that provision / Which

shall be needful for your entertainment' (II. iv. 205–6). There follows Goneril and Regan's bargaining down of his retinue, Lear's
angry exit, not to France but into the storm, the sisters' smug
agreement that Lear 'must needs taste his folly' (II. iv. 291). The
scene closes with the twice repeated admonition to Gloucester,
'Shut up your doors' (304, 308).

Departing from his usual sources, Shakespeare here refashions
the comedic lock-out of the errors plays. Like Menaechmus, shut
out by his wife and then by Erotium, Lear, doubly rejected, finds
himself 'exclusissumus' (698). 'In such a night / To shut me out?'
(III. iv. 17–18), he muses incredulously. Shakespeare's first version
of the scene in *The Comedy of Errors* appropriates also the darker
anger of Amphitruo, mistook, locked-out, taunted. Later variations
in *Twelfth Night* explore the lock-out as metaphor for spiritual dis-
tempers. In *Lear* Shakespeare draws on this past experience to
stunning effect: Lear feels Amphitruo's righteous wrath at betrayal;
and his lock-out poignantly symbolizes loss of family, home, and
identity. Now with nowhere to go, the King confronts the raw elements of nature as well as his unaccommodated self.

The inscribed comedic model, of course, appears here in complex form. Lear is not merely a victim, but also an agent, not
merely rejected, but also and emphatically rejecting. Refusing their
terms, Lear in a sense locks out his daughters, choosing self-vali-
dating isolation to self-degrading society. As ancient Greek and
later playwrights well recognized, such a choice could furnish
ample material for comedy.[45] A fragment from an early Greek
comedy, Phrynichus' *Monotropos*, pithily summarizes the lead
character:

> ὄνομα δὲ μοῦστι Μονότροπος
>   ζῶ δὲ Τίμωνος βίον
> ἄγαμον, ἄζυγον, ὀξύθυμον, ἀπρόσοδον,
> ἀγέλαστον, ἀδιάλεκτον, ἰδιογνώμονα.   (Kassel–Austin, vii. 4040; cf.
> Antiphanes, ed. Edmonds, ii. 270–1)

My name is Solitary Man. I live the life of Timon—unwed, unyoked,
sharp-tempered, unapproachable, laughless, silently self-contained, holding
to my own opinions.

---

[45] See Handley's edn. of *Dyskolos*, 129–30; Henderson's edn. of *Lysistrata*, 172;
and the fuller treatments of Photiadès, 'Le Type du Misanthrope dans la littérature
grecque', and Préaux, 'Réflexions sur la Misanthropie au Théâtre'.

The anonymous academic *Timon* provided a comic treatment of the character in English which Shakespeare probably knew around 1602.[46] Early and late, angry withdrawal and fulminating misanthropy characterize the comedic *idiotes*—self-important, isolated, inflexible, anti-festive, and ridiculous. Frye well remarked that Shakespeare's *Timon* 'has many features making for an *idiotes* comedy rather than a tragedy'.[47] The same must be said of *King Lear*, especially when we recall that the traditional *idiotes* has a curious but consistent relationship with a clown, in this case, a fool. Lear's angry withdrawal to the heath and his declamatory rage against the world thus describes a progress archetypally comic as well as tragic. Lear suffers from the δυσκολία of the earliest New Comedic *idiotes*, Menander's Knemon, ἀπάνθρωπός τις ἄνθρωπος (6, 'a man far from men'); and at the same time he experiences the terrible isolation of Oedipus or another Sophoclean tragic hero, μόνος ('alone'), and ἐρῆμος ('desolate').

The end of *Lear* likewise displays New Comedic configuration, though more specific and familiar. Commentators have long observed that the second half of the play incorporates and subverts the features of pastoral romance;[48] they have not noted as well that this genre is intimately indebted to New Comedy for its development. Indirectly through romance drama or fiction or directly, Plautus and Terence supply many of the romance features of *Lear*. As observed in earlier discussion of *Pericles* and *The Tempest*, New Comedic romance generally features a pure female figure variously assaulted, journeys over sea and long time, reunions of parents and children. Shakespeare incorporates all these structural features into this play, locating them at the centre of *Lear*'s closing movement. This movement features the rejected Cordelia, who journeys to England to rescue her father. The reunion of Lear and Cordelia, played over three separate moments—IV. vii, the beginning and end of v. iii—represents a tragic reworking of comedic material, one that draws power and emotion from the models it subsumes and, finally, subverts.

At the centre of Shakespeare's tragic romance stands Cordelia,

---

[46] So argues Bulman, 'The Date and Production of "Timon" Reconsidered'; 'Shakespeare's Use of the "Timon" Comedy'.

[47] *Natural Perspective*, 98.

[48] See Mack, *King Lear in our Time*, 63–6; Young, *The Heart's Forest*, 73–103; Salingar, *Dramatic Form in Shakespeare and the Jacobeans*, 91–106.

herself a version of the Italianate 'woman as wonder'. Throughout
the play Cordelia exhibits the luminous spirituality of that comedic
and redemptive figure we glimpsed in Lucrezia, Elfenice, Drusilla,
Carizia, Hero, Isabella, Helena, Marina, and Miranda. Constant
and self-sacrificing, Cordelia weeps 'holy water' from 'heavenly
eyes' (Quarto only, IV. iii. 30), 'Redeems nature from the general
curse' (IV. vi. 206). Like the Italian *donna* she shines all the brighter
for contrast with foils, the base Agnoletta of Piccolomini's *Amor
costante*, the earthy Violante of Bargagli's *La pellegrina*, Mistress
Overdone, Dionyza, here the dog-hearted daughters, Goneril and
Regan. Like Drusilla or Helena and unlike her counterpart in the
chronicles and *Leir*, she is a miraculous healer: 'O my dear father,
restoration hang / Thy medicine on my lips, and let this kiss /
Repair those violent harms that my two sisters / Have in thy reverence made' (IV. vii. 25–8). The Doctor (Gentleman in Folio) yields
to her ministrations at the moment of Lear's awakening. As in the
commedia erudita the dazed and bewildered beholder first thinks
the miraculous lady a spirit:

ARISTIDE: Crederrò bene che siate lo spirito d'Elfenice, ma non Elfenice
istessa, poich'ella è morta.   (*La donna costante*, 99).

LUCRETIO: Ma voi chi sete? ò spirito, ò donna, che viue? Sete voi Drusilla?
(*La pellegrina*, 151).

LEAR: You are a spirit, I know; when did you die?   (IV. vii. 48)

Recognizing his daughter Cordelia, Lear experiences a thoroughly
Shakespearean *cognitio*, the discovery of moral and spiritual identity, not merely social status. This *cognitio* brings concomitant discovery of self, the one who wronged Cordelia, the father 'old and
foolish'. Like Bargagli's Drusilla, Shakespeare's Isabella, and many
others, Cordelia forgives, thus allowing for a temporary reconciliation and the restoration of harmony.

In the beginning of v. iii the New Comedic themes of lost identity, false accusation, and arrest—fundamental to the errors
plays—wear their rue with a difference. Here the revelation of
identity does not cancel the tragic impulses but enables them: Lear
and Cordelia enter as prisoners of the victorious Edmund. Yet, the
surging joy of their reunion continues unabated, as Lear basks in
Cordelia's love and forgiveness, looking forward to singing 'like
birds i' th' cage', to taking on 'the mystery of things' as God's

spies, to wearing out 'packs and sects of great ones' (v. iii. 9 ff.). 'Have I caught thee? / He that parts us shall bring a brand from heaven / And fire us hence like foxes' (21–3). Such language reifies in a startling way the conventional rhetoric of New Comedic reunions. In *Poenulus*, for example, Hanno recovers his daughters and exclaims, 'nunc ego sum fortunatus, / multorum annorum miserias nunc hac uoluptate sedo' (1262–3, 'Now I am a lucky man! And this joy now relieves the miseries of many a year'). Including Agorastocles in the embrace Hanno says, 'condamus alter alterum ergo in neruom bracchialem. / quibu' nunc in terra melius est?' (1269–70, 'Let's each of us lock up the other in our arms. Who now on earth is happier?'). In *Rudens* Daemones responds similarly to the discovery of his daughter Palaestra: 'contineri quin complectar non queo. / filia mea, salue. ego is sum qui te produxit pater, / ego sum Daemones' (1172–4, 'I can't keep from hugging her. Greetings, my daughter! I am the father who brought you up. I am Daemones!'). Italian variations express in similar terms the 'grande allegrezza' (*La donna costante*, 161) of reunion. Lear's reappropriation of this New Comedic rhetoric defies the unresolved tragic error that entraps him, signalling his liberation from Fortune's power and his attainment of transcendent joy.

The New Comedic reverie is evoked, of course, only to be shattered: '*Enter Lear with Cordelia in his arms*' (v. iii. 257 s.d.). The dramatic entrance at the end of the play, itself a stroke from the errors plays, dashes audience expectation, cruelly violating the closure that the inscribed comedic model warrants and signifies. The inert figure of Cordelia evokes the inert figures of those wondrous Italian heroines—Lucrezia, Elfenice, Carizia, and Drusilla—as well as Hero, Helena, Marina—all reported dead, all miraculously returning to life. Lear desperately hopes that Cordelia lives: 'If it be so, / It is a chance which does redeem all sorrows / That ever I have felt' (266–8). But the found daughter is again lost, this time forever; the *donna tanto mirabile* has no breath at all. Mutely disallowing such resurrections, the world of the play leaves Lear and the audience all the more disappointed and darkling. The daughter is lost not found, or more precisely and painfully, found then lost again. The death of Cordelia represents Shakespeare's final, most profound, and most moving inversion of New Comedy.

Lear's use of the word 'chance' above echoes with previous significations. It recalls France speaking of Cordelia, 'thrown' to his 'chance' (I. i. 256), either accidentally fallen to his lot or purposefully placed there. Kent asks the Fool, 'How chance the King comes with so small a number?' (II. iv. 63). The chance here is no chance at all but Goneril's wilfulness and, as the Fool's reference to the great wheel running down a hill implies, the laws that govern power relations. In one of the most heartening moments in a bleak play the nameless First Servant challenges Cornwall: 'Nay then come on, and take the chance of anger' (III. vii. 79); 'The chance of anger' here denotes the potential consequence of both Cornwall's evil anger and the servant's righteous indignation, while suggesting the risk and uncertainty both men face. Regan tells Oswald, 'If you do chance to hear of that blind traitor, / Preferment falls on him that cuts him off' (IV. v. 37–8). Ironically, Oswald's chance becomes his own occasion of death and the instrument of Edgar's advancement. In *Lear* 'chance' refers to the human capacity for wilful action—evil and good—as well as to the unfathomable powers that rule our lives; it occupies that hazy area between accident, volition, and destiny, a region of shifting ground and deceptive constellations.

Lear's invocation of chance, rather than God or the gods, at the most poignant and powerful moment of the play must give us pause. For chance not only fails to provide Lear with the promised end, but it has already supplied the unexpected disaster. As many have remarked, Cordelia's death seems entirely fortuitous, entirely a matter of chance. It comes after our attention has been diverted to the duel, Edgar's revelation, the multiple deaths, after Edmund has cancelled the order for the murders, after the logic of the action has been completed, after the ceremonies of reconciliation and conclusion seem at an end. As Booth comments:

Shakespeare has already presented an action that is serious, of undoubted magnitude, *and complete*; he thereupon continues that action beyond the limits of the one category that no audience can expect to see challenged: Shakespeare presents the culminating events of his *story* after his *play* is over.[49]

So doing, Shakespeare violates Aristotle's recommendation for anagnorisis and peripeteia in a complex tragic action:

ταῦτα δὲ δεῖ γίνεσθαι ἐξ αὐτῆς τῆς συστάσεως τοῦ μύθου, ὥστε ἐκ τῶν προγεγενημένων συμβαίνειν ἢ ἐξ ἀνάγκης ἢ κατὰ τὸ εἰκὸς γίγνεσθαι ταῦτα·

[49] *King Lear, Macbeth, Indefinition, and Tragedy*, 11.

διαφέρει γὰρ πολὺ τὸ γίγνεσθαι τάδε διὰ τάδε ἢ μετὰ τάδε.

(*Poet.* 1452a18–21)

These should derive from the actual structure of the plot so as to accord with things that have happened, and to happen themselves either from necessity or probability; for there is, in fact, a great difference between what happens because of something and what happens simply after something.

The death of Cordelia is manifestly *post hoc*; it strikes no one as happening from necessity or probability, ἐξ ἀνάγκης ἢ κατὰ τὸ εἰκὸς; the climax of the fabula destroys rather than completes its internal coherence, its logic of cause and effect. This chance seems to render all human action pointless and futile; it is again the dark side of comedic *tyche*.

This *tyche*, manifesting itself not as a principle of cosmic randomness but as an accident of plot, normally effects anagnorisis and peripeteia in comedy. We recall the many coincidences, happy accidents, and implausible serendipities that lead to resolutions in Greek and Latin comedy—the fortuitous entrance, the chance eavesdropping or sighting, the fortunate happenstance. Appearing as a delayed prologue in Menander's *Aspis*, *Tyche* introduces herself by announcing her incompatibility with tragic action and by claiming complete responsibility for the events of the play. As Lloyd-Jones observes, *Tyche* does not mean here and elsewhere blind chance but 'whatever happens', usually through the incomprehensible workings of a divine agency.[50] Perhaps the cleverest trickster in Roman comedy pays homage to this goddess, or to a Roman equivalent:

> sed profecto hoc sic erit:
> centum doctum hominum consilia sola haec deuincit dea,
> Fortuna.   (*Pseud.* 677–9)

But surely it will go this way: Fortune—this one lone goddess—smashes the schemes of one hundred learned men.

As we have observed, Renaissance theorists and playwrights repeatedly recast such chance as divine providence and discerned in

---

[50] Lloyd-Jones, *Greek Comedy*, 24; see also Gomme and Sandbach, 73–4, 711–12. In the absence of Poetics II, Renaissance commentators on Aristotle conceded the role of chance 'only—and then by no means universally—in the case of comedy, where the example of Terence no doubt justifies Robortello's contention that comedies may give pleasure even though their peripeteia and anagnorisis do not arise from the action' (Cave, *Recognitions*, 59).

its resolutions celestial harmonies. Recognizing the prevailing hermeneutic, one can fully savour Machiavelli's brilliant inversion in *La mandragola*: there the virtuous young wife, seduced by an elaborate deception, credits the success of the plan to divine providence and decides to retain her new lover permanently, 'io voglio iudicare che e' venga da una celeste disposizione che abbi voluto così, e non sono sufficiente a recusare quello che 'l cielo vuole che io accetti' (165, 'I have decided that this has happened through a heavenly disposition that has wished it thus, and I am not able to refuse that which heaven wills I accept').

In *Lear* Shakespeare too confronts and contradicts the providential view, though his purposes are tragic not satiric. On occasion characters in the play, like contemporary editors and commentators, attempt to see divine order in sublunary chaos. Albany, for example, hearing of Gloucester's blinding and Cornwall's death, supplies the conventional gloss: 'This shows you are above, / You justicers, that these our nether crimes / So speedily can venge!' (IV. ii. 78–80). Futilely, Albany invokes these same just divinities in his exclamation, 'The gods defend her!' (V. iii. 257), just before Lear enters with Cordelia in his arms. In one appalling moment comedic chance becomes tragic *tyche*. Cordelia's death confounds the efforts of mortals to justify human events *sub specie aeternitatis*, to contain fact and fiction in a comfortable moral framework. Albany's hope, along with the entire humanist project, lies in ruins. Instead, *Lear* offers the audience the terrible possibility that chance rules all, and that it is entirely indifferent (or malevolent) to justice or human needs. In so doing, the play exactly reverses the conventional dynamics of comedy, clearly outlined in the Prologo to Borghini's *La donna costante*:

Comincia di notte, e finisce di giorno, perche si come nel principio del mondo, come dicono i filosofi, furono prima le tenebre, & il Caos, ove gli elementi stauano in confuso, e poi venuta la luce ne segui questo bell'ordine del mondo; Così la nostra Comedia comincia di notte tutta confusa, e trauagliata, e poi venuto il giorno tutta quieta, e pacifica diuiene.　　(sig. A6)

It starts in night and ends in daylight, just as in the beginning of the world, the philosophers explain, there was first darkness and Chaos, in which all the elements mixed in confusion, and then came light and, following, the beautiful order of creation. So our comedy begins in a night all confused and distressed and then ends in a daylight all quiet, peaceful, and divine.

Borghini's rhetoric here links the play world and the real one: the action on stage imitates *la divina commedia* written by God and inscribed in creation. Reversing Borghini's comedic sequence from night to day, *Lear* also confounds the underlying metaphysic. This play uncreates the world, returning it again to 'le tenebre, & il Caos'. Of course, this reversal is not absolute; we may value all the more the virtuous who are trapped in the surrounding darkness.[51] Yet Shakespeare's bold inversion of New Comedic practices and expectations greatly augments *Lear*'s power to shock and disturb.

---

[51] Attending to the affective power of the play in the theatre, McAlindon ('Tragedy, *King Lear*, and the Politics of the Heart') well argues this point against political readings, such as that of Dollimore (*Radical Tragedy*, 189–203).

Bibliography

I cite throughout *The Riverside Shakespeare*, but with caution and supplementary materials when referring to multiple-text plays like *Hamlet* and *Lear*; for Menander, Plautus, and Terence, I cite the Oxford Classical Texts editions. Unless otherwise noted all translations in the text are my own.

(i) Primary Sources

ACCADEMIA DEGLI INTRONATI, *La commedia degli ingannati* (*Gl'ingannati*), ed. Florindo Cerreta (Florence, 1980).

ACCOLTI, BERNARDO, *Verginia* (Venice, 1530).

ANDREINI, FRANCESCO, *Le bravure del Capitano Spauento; divise in molti ragionamenti in forma di dialogo* (Venice, 1607).

ARETINO, PIETRO, *Talanta*, tr. Christopher Cairns, *Three Renaissance Comedies*, ed. Christopher Cairns (Lewiston, NY, 1991).

ARIOSTO, LUDOVICO, *Orlando furioso* (Venice, 1542) [annotations by Aluigi Gonzaga]; (Venice, 1580) [annotations by Tomasso Porcacchi]; (Venice, 1585) [annotations by Ieronimo Ruscelli].

—— *Orlando Furioso in English Heroical Verse by John Harington* (1591; repr. Amsterdam, 1970).

—— *Gli soppositi* (Venice, 1525) [prose].

—— *I svppositi* (Venice, 1551) [verse].

ARISTOPHANES, *Comoediae*, eds. F. W. Hall and W. M. Geldart, 2 vols., 2nd edn., (OCT, 1906–7).

—— *Clouds*, ed. K. J. Dover (Oxford, 1968).

—— *Lysistrata*, ed. Jeffrey Henderson (Oxford, 1987).

—— *Wasps*, ed. Douglas M. MacDowell (Oxford, 1971).

ARISTOTLE, *Ars Rhetorica*, ed. W. D. Ross (OCT, 1959).

—— *De Arte Poetica Liber*, ed. Rudolph Kassel (OCT, 1965; repr. 1980); tr. W. Hamilton Fyfe (LCL, 1927; rev. 1932).

—— *The Nicomachean Ethics*, tr. H. Rackham (LCL, 1926; rev. 1934).

AUGUSTINE, SAINT, *Confessions*, tr. William Watts (1631), 2 vols. (LCL, 1912).

AXTON, MARIE ed., *Three Tudor Classical Interludes* (Cambridge, 1982).

BAÏF, JEAN-ANTOINE DE, *Le Brave*, ed. Simone Maser (Geneva, 1979).

—— *L'Eunuque, Evres en rime*, vol. iv, ed. Ch. Marty-Laveux (Paris, 1887).

BANDELLO, MATTEO, *La prima parte de le novelle del Bandello*, vol. i (Lucca, 1554).

BARGAGLI, GIROLAMO, *La pellegrina* (Siena, 1589); tr. Bruno Ferraro, *The Female Pilgrim* (CRPT, 1988).

BEAUMARCHAIS, CARON DE, *The Barber of Seville and The Marriage of Figaro*, tr. John Wood (1964; repr. Baltimore, 1967).

BEAUMONT, FRANCIS, and FLETCHER, JOHN, *The Dramatic Works*, ed. Fredson Bowers, 9 vols. (Cambridge, 1966–93).

BECKETT, SAMUEL, *Waiting for Godot* (New York, 1954).

BELLEAU, REMY, *La Reconnue*, ed. Jean Braybrook (Geneva, 1989).

BENTIVOGLIO, HERCOLE, *I fantasmi* (Venice, 1544).

BEOLCO, ANGELO, *La piovana* (Venice, 1548).

BERRARDO, G., *Cassina* (Venice, 1530) [tr. of Plautus].

—— *Mustellaria* (Venice, 1530) [tr. of Plautus].

BIBBIENA (see Dovizi).

The Birthe of Hercules (with an 'Introduction on the Influence of Plautus'), ed. Malcolm William Wallace (Chicago, 1903); ed. R. Warwick Bond, (MSR, 1911).

BOCCACCIO, GIOVANNI, *Tutte le opere*, ed. Vittore Branca, 12 vols. (Milan, 1964–) [incomplete].

BOND, R. WARWICK ed., *Early Plays from the Italian* (Oxford, 1911).

BONINO, GUIDO DAVICO ed., *Il teatro italiano II, la commedia del cinquecento*, 3 vols., paper (Turin, 1977–8) [Appendice: Cronache e descrizioni di spettacoli].

BORGHINI, RAFFAELLO, *La donna costante* (Florence, 1582).

BROOKE, SAMUEL, *Adelphe, Scyros, Melanthe*, ed. Götz Schmitz (RLDE, 1991).

BRUNO, GIORDANO, *Il candelaio*, tr. J. R. Hale, *The Genius of the Italian Theatre*, ed. Eric Bentley (New York, 1964).

BULLOUGH, GEOFFREY ed., *Narrative and Dramatic Sources of Shakespeare*, 8 vols. (London, 1957–75).

CALDERÓN, PEDRO, *Four Comedies*, tr. Kenneth Muir (Lexington, Ky., 1980).

—— *Three Comedies*, tr. Kenneth Muir and Ann L. Mackenzie (Lexington, Ky., 1985).

CARO, ANNIBAL, *Gli straccioni*, tr. Massimo Ciavolella and Donald Beecher, *The Scruffy Scoundrels* (CRPT, 1980).

CASTELVETRO, LODOVICO, *Poetica d'Aristotele vulgarizzata, et sposta* (1570; repr. Munich, 1968).

—— 'Parere di Ludovico Castelvetro sopra ciascuna comedia di Plauto', ed. Giuseppe Spezi, *Il propugnatore*, 1 (1868), 61–74.

CECCHI, GIOVANNI MARIA, *La moglie* (Venice, 1585).

—— *Commedie*, ed. Gaetano Milanesi, 2 vols. (Florence, 1856).

CECCHI, GIOVANNI MARIA, *L'assiuolo*, tr. Konrad Eisenbichler, *The Horned Owl* (CRPT, 1981).

CERVANTES, MIGUEL DE, *Interludes*, tr. Edwin Honig (New York, 1964).

CHAPMAN, GEORGE, *Plays: The Comedies*, ed. Thomas Marc Parrott, 2 vols. (New York, 1961); ed. Allan Holaday (Urbana, Ill., 1970) [references are cited to the later edn.].

CIBBER, COLLEY, *Dramatic Works*, 5 vols. (1777; repr. New York, 1966).

Clyomon and Clamydes, ed. Betty J. Littleton (The Hague, 1968).

CONGREVE, WILLIAM, *Complete Plays*, ed. Herbert Davis (Chicago, 1967).

CORNEILLE, PIERRE, *The Liar, The Illusion*, tr. Ranjit Bolt (Bath, 1989).

CRAWFORD, JAMES M. tr., *The Secular Latin Comedies of Twelfth-century France*, Diss., Indiana University, 1977.

DAVIES, JOHN, *Complete Works*, ed. Alexander B. Grosart, 2 vols. (Edinburgh, 1878).

DAY, JOHN, *Works*, ed. A. H. Bullen (London, 1881).

DEKKER, THOMAS, *Dramatic Works*, ed. Fredson Bowers, 4 vols. (Cambridge, 1953–61); Cyrus Hoy, *Introductions, Notes, and Commentaries* [to Bowers's edn.], 4 vols. (Cambridge, 1980).

DELLA PORTA, GIAMBATTISTA, *Le commedie*, ed. Vincenzo Spampanato, vol. i (Bari, 1910).

—— *Gli duoi fratelli rivali / The Two Rival Brothers*, tr. Louise George Clubb (Berkeley, 1980).

DENNIS, JOHN, *The Comical Gallant* (London, 1702).

DENOMY, ALEXANDER JOSEPH ed., *The Old French Lives of Saint Agnes* (Cambridge, Mass., 1938).

DODSLEY, ROBERT ed., *A Select Collection of Old English Plays*, rev. W. Carew Hazlitt, 7 vols. (1874–6; repr. New York, 1964).

DOLCE, LODOVICO, *Comedie* (Venice, 1560).

—— *Il marito* (Venice, 1586).

—— *Il ragazzo* (Venice, 1586).

DONATUS, AELIUS, *Commentum Terenti*, ed. P. Wessner, 3 vols. (1902–8; repr. Stuttgart, 1962–3) [with Evanthius and Eugraphius].

DOVIZI, BERNARDO DI BIBBIENA, *Calandra* (Venice, 1553) [*La calandria*].

DRYDEN, JOHN, *Works*, ed. Edwards Niles Hooker *et al.*, 20 vols. (Berkeley, 1956–89).

EDMONDS, JOHN MAXWELL tr., *The Fragments of Attic Comedy*, 4 vols. (Leiden, 1957–61).

ELLIOTT, ALISON GODDARD tr., *Seven Medieval Latin Comedies* (New York, 1984).

ERASMUS DESIDERIUS, *Opera Omnia*, 1–2 (Amsterdam, 1971).

—— *Collected Works*, vol. xxiv, *Literary and Educational Writings 2: De Copia / De Ratione Studii*, tr. Craig R. Thompson (Toronto, 1978).

ETHEREGE, SIR GEORGE, *Plays*, ed. Michael Cordner (Cambridge, 1982).

EVANTHIUS (see Donatus).

FARQUHAR, GEORGE, Works, ed. Shirley Strum Kenny, 2 vols. (Oxford, 1988).

FIELDING, HENRY, Complete Works, ed. William Ernest Henley, 16 vols. (1903; repr. New York, 1967).

FIRENZUOLA, AGNOLO, I lucidi (Venice, 1560).

FLETCHER, JOHN (see Beaumont, Francis).

FORSETT, EDWARD, Pedantius, ed. G. C. Moore Smith (Louvain, 1905); ed. E. F. J. Tucker (RLDE, 1989) [perhaps by A. Wingfield].

FOXE, JOHN, Two Latin Comedies, ed. John Hazel Smith (Ithaca, NY, 1973) [Titus et Gesippus, Christus Triumphans].

FRACASTORO, GIROLAMO, La Venexiana, tr. Matilde Valenti Pfeiffer (New York, 1950).

FRAUNCE, ABRAHAM, Victoria, ed. G. C. Moore Smith (Louvain, 1906); ed. Horst-Dieter Blume (RLDE, 1991) [with Hymenaeus and Laelia].

FULLONIUS, The Comedy of Acolastus, tr. John Palsgrave, ed. P. L. Carver (London, 1937).

GARNIER, ROBERT, Oeuvres complètes, ed. Lucien Pinvert, 2 vols. (Paris, 1923).

GASCOIGNE, GEORGE, Complete Works, ed. John W. Cunliffe, 2 vols. (1907–10; repr. Grosse Pointe, Mich., 1969).

GELLI, GIOVANNI BATTISTA, Lo errore (Florence, 1603).

GELLIUS, AULUS, Attic Nights, tr. John C. Rolfe, 3 vols. (LCL, 1927–8; rev. 1946–52).

GNAPHEUS (see Fullonius).

GOLDONI, CARLO, Four Comedies, tr. Frederick Davies (London, 1968).

GOLDSMITH, OLIVER, Collected Works, ed. Arthur Friedman, 5 vols. (Oxford, 1966).

GOSSON, STEPHEN, Playes Confuted in Five Actions (1582), ed. Arthur Freeman (New York, 1972).

GOWER, JOHN, Confessio Amantis, ed. Russell A. Peck (1968; repr. Toronto, 1980).

GRÉVIN, JACQUES, La Trésorière, Les Esbahis, Comédies, ed. Élisabeth Lapeyre (Paris, 1980).

—— Les Esbahis, tr. Leanore Lieblein and Russell McGillivray, Taken by Surprise (CRPT, 1985).

GRIMALD, NICHOLAS, Christus Redivivus (printed 1543), Archipropheta (printed 1548), ed. Kurt Tezeli von Rosador (RLDE, 1982).

HAWKESWORTH, WALTER, Leander Labyrinthus, ed. Susan Brock (RLDE, 1987).

HEYWOOD, THOMAS, Dramatic Works, ed. R. H. Shepherd for John Pearson, 6 vols. (1874; repr. New York, 1964) [cited to volume, page].

—— The Captives; or The Lost Recovered, ed. Alexander Corbin Judson (New Haven, Conn., 1921).

HORACE, *Opera*, ed. Stephanus Borsák (Leipzig, 1984).

HROSVIT OF GANDERSHEIM, *Plays*, tr. Katharina Wilson (New York, 1989).

Hymenaeus, ed. G. C. Moore Smith (Cambridge, 1908) [see Fraunce].

INGELEND, THOMAS, *The Disobedient Child*, ed. John S. Farmer (London, 1908).

IONESCO, EUGÈNE, *Four Plays*, tr. Donald M. Allen (New York, 1958).

—— *Rhinoceros and Other Plays*, tr. Derek Prouse (New York, 1960).

Jack Juggler, ed. John S. Farmer, *Early English Dramatists: Anonymous Plays* (1906; repr. Guildford, 1966) [see also Axton, Marie ed.].

JANKO, RICHARD ed., *Aristotle on Comedy: Towards a Reconstruction of Poetics II* (Berkeley, 1984).

JEFFERAY, JOHN, *The Bugbears*, ed. James D. Clark (New York, 1979).

JODELLE, ESTIENNE, *L'Eugène*, tr. Arthur P. Stabler, *Four French Renaissance Plays*, ed. Arthur P. Stabler (Pullman, Wash., 1978).

JONSON, BEN: complete critical edition by C. H. Herford and Percy and Evelyn Simpson, 11 vols. (Oxford, 1925–52).

—— *The Staple of News*, ed. Anthony Parr (Revels, 1988).

KASSEL, R. and AUSTIN, C. (eds.), *Poetae Comici Graeci*, 5 vols. (Berlin, 1983–91).

Laelia, ed. G. C. Moore Smith (Cambridge, 1910) [see Fraunce].

LANCI, CORNELIO, *La ruchetta* (Florence, 1584).

LANGBAINE, GERARD, *An Account of the English Dramatick Poets*, ed. Arthur Freeman (1691; repr. New York, 1973).

LARIVEY, PIERRE DE, *Les Esprits*, tr. Jean-Charles Seigneuret, *Four French Renaissance Plays*, ed. Arthur P. Stabler (Pullman, Wash., 1978).

—— *Le Laquais comédie*, eds. Madeleine Lazard and Luigia Zilli (Paris, 1987).

LATAILLE, JEAN DE, *Les Corrivaus*, tr. H. P. Clive, *The Rivals* (CRPT, 1981).

LAWTON, H. W. ed., *Handbook of French Renaissance Dramatic Theory* (Manchester, 1949).

LUCIAN, tr. A. M. Harmon *et al.*, 8 vols. (LCL, 1913–67).

LYLY, JOHN, *The Complete Works*, ed. R. Warwick Bond, 3 vols. (1902; repr. Oxford, 1967).

MACHIAVELLI, NICCOLÒ *Opere*, vol. iv, *Teatro e scritti letterari* (Milan, 1969).

—— *The Comedies*, eds. David Sices and James B. Atkinson (Hanover, NH, 1985).

MACROPEDIUS, *Two Comedies: Rebelles (The Rebels), Bassarus*, tr. Yehudi Lindeman (Nieuwkoop, The Netherlands, 1983).

MARIVAUX, PIERRE, *Plays*, introd. Claude Schumacher (London, 1988) [various translators].

MARLOWE, CHRISTOPHER, *The Complete Works*, ed. Fredson Bowers, 2 vols., 2nd edn. (Cambridge, 1981).

MAROWITZ, CHARLES, *The Shrew* (London, 1975).

MARSTON, JOHN, *Works*, ed. Arthur Henry Bullen, 3 vols. (1877; repr. Hildesheim, 1970).

—— *Parasitaster or The Fawn*, ed. David A. Blostein (Revels, 1978).

MASSINGER, JOHN, *Plays and Poems*, ed. Philip Edwards and Colin Gibson, 5 vols. (Oxford, 1976).

MENANDER, *Reliqviae Selectae*, ed. F. H. Sandbach (OCT, 1972; rev. 1990).

—— *The Dyskolos of Menander*, ed. E. W. Handley (Cambridge, Mass., 1965).

—— *Menander*, tr. W. G. Arnott, vol. i (LCL, 1979).

—— *Plays and Fragments*, tr. Norma Miller (London, 1987).

MIDDLETON, THOMAS, *Works*, ed. A. H. Bullen, 8 vols. (1885–6; repr. New York, 1964).

MINTURNO, ANTONIO SEBASTIANO, *L'arte poetica* (1564; repr. Munich, 1971).

Misogonus, ed. Lester E. Barber (New York, 1979).

MOLIÈRE, JEAN BAPTISTE POQUELIN, *Oeuvres complètes*, ed. Robert Jouanny, 2 vols. (Paris, 1962).

MOLINA, TIRSO DE, *The Trickster of Seville and the Stone Guest (El burlador de Sevilla y el convidado de piedra)*, tr. Gwynne Edwards (Warminster, 1986).

MONTAIGNE, MICHEL DE, *Essays & Belles-Lettres*, tr. John Florio, introd. A. R. Waller, 3 vols. (1910; repr. London, 1938).

MOUNTFORD, J. F. ed., *The Scholia Bembina* (Liverpool, 1934).

Mucedorus, ed. Arvin H. Jupin (New York, 1987).

MUNDAY, ANTHONY, *Fedele and Fortunio*, ed. Richard Hosley (New York, 1981).

—— *John a Kent and John a Cumber*, ed. Arthur E. Pennell (New York, 1980).

Nice Wanton, ed. Leonard Tennenhouse, *The Tudor Interludes* (New York, 1984) [with *Impatient Poverty*].

ODDI, SFORZA, *I morti vivi* (Venice, 1578) [bound with *L'erofilomachia* and Pino's *Breve considerationel*].

OVID, *Metamorphoses*, ed. W. S. Anderson (Leipzig, 1977); tr. Arthur Golding, *The XV Bookes Entytuled Metamorphosis* (1567; repr. Amsterdam, 1977).

PEELE, GEORGE, *Life and Works*, ed. Charles Tyler Prouty *et al.*, 3 vols. (New Haven, Conn., 1952–70).

PETRARCA, FRANCESCO, *Le familiari*, ed. Vittorio Rossi, 4 vols. (Florence, 1933–42).

PICCOLOMINI, ALESSANDRO, *Alessandro* (Venice, 1562); tr. Rita Belladonna, *Alessandro* (CRPT, 1984).

PICKERING, JOHN, *The Interlude of Vice (Horestes)*, ed. Daniel Seltzer (MSR, 1961).

PINO DA CAGLI, BERNARDO, *Breve consideratione intorno al componimento de la comedia de' nostri tempi* (Venice, 1548) [with Oddi].

PLATO, *Opera*, ed. Joannes Burnet, 5 vols. (OCT, 1900–7).

PLAUTUS, *Comoediae*, ed. W. M. Lindsay, 2 vols. (OCT, 1904–5; repr. 1989).

PLAUTUS, *Comoediae XX* (Basle, 1558).

—— *Opera* (Paris, 1577).

—— *Plautus*, tr. Paul Nixon, 5 vols. (LCL, 1916–38).

—— *Amphitruo*, ed. W. B. Sedgwick (Manchester, 1960).

—— *Captivi*, ed. W. M. Lindsay, 2nd edn. (Oxford, 1926).

—— *Casina*, ed. W. T. MacCary and M. M. Willcock (Cambridge, 1976).

—— *Menaechmi*, tr. William Warner (1595), ed. W. H. D. Rouse (London, 1912).

—— *Menaechmi*, ed. A. S. Gratwick (Cambridge, 1993).

—— *Mostellaria*, ed. Edward A. Sonnenschein, 2nd edn. (Oxford, 1907).

—— *Plautus: Three Comedies*, tr. Erich Segal (New York, 1969).

PLUTARCH, *Moralia*, tr. Frank C. Babbitt *et al.*, 17 vols. (LCL, 1927–   ) [incomplete].

POLIZIANO, ANGELO, *Prose volgari inedite e poesie Latine e Greche*, ed. Isidoro del Lungo (Florence, 1867).

PRESTON, THOMAS, *Cambyses*, ed. Robert Carl Jonson (Salzburg, 1975).

QUINTILIAN, *Institutio Oratoria*, tr. H. E. Butler, 4 vols. (LCL, 1921–2).

RAINOLDES, JOHN, *Th'overthrow of Stage-Playes* (1599), ed. Arthur Freeman (New York, 1974) [with William Gager and Alberico Gentili].

The Rare Triumphs of Love and Fortune, ed. John Isaac Owen (New York, 1979).

RASTELL, JOHN, *Three Rastell Plays*, ed. Richard Axton (Cambridge, 1979).

RIBBECK, OTTO ed., *Scaenicae*, vol. ii, *Comicorum Romanorum Fragmenta*, 3rd edn. (Leipzig, 1898).

ROJAS, FERNANDO DE, *Celestina with the Translation of James Mabbe (1631)*, ed. Dorothy Sherman Severin (Warminster, 1987).

ROTROU, JEAN, *Oeuvres*, ed. Viollet-le-Duc, 5 vols. (Paris, 1820).

RUEDA, LOPE DE, *The Interludes*, tr. Randall W. Listerman (CRPT, 1988).

RUGGLE, GEORGE, *Ignoramus*, ed. E. F. J. Tucker (RLDE, 1987); tr. Ferdinando Parkhurst, ed. E. F. J. Tucker (New York, 1987).

RUSCELLI, GIROLAMO (ed.), *Delle comedie elette* (Venice, 1554).

SANESI, IRENEO (ed.), *Commedie del cinquecento*, 2 vols. (Bari, 1912).

SCALA, FLAMINIO, *Il teatro delle favole rappresentative*, ed. Ferruccio Marotti, 2 vols. (Milan, 1976); tr. Henry F. Salerno, *Scenarios of the Commedia dell'Arte* (New York, 1967).

SCALIGER, JULIUS CAESAR, *Poetices Libri Septem* (1561; repr. Stuttgart, 1964).

SCHONAEUS, CORNELIUS, *Terentivs Christianus* (Wittenberg, 1599).

SEDLEY, SIR CHARLES, *The Poetical and Dramatic Works*, ed. V. de Sola Pinto, 2 vols. (London, 1928).

SHADWELL, THOMAS, *Complete Works*, ed. Montague Summers, 5 vols. (1927; repr. New York, 1968).

SHAKESPEARE, WILLIAM, *The Riverside Shakespeare*, ed. G. Blakemore Evans (Boston, 1974) [brackets omitted].

SHAKESPEARE, WILLIAM, *The Norton Facsimile: The First Folio of Shakespeare*, ed. Charlton Hinman (New York, 1968).

—— *Shakespeare's Plays in Quarto*, ed. Michael J. B. Allen and Kenneth Muir (Berkeley, 1981).

—— *The Parallel King Lear 1608–1623*, ed. Michael Warren (Berkeley, 1989).

SHAW, G. BERNARD, *Collected Plays with their Prefaces*, ed. Dan H. Laurence, 7 vols. (London, 1970–4).

SHERIDAN, RICHARD BRINSLEY, *Plays and Poems*, ed. R. Crompton Rhodes, 3 vols. (Oxford, 1928).

SIDNEY, SIR PHILIP, *Poems*, ed. William A. Ringler, jun. (Oxford, 1962).

—— *The Countess of Pembroke's Arcadia (The Old Arcadia)*, ed. Jean Robertson (Oxford, 1973).

SMITH, G. GREGORY ed., *Elizabethan Critical Essays*, 2 vols. (1904; repr. Oxford, 1971).

SPENSER, EDMUND, *Works*, ed. Edwin Greenlaw *et al.*, 11 vols. (Baltimore, 1932–57).

SPINGARN, J. E. ed., *Critical Essays of the Seventeenth Century*, 3 vols. (1908–9; repr. Bloomington, Ind., 1957).

STEELE, RICHARD, *The Conscious Lovers*, ed. Shirley Strum Kenney (Lincoln, Nebr., 1968).

STOPPARD, TOM, *Rosencrantz and Guildenstern Are Dead* (London, 1967).

SUETONIUS: tr. J. C. Rolfe, 2 vols. (LCL, 1914).

SYNGE, J. M., *Collected Works*, ed. Robin Skelton *et al.*, 4 vols. (1962–8; repr. Washington, DC, 1982).

TERENCE, *Comoediae*, ed. Robert Kauer, Wallace M. Lindsay, Otto Skutsch (OCT, 1926; rev. 1979).

—— *Terentius Comico Carmine* (Argentia, 1503).

—— *Comoediae* (Paris, 1552).

—— *Terentivs, in Quem Triplex Edita Est P. Antesignani Rapistagnensis Commentatio* (Lyon, 1560).

—— *In P. Terentii Comoedias Sex Nouus Commentarius*, ed. M. Stephano Riccii (Mulhausen, 1568) [*Andria* and *Eunuchus*].

—— *Terence in English*, tr. R. Bernard (Cambridge, 1598).

—— *Terence*, tr. John Sargeaunt, 2 vols. (LCL, 1912; repr. 1979).

—— *Adelphoe*, ed. R. H. Martin (Cambridge, 1976); *The Brothers*, tr. A. S. Gratwick (Warminster, 1987).

—— *Andria*, tr. Maurice Kyffin (London, 1588).

THEOPHRASTUS, *Characters*, tr. J. M. Edmonds, (LCL, 1929).

TIMON, ed. J. C. Bulman and J. M. Nosworthy, (MSR, 1980).

Tractatus Coislinianus (see Janko).

TRISSINO, GIOVANNI GIORGIO, *I simillimi* (Venice, 1548).

The True Tragedy of Richard the Third (1594), ed. W. W. Greg (MSR, 1929).

TURNÈBE, ODET DE, *Les contens*, tr. Donald Beecher, *Satisfaction All Around* (CRPT, 1979).

UDALL, NICHOLAS, *Flowres for Latine Speaking Selected and Gathered out of Terence* (London, 1568).

—— *Dramatic Writings*, ed. John S. Farmer (1906; repr. New York, 1966).

VANBRUGH, JOHN SIR, *The Relapse*, ed. Curt A. Zimansky (Lincoln, Nebr., 1970).

VEGA, LOPE DE, *Five Plays*, tr. Jill Booty (New York, 1961).

VICKERS, BRIAN (ed.), *Shakespeare: The Critical Heritage*, 6 vols. (London, 1974–81).

WARMINGTON, E. H. (tr.), *Remains of Old Latin*, 4 vols. (LCL, 1935–40).

WEINBERG, BERNARD (ed.), *Critical Prefaces of the French Renaissance* (Evanston, Ill., 1950).

—— (ed.), *Trattati di poetica e retorica del cinquecento*, 4 vols. (Bari, 1970–4).

WILDE, OSCAR, *The Oxford Authors: Oscar Wilde*, ed. Isobel Murray (Oxford, 1989).

WILSON, JOHN, *Dramatic Works*, ed. James Maidment and W. H. Logan (Edinburgh, 1874).

WYCHERLEY, WILLIAM, *Plays*, ed. Arthur Freidman (Oxford, 1979).

(ii) Critical Commentary

ALTMAN, JOEL, *The Tudor Play of Mind* (Berkeley, 1978).

ANDERSON, GRAHAM, *Ancient Fiction: The Novel in the Graeco-Roman World* (Totowa, NJ, 1984).

ANDERSON, WILLIAM S., 'Love Plots in Menander and his Roman Adapters', *Ramus* 13 (1984), 124–34.

ARCHIBALD, ELIZABETH, ' "Deep clerks she dumbs": The Learned Heroine in *Apollonius of Tyre* and *Pericles*', CD 22 (1988–9), 289–303.

—— *Apollonius of Tyre: Medieval and Renaissance Themes and Variations* (Cambridge, 1991).

ARNOTT, W. GEOFFREY, *Menander, Plautus, Terence* (Oxford, 1975).

—— 'Time, Plot and Character in Menander', *Papers of the Liverpool Latin Seminar 1979*, ed. Francis Cairns (Liverpool, 1979), 343–60.

ARTHOS, JOHN, 'Shakespeare's Transformation of Plautus', CD 1 (1967–8), 239–53.

ASTINGTON, JOHN H., 'Malvolio and the Dark House', *ShS* 41 (1988), 55–62.

BAIN, DAVID, *Actors and Audience: A Study of Asides and Related Conventions in Greek Drama* (Oxford, 1977).

BAKHTIN, M. M., *Speech Genres and Other Late Essays*, tr. Vern W. McGee (Austin, Tx., 1986).

BALDWIN, T. W., *The Organization and Personnel of the Shakespearean Company* (1927; repr. New York, 1961).

—— *William Shakespere's Small Latine and Lesse Greek*, 2 vols. (Urbana, Ill., 1944).

—— *Shakespere's Five-Act Structure* (Urbana, Ill., 1947).

—— *On the Literary Genetics of Shakespere's Plays 1592–1594* (Urbana, Ill., 1959).

—— *On the Compositional Genetics of 'The Comedy of Errors'* (Urbana, Ill., 1965).

BALLENTINE, FLOYD G., 'The Influence of Terence upon English Comedy', *TAPA* 37 (1906), xiii–xiv.

BARBER, C. L., *Shakespeare's Festive Comedy* (Princeton, 1959).

BARBER, LESTER E., '*The Tempest* and New Comedy', *SQ* 21 (1970), 207–11.

BARKAN, LEONARD, 'Diana and Actaeon: The Myth as Synthesis', *ELR* 10 (1980), 317–59.

BARNET, SYLVAN, 'Charles Lamb and the Tragic Malvolio', *PQ* 33 (1954), 178–88.

BARTON, ANNE, *Ben Jonson: Dramatist* (Cambridge, 1984).

BATE, JONATHAN, *Shakespeare and Ovid* (Oxford, 1993).

BATE, KEITH, 'Twelfth-century Latin Comedies and the Theatre', *Papers of the Liverpool Latin Seminar 1979*, ed. Francis Cairns (Liverpool, 1979), 249–62.

BEACHAM, RICHARD C., *The Roman Theatre and its Audience* (London, 1991).

BEARE, W., *The Roman Stage*, 3rd edn. (London, 1964).

BEAURLINE, L. A., *Jonson and Elizabethan Comedy* (San Marino, Calif., 1978).

BECK, ERVIN, 'Terence Improved: The Paradigm of the Prodigal Son in English Renaissance Comedy', *RD* 6 (1973), 107–22.

BEECHER, DONALD, and CIAVOLELLA, MASSIMO (eds.), *Comparative Critical Approaches to Renaissance Comedy* (Ottawa, 1986).

BENHAM, ALLEN R., 'A Note on the *Comedy of Errors*', *MLN* 36 (1921), 377–8.

BENSON, LARRY D. ed., *The Learned and the Lewed: Studies in Chaucer and Medieval Literature* (Cambridge, Mass., 1974).

BERGER, JUN., HARRY, 'Miraculous Harp: A Reading of Shakespeare's Tempest', *ShakS* 5 (1969), 253–83.

—— 'Against the Sink-a-Pace: Sexual and Family Politics in *Much Ado About Nothing*', *SQ* 33 (1982), 302–13.

BERNARD, JOHN D. ed., *Vergil at 2000* (New York, 1986).

BERRY, EDWARD I., *Shakespeare's Comic Rites* (Cambridge, 1984).

BERRY, PHILIPPA, *Of Chastity and Power: Elizabethan Literature and the Unmarried Queen* (London, 1989).

BERRY, RALPH, '*Twelfth Night*: The Experience of the Audience', *ShS* 34 (1981), 111–19.

BEVINGTON, DAVID, *Action is Eloquence: Shakespeare's Language of Gesture* (Cambridge, Mass., 1984).

BOAS, FREDERICK S., *University Drama in the Tudor Age* (Oxford, 1914).

BOLGAR, R. R., *The Classical Heritage and its Beneficiaries* (Cambridge, 1954).

BOND, R. WARWICK, *Studia Otiosa: Some Attempts in Criticism* (London, 1938).

BONHEIM, HELMUT ed., *The King Lear Perplex* (San Francisco, 1960).

BOOSE, LYNDA E., 'The Father and the Bride in Shakespeare', *PMLA* 97 (1982), 325–47.

—— 'Scolding Brides and Bridling Scolds: Taming the Woman's Unruly Member', *SQ* 42 (1991), 179–213.

BOOTH, STEPHEN, *King Lear, Macbeth, Indefinition, and Tragedy* (New Haven, Conn., 1983).

BOUGHNER, DANIEL C., *The Braggart in Renaissance Comedy* (Minneapolis, 1954).

—— 'Jonsonian Structure in *The Tempest*', *SQ* 21 (1970), 3–10.

BRADBROOK, M. C., 'Dramatic Role as Social Image: a Study of the Taming of the Shrew', *SJ* 94 (1958), 132–50.

—— 'Romance, Farewell!: *The Tempest*', *ELR* 1 (1971), 239–49.

BRADBURY, MALCOLM and PALMER, DAVID (eds.), *Shakespearian Comedy* (London, 1972).

BRADLEY, A. C., *Shakespearean Tragedy*, 2nd edn. (1905; repr. London, 1926).

BRADNER, LEICESTER, 'The First Cambridge Production of *Miles Gloriosus*', *MLN* 70 (1955), 400–3.

—— 'The Latin Drama of the Renaissance (1314–1650)', *Studies in the Renaissance* 4 (1957), 31–70.

BRERETON, GEOFFREY, *French Comic Drama from the Sixteenth to the Eighteenth Century* (London, 1977).

BRINK, C. O., *Horace on Poetry*, 3 vols. (Cambridge, 1963–82).

BROCKBANK, J. P., ' "Pericles" and the Dream of Immortality', *ShS* 24 (1971), 105–16.

—— ed., *Players of Shakespeare* (Cambridge, 1985).

BROWN, JOHN RUSSELL, and HARRIS, BERNARD (eds.), *Early Shakespeare* (New York, 1961).

—— and —— (eds.), *Elizabethan Theatre* (New York, 1967).

—— and —— (eds.), *Later Shakespeare* (New York, 1967).

BROWN, P. G. McC., 'Plots and Prostitutes in Greek New Comedy', *Papers of the Leeds International Latin Seminar 1990*, ed. Francis Cairns and Malcolm Heath (Leeds, 1990), 241–66.

BROWN, PETER, *The Body and Society: Men, Women, and Sexual Renunciation in Early Christianity* (New York, 1988).

BRUNVAND, JAN HAROLD, 'The Folktale Origin of *The Taming of the Shrew*', *SQ* 17 (1966), 345–59.

BRYANT, JUN., J. A., 'Falstaff and the Renewal of Windsor', *PMLA* 89 (1974), 296–301.

BULMAN, JAMES C., 'The Date and Production of "Timon" Reconsidered', *ShS* 27 (1974), 111–27.

—— 'Shakespeare's Use of the "Timon" Comedy', *ShS* 29 (1976), 103–16.

—— *The Heroic Idiom of Shakespearean Tragedy* (Newark, NJ, 1985).

—— *Shakespeare in Performance: 'The Merchant of Venice'* (Manchester, 1991).

CALDERWOOD, JAMES L., 'Hamlet's Readiness', *SQ* 35 (1984), 267–73.

CALIUMI, GRAZIA, *Studi e ricerche sulle fonti italiane del teatro elisabettiano* — Vol. I: *Il bandello* (Rome, 1984).

The Cambridge History of Classical Literature II: Latin Literature, ed. E. J. Kenney and W. V. Clausen (Cambridge, 1982).

The Cambridge History of Classical Literature I: Greek Literature, ed. P. E. Easterling and B. M. W. Knox (Cambridge, 1985).

CAMPBELL, OSCAR JAMES, 'The Relation of *Epicoene* to Arentino's *Il marescalco*', *PMLA* 46 (1931), 752–62.

—— '*Love's Labour's Lost* Re-studied', University of Michigan Publications, Language and Literature, 1 (1925), 3–45.

—— 'The Italianate Background of *The Merry Wives of Windsor*', Univ. of Michigan Publications, Language and Literature, 8 (1932), 81–117.

CAPPELLETTO, RITA, *La lectura Plauti del Pontano* (Urbino, 1988).

CARROLL, WILLIAM C., *The Metamorphoses of Shakespearean Comedy* (Princeton, 1985).

CAVE, TERENCE, *Recognitions* (Oxford, 1988).

CHALIFOUR, CLARK L., 'Sir Philip Sidney's *Old Arcadia* as Terentian Comedy', *SEL* 16 (1976), 51–63.

CHAMPION, LARRY S., *The Evolution of Shakespeare's Comedy* (Cambridge, Mass., 1970).

CHANDLER, RICHARD E., and SCHWARTZ, KESSEL, *A New History of Spanish Literature* (Baton Rouge, La., 1991).

CHARLTON, H. B., *Shakespearian Comedy* (London, 1938).

CHARNEY, MAURICE ed., *Shakespearean Comedy* (New York, 1980).

—— *Hamlet's Fictions* (New York, 1988).

CHIAPPELLI, FREDI *et al.* (eds.), *First Images of America*, 2 vols. (Berkeley, 1976).

CHURCHILL, GEORGE B. and KELLER, WOLFGANG, 'Die lateinischen Universitäts-Dramen Englands in der Zeit der Königin Elisabeth', *SJ* 34 (1898), 221–323 [supplemented by Morgan].

CLAYTON, THOMAS ed., *The 'Hamlet' First Published (Q1, 1603)* (Newark, NJ, 1992).

CLUBB, LOUISE GEORGE, *Giambattista Della Porta, Dramatist* (Princeton, 1965).

—— *Italian Drama in Shakespeare's Time* (New Haven, Conn., 1989).

COHEN, WALTER, 'Intrigue Tragedy in Renaissance England and Spain', *RD* 15 (1984), 175–200.

COLE, HELEN WIEAND, 'The Influence of Plautus and Terence upon "The Stonyhurst Pageants"', *MLN* 38 (1923), 393–9.

COLE, HOWARD C., *The 'All's Well' Story from Boccaccio to Shakespeare* (Urbana, Ill., 1981).

COOK, CAROL, ' "The Sign and Semblance of Her Honor": Reading Gender Difference in *Much Ado About Nothing*', *PMLA* 101 (1986), 186–202.

COPLEY, FRANK O., *Exclusus Amator: A Study in Latin Love Poetry* (Baltimore, 1956).

CORNFORD, FRANCIS MACDONALD, *The Origin of Attic Comedy*, ed. Theodor H. Gaster (1934; repr. Gloucester, Mass., 1968).

CORRIGAN, BEATRICE M., *'Il capriccio*: an Unpublished Italian Renaissance Comedy and its Analogues', *Studies in the Renaissance* 5 (1958), 74–86.

COULTER, CORNELIA C., 'The Plautine Tradition in Shakespeare', *JEGP* 19 (1920), 66–83.

COX, J. F., 'The Stage Representations of the "Kill Claudio" Sequence in *Much Ado About Nothing*', *ShS* 32 (1979), 27–36.

CREIZENACH, WILHELM, *The English Drama in the Age of Shakespeare* (1916; repr. New York, 1964).

CUPAIUOLO, GIOVANNI, *Bibliografia Terenziana (1470–1983)* (Naples, 1984).

DANIELL, DAVID, 'The Good Marriage of Katherine and Petruchio', *ShS* 37 (1984), 23–31.

DAVIDSON, CLIFFORD et al. (eds.), *Drama in the Renaissance* (New York, 1986).

DAVISON, PETER, *'Hamlet': Text and Performance* (London, 1983).

DAWSON, ANTHONY B., *Indirections: Shakespeare and the Art of Illusion* (Toronto, 1978).

DEAN, LEONARD F. ed., *Shakespeare: Modern Essays in Criticism* (1957; repr. New York, 1967).

DÉR, KATALIN, *'Vidularia*: Outlines of a Reconstruction', *CQ* 37 (1987), 432–43.

DESSEN, ALAN C., *Shakespeare and the Late Moral Plays* (Lincoln, Nebr., 1986).

DIBDIN, THOMAS FROGNALL, *An Introduction to the Knowledge of Rare and Valuable Editions of the Greek and Latin Classics*, 2 vols., 4th edn. (London, 1827).

DOLLIMORE, JONATHAN, *Radical Tragedy: Religion, Ideology and Power in the Drama of Shakespeare and his Contemporaries* (Chicago, 1984).

—— and ALAN SINFIELD (eds.), *Political Shakespeare* (Ithaca, NY, 1985).

DORAN, MADELEINE, *Endeavors of Art* (Madison, Wis., 1954).

DOREY, T. A., and DUDLEY, R. DONALD (eds.), *Roman Drama* (New York, 1965).

DOVER, K. J., *Aristophanic Comedy* (London, 1972).

DRAPER, JOHN W., 'Falstaff and the Plautine Parasite', *Classical Journal* 33 (1938), 390–401.

DUBROW, HEATHER, and STRIER, RICHARD (eds.), *The Historical Renaissance: New Essays on Tudor and Stuart Literature and Culture* (Chicago, 1988).

DUCKWORTH, GEORGE E., *The Nature of Roman Comedy* (Princeton, 1952).

DUSINBERRE, JULIET, 'Women and Boys: Stealing the Show?', a paper presented to a seminar of the Twenty-fifth International Shakespeare Conference, Stratford-upon-Avon, 1992.

EDWARDS, PHILIP *et al.* (eds.), *Shakespeare's Styles: Essays in Honour of Kenneth Muir* (Cambridge, 1980).

ELSE, GERALD F., *Aristotle's Poetics: The Argument* (Cambridge, Mass., 1957).

—— *Plato and Aristotle on Poetry*, ed. Peter Burian (Chapel Hill, NC, 1986).

EMPSON, WILLIAM, *Essays on Shakespeare*, ed. David B. Pirie (Cambridge, 1986).

ENK, P. J., 'Shakespeare's "Small Latin"', *Neophilologus* 5 (1920), 359–65.

ERICKSON, PETER and KAHN, COPPÉLIA (eds.), *Shakespeare's 'Rough Magic': Renaissance Essays in Honor of C. L. Barber* (Newark, NJ, 1985).

EVANS, BERTRAND, *Shakespeare's Comedies* (Oxford, 1960).

FANTHAM, ELAINE, '*Hautontimorumenos* and *Adelphoe*: A Study of Fatherhood in Terence and Menander', *Latomus* 30 (1971), 970–98.

—— 'Towards a Dramatic Reconstruction of the Fourth Act of Plautus' *Amphitruo*', *Philologus* 117 (1973), 197–214.

FAY, EDWIN W., 'Further Notes on the Mostellaria of Plautus', *AJP* 24 (1903), 245–77.

FELPERIN, HOWARD, *Shakespearean Romance* (Princeton, 1972).

FERGUSON, MARGARET *et al.* (eds.), *Rewriting the Renaissance* (Chicago, 1986).

FOREHAND, WALTER E., 'Plautus' *Casina*: An Explication', *Arethusa* 6 (1973), 233–56.

—— *Terence* (Boston, 1985).

FORSYTHE, R. S., 'A Plautine Source of *The Merry Wives of Windsor*', *MP* 18 (1920), 401–21.

FOTHERGILL-PAYNE, LOUISE and PETER (eds.), *Parallel Lives: Spanish and English National Drama 1580–1680* (Lewisburg, Pa., 1991).

FOUCAULT, MICHEL, *Madness and Civilization*, tr. Richard Howard (London, 1965).

FOUCAULT, MICHEL, *The History of Sexuality*, tr. Robert Hurley, vol. i (New York, 1978).

FRAENKEL, EDUARD, *Plautinisches im Plautus* (1922), rev., Italian tr. Franco Munari, *Elementi Plautini in Plauto* (Florence, 1960) [references to Italian version].

FRANTZ, DAVID O., *Festum Voluptatis: A Study of Renaissance Erotica* (Columbus, OH, 1989).

FREEDMAN, BARBARA, 'Falstaff's Punishment; Buffoonery as Defensive Posture in *The Merry Wives of Windsor*', *ShakS* 14 (1981), 163–74.

—— *Staging the Gaze: Postmodernism, Psychoanalysis, and Shakespearean Comedy* (Ithaca, NY, 1991).

FROST, K. B., *Exits and Entrances in Menander* (Oxford, 1988).

FRYE, NORTHROP, 'The Argument of Comedy', *English Institute Essays 1948* (New York, 1949), 58–73.

—— 'Characterization in Shakespearian Comedy', *SQ* 4 (1953), 271–7.

—— *Anatomy of Criticism: Four Essays* (Princeton, 1957).

—— *A Natural Perspective* (New York, 1965).

FRYE, ROLAND MUSHAT, *The Renaissance Hamlet* (Princeton, 1984).

GALINSKY, G. KARL, 'Scipionic Themes in Plautus' *Amphitruo*', *TAPA* 97 (1966), 203–35.

GALLENCA, CHRISTIANE, 'Ritual and Folk Custom in *The Merry Wives of Windsor*', *Cahiers Élisabéthains* 27 (1985), 27–41.

GESNER, CAROL, '*The Tempest* as Pastoral Romance', *SQ* 10 (1959), 531–9.

—— *Shakespeare and the Greek Romance* (Lexington, Ky., 1970).

GILBERT, ALLAN, 'Two Margarets: The Composition of *Much Ado About Nothing*', *PQ* 41 (1962), 61–71.

GILBERT, ALLAN H., 'Thomas Heywood's Debt to Plautus', *JEGP* 12 (1913), 593–611.

GILL, ERMA, 'A Comparison of the Characters in *The Comedy of Errors* with Those in the *Menaechmi*', *Texas Studies in English* 5 (1925), 79–95.

—— 'The Plot-Structure of *The Comedy of Errors* in Relation to its Sources', *Texas Studies in English* 10 (1930), 13–65.

GODMAN, PETER, and MURRAY, OSWYN (eds.), *Latin Poetry and the Classical Tradition: Essays in Medieval and Renaissance Literature* (Oxford, 1990).

GODSHALK, W. L., '*All's Well That Ends Well* and the Morality Play', *SQ* 25 (1974), 61–70.

GOLDBERG, SANDER M., *The Making of Menander's Comedy* (Berkeley, 1980).

—— 'Scholarship on Terence and the Fragments of Roman Comedy 1959–1980', *CW* 75 (1981), 77–115.

—— *Understanding Terence* (Princeton, 1986).

GOMME, A. W., and SANDBACH, F. H., *Menander: A Commentary* (1973; repr. Oxford, 1983).

GORDON, D. J., 'Much Ado About Nothing: A Possible Source for the Hero-Claudio Plot', SP 39 (1942), 279–90.

GOSSETT, SUZANNE, ' "Best Men are Molded out of Faults": Marrying the Rapist in Jacobean Drama', ELR 14 (1984), 305–27.

GOTTSCHALK, PAUL, 'Hamlet and the Scanning of Revenge', SQ 24 (1973), 155–70.

GREENBLATT, STEPHEN ed., The Power of Forms in the English Renaissance (Norman, Okla., 1982).

—— Shakespearean Negotiations (Berkeley, 1988).

GREENE, EDWARD J. H., Menander to Marivaux: The History of a Comic Structure (Edmonton, 1977).

GREENE, THOMAS M., The Light in Troy: Imitation and Discovery in Renaissance Poetry (New Haven, Conn., 1982).

—— The Vulnerable Text: Essays on Renaissance Literature (New York, 1986).

GREIF, KAREN, 'A Star is Born: Feste on the Modern Stage', SQ 39 (1988), 61–78.

GRENDLER, PAUL F., Schooling in Renaissance Italy: Literacy and Learning 1300–1600 (Baltimore, 1989).

GRIMALDI, WILLIAM M. A., SJ, Aristotle, Rhetoric: A Commentary, 2 vols. (New York, 1980–8).

GRISMER, RAYMOND LEONARD, The Influence of Plautus in Spain before Lope de Vega (New York, 1944).

GUILFOYLE, CHERRELL, Shakespeare's Play within Play (Kalamazoo, Mich., 1990).

GUM, COBURN, The Aristophanic Comedies of Ben Jonson (The Hague, 1969).

GURR, ANDREW, 'Intertextuality at Windsor', SQ 38 (1987), 189–200.

HAMILTON, DONNA, Virgil and 'The Tempest': The Politics of Imitation (Columbus, OH, 1990).

HANDLEY, ERIC, and HURST, ANDRÉ (eds.), Relire Ménandre (Geneva, 1990).

HANKINS, JOHN E., 'Caliban the Bestial Man', PMLA 62 (1947), 793–801.

HANSEN, WILLIAM F., 'An Oral Source for the Menaechmi', CW 70 (1977), 385–90.

HANSON, JOHN ARTHUR, 'Scholarship on Plautus since 1950', CW 59 (1965–6), 103–7, 126–9, 141–8.

HARING-SMITH, TORI, From Farce to Metadrama: A Stage History of 'The Taming of the Shrew' 1594–1983 (Westport, Conn., 1985).

HARROLD, WILLIAM E., 'Shakespeare's Use of Mostellaria in The Taming of the Shrew', Deutsche Shakespeare-Gesellschaft West (1970), 188–94.

HARTIGAN, KARELISA V. ed., From Pen to Performance (Lanham, Md., 1983).

HASSEL, JUN., R. CHRIS, Faith and Folly in Shakespeare's Romantic Comedies (Athens, Ga., 1980).

HAWKINS, SHERMAN, 'The Two Worlds of Shakespearean Comedy', *ShakS* 3 (1967), 62–97.

HEATH, MALCOLM, 'Aristotelian Comedy', *CQ* 39 (1989), 344–54.

HECK, THOMAS F., *Commedia dell'Arte: A Guide to the Primary and Secondary Literature* (New York, 1988).

HECKSCHER, WILLIAM S., 'Shakespeare in his Relationship to the Visual Arts: A Study in Paradox', *RORD* 13 (1970), 5–71.

HEILMAN, ROBERT B., 'The *Taming* Untamed, or, The Return of the Shrew', *MLQ* 27 (1966), 147–61.

HELMS, LORRAINE, 'The Saint in the Brothel: Or, Eloquence Rewarded', *SQ* 41 (1990), 319–32.

HENNINGS, THOMAS P., 'The Anglican Doctrine of the Affectionate Marriage in *The Comedy of Errors*', *MLQ* 47 (1986), 91–107.

HENZE, RICHARD, '*The Comedy of Errors*: A Freely Binding Chain', *SQ* 22 (1971), 35–41.

HERFORD, CHARLES H., *Studies in the Literary Relations of England and Germany in the Sixteenth Century* (Cambridge, 1886).

HERRICK, MARVIN T., *Comic Theory in the Sixteenth Century* (Urbana, Ill., 1950).

—— *Tragicomedy: Its Origin and Development in Italy, France, and England* (Urbana, Ill., 1955).

—— *Italian Comedy in the Renaissance* (Urbana, Ill., 1960).

HIGHET, GILBERT, *The Classical Tradition* (Oxford, 1949).

HILLMAN, RICHARD, 'Shakespeare's Gower and Gower's Shakespeare: The Larger Debt of *Pericles*', *SQ* 36 (1985), 427–37.

HINDLEY, ALAN, 'Medieval French Drama: A Review of Recent Scholarship, Part II: Comic Drama', *RORD* 23 (1980), 93–126.

HODGDON, BARBARA, 'Katherina Bound; or, Play(K)ating the Strictures of Everyday Life', *PMLA* 107 (1992), 538–53.

HOLDERNESS, GRAHAM, *Shakespeare in Performance: 'The Taming of the Shrew'* (Manchester, 1989).

HOSLEY, RICHARD, 'Was There a "Dramatic Epilogue" to *The Taming of the Shrew*', *SEL* 1 (1961), 17–34.

—— ed., *Essays on Shakespeare and Elizabethan Drama in Honour of Hardin Craig* (London, 1963).

—— 'Sources and Analogues of *The Taming of the Shrew*', *HLQ* 27 (1964), 289–308.

—— 'The Formal Influence of Plautus and Terence', *Elizabethan Theatre*, ed. John Russell Brown and Bernard Harris (New York, 1967), 130–45.

HOTSON, LESLIE, *The First Night of 'Twelfth Night'* (London, 1954).

HOWARD, JEAN E., 'Crossdressing, the Theatre, and Gender Struggle in Early Modern England', *SQ* 39 (1988), 418–40.

——, and O'CONNOR, MARION F. (eds.), *Shakespeare Reproduced: The Text in History and Ideology* (New York, 1987).

HOY, CYRUS, 'Fletcherian Romantic Comedy', *RORD* 27 (1984), 3–11.

HUGHES, J. DAVID, *A Bibliography of Scholarship on Plautus* (Amsterdam, 1975).

HUNTER, R. L., *A Study of 'Daphnis and Chloe'* (Cambridge, 1983).

—— *The New Comedy of Greece and Rome* (Cambridge, 1985).

HUNTER, ROBERT GRAMS, *Shakespeare and the Comedy of Forgiveness* (New York, 1965).

HUTTON, EDWARD, *Giovanni Boccaccio: A Biographical Study* (London, 1910).

JACKSON, RUSSELL, and SMALLWOOD, ROBERT (eds.), *Players of Shakespeare 2* (Cambridge, 1988).

JARDINE, LISA, *Still Harping on Daughters: Women and Drama in the Age of Shakespeare* (Sussex, 1983).

JEFFERY, BRIAN, *French Renaissance Comedy 1552–1630* (Oxford, 1969).

JONES, EMRYS, *Scenic Form in Shakespeare* (Oxford, 1971).

—— *The Origins of Shakespeare* (Oxford, 1977).

JORDAN, CONSTANCE, *Renaissance Feminism: Literary Texts and Political Models* (Ithaca, NY, 1990).

JORGENSEN, PAUL A., 'Much Ado About Nothing', *SQ* 5 (1954), 287–95.

KAHN, COPPÉLIA, *Man's Estate: Masculine Identity in Shakespeare* (Berkeley, 1981).

KASTAN, DAVID SCOTT, 'All's Well That Ends Well and the Limits of Comedy', *ELH* 52 (1985), 575–89.

—— ' "His semblable is his mirror": Hamlet and the Imitation of Revenge', *ShakS* 19 (1987), 111–24.

KATSOURIS, ANDREAS G., *Tragic Patterns in Menander* (Athens, 1975).

KAUFMAN, HELEN ANDREWS, 'Nicolò Secchi as a Source of Twelfth Night', *SQ* 5 (1954), 271–80.

KAY, CAROL McGINNIS, and JACOBS, HENRY E. (eds.), *Shakespeare's Romances Reconsidered* (Lincoln, Nebr., 1978).

KING, WALTER N., 'Much Ado About Something', *SQ* 15 (1964), 143–55.

KINNEY, ARTHUR F., 'Shakespeare's Comedy of Errors and the Nature of Kinds', *SP* 85 (1988), 29–52.

KNIGHT, G. WILSON, *The Wheel of Fire*, 4th edn. (1949; repr. London, 1965).

—— *The Sovereign Flower* (New York, 1958).

KNOWLES, RICHARD PAUL, ' "The More Delay'd, Delighted": Theophanies in the Last Plays', *ShakS* 15 (1982), 269–80.

KNOX, BERNARD, ' "The Tempest" and the Ancient Comic Tradition', *English Institute Essays 1954* (New York, 1955), 52–73.

—— *Word and Action: Essays on the Ancient Theatre* (Baltimore, 1979).

KONSTAN, DAVID, *Roman Comedy* (Ithaca, NY, 1983).

KRISTEVA, JULIA, *Desire in Language*, tr. Leon S. Roudiez *et al.* (New York, 1980).

LANCASTER, HENRY CARRINGTON, *A History of French Dramatic Literature in the Seventeenth Century*, 5 vols. (Baltimore, 1929–42).

LAWRENCE, WILLIAM WITHERLE, *Shakespeare's Problem Comedies* (New York, 1931).

LAWRY, JON S., '*Twelfth Night* and "Salt Waves Fresh in Love"', *ShakS* 6 (1970), 89–108.

LAWTON, HAROLD WALTER, *Térence en France au XVIe siècle: éditions et traductions* (Paris, 1926).

LEA, K. M., *Italian Popular Comedy: A Study in the Commedia dell'Arte, 1560–1620, with Special Reference to the English Stage*, 2 vols. (1934; repr. New York, 1962) [continuous pagination].

LEACH, ELEANOR WINSOR, '*Meam Quom Formam Noscito*: Language and Characterization in the *Menaechmi*', *Arethusa* 2 (1969), 30–45.

—— 'Plautus' *Rudens*: Venus Born from a Shell', *Texas Studies in Literature and Language* 15 (1974), 915–31.

LEBÈGUE, RAYMOND, *Le Théâtre comique en France de Pathelin à Mélite* (Paris, 1972).

LEE, A. C., *The Decameron: Its Sources and Analogues* (London, 1909).

LEGGATT, ALEXANDER, *Shakespeare's Comedy of Love* (London, 1974).

—— *Shakespeare in Performance: 'King Lear'* (Manchester, 1991).

LEGRAND, P. E., *The New Greek Comedy*, tr. James Loeb (London, 1917).

LELYVELD, TOBY, *Shylock on the Stage* (Cleveland, 1960).

LENZ, CAROLYN RUTH SWIFT et al. (eds.), *The Woman's Part: Feminist Criticism of Shakespeare* (Urbana, Ill., 1980).

LEO, FRIEDRICH, *Plautinische Forschungen: Zur Kritik und Geschichte der Komödie*, 2nd edn. (1912; repr. Darmstadt, 1966).

LEVIN, CAROLE, and ROBERTSON, KAREN (eds.), *Sexuality and Politics in Renaissance Drama* (Lewiston, NY, 1991).

LEVIN, HARRY, *The Question of Hamlet* (New York, 1959).

—— *Refractions: Essays in Comparative Literature* (London, 1966).

—— *Playboys and Killjoys: An Essay on the Theory and Practice of Comedy* (New York, 1987).

LEVIN, RICHARD, *The Multiple Plot in English Renaissance Drama* (Chicago, 1971).

LEWALSKI, B. K., 'Love, Appearance and Reality: Much Ado About Something', *SEL* 8 (1968), 235–51.

LEWIS, CYNTHIA, ' "Derived Honesty and Achieved Goodness": Doctrines of Grace in *All's Well That Ends Well*', *Renaissance and Reformation* 26 (1990), 147–70.

LINDHEIM, NANCY, *The Structures of Sidney's Arcadia* (Toronto, 1982).

LLOYD-JONES, HUGH, 'The Structure of Menander's Comedies', *Dioniso* 57 (1987), 313–21.

—— *Greek Comedy, Hellenistic Literature, Greek Religion, and Miscellanea* (Oxford, 1990).

LODGE, GONZALES, *Lexicon Plautinvm*, 2 vols. (Leipzig, 1924–33).

LOMAX, MARION, *Stage Images and Traditions* (Cambridge, 1987).

LORD, GISELA, 'Die Figur des Pedanten bei Shakespeare', *Deutsche Shakespeare-Gesellschaft West* (1969), 213–44.

LOWE, J. C. B., 'The *Virgo Callida* of Plautus, *Persa*', *CQ* 39 (1989), 390–9.

LUMLEY, ELEANOR P., *The Influence of Plautus on the Comedies of Ben Jonson* (New York, 1901).

MCALINDON, TOM, 'Tragedy, *King Lear*, and the Politics of the Heart', *ShS* 44 (1991), 85–90.

MACCARY, W. THOMAS, 'Menander's Characters: Their Names, Roles and Masks', *TAPA* 101 (1970), 277–90.

—— *Friends and Lovers: The Phenomenology of Desire in Shakespearean Comedy* (New York, 1985).

—— Review of Konstan, *Roman Comedy*, *AJP* 107 (1986), 448–52.

MACK, MAYNARD, *King Lear in our Time* (Berkeley, 1965).

MCGARRITY, TERRY, 'Reputation vs. Reality in Terence's *Hecyra*', *Classical Journal* 76 (1980–1), 149–56.

MCGLYNN, PATRICK, *Lexicon Terentianvm*, 2 vols. (London, 1963–7).

MACINTYRE, JEAN, 'Hamlet and the Comic Heroine', *Hamlet Studies* 4 (1982), 6–18.

MCKENDRICK, MELVEENA, *Theatre in Spain 1490–1700* (Cambridge, 1989).

MCPHERSON, DAVID, 'Ben Jonson's Library and Marginalia: An Annotated Catalogue', *SP* 71 (1974).

—— 'Roman Comedy in Renaissance Education: The Moral Question', *Sixteenth Century Journal* 12 (1981), 19–30.

MARSHALL, BRUCE ed., *Vindex Humanitatis: Essays in Honour of John Huntly Bishop* (Armidale, NSW, 1980).

MARTI, HEINRICH, 'Terenz 1909–1959', *Lustrum* 6 (1961), 114–238; 8 (1963), 5–101, 244–64.

MELZI, ROBERT C., 'From Lelia to Viola', *RD* 9 (1966), 67–81.

Ménandre, Fondation Hardt Entretiens, ed. Eric G. Turner, 16 (1970).

MIKO, STEPHEN, 'Tempest', *ELH* 49 (1982), 1–17.

MILLER, RONALD F., 'King Lear and the Comic Form', *Genre* 8 (1975), 1–25.

MINCOFF, M., 'The Dating of *The Taming of the Shrew*', *English Studies* 54 (1973), 554–65.

MIOLA, ROBERT S., *Shakespeare and Classical Tragedy: The Influence of Seneca* (Oxford, 1992).

MORGAN, LOUISE B., 'The Latin University Drama', *SJ* 47 (1911), 69–91 [supplement to Churchill and Keller].

MORGANN, MAURICE, *An Essay on the Dramatic Character of Sir John*

Falstaff (1777; rev. 1789–90), *Maurice Morgann: Shakespearian Criticism*, ed. Daniel A. Fineman (Oxford, 1972).

MOUFLARD, MARIE-MADELEINE, *Robert Garnier 1545–90*, vol. iii, *Les Sources* (Paris, 1964).

MUIR, KENNETH, *The Sources of Shakespeare's Plays* (New Haven, Conn., 1978).

—— *Shakespeare's Comic Sequence* (New York, 1979).

—— *et al.* (eds.), *Shakespeare: Man of the Theater* (Newark, NJ, 1983).

MULRYNE, J. R., *Shakespeare: 'Much Ado About Nothing'* (London, 1965).

—— 'To glad your ear and please your eyes: Pericles at The Other Place', *Critical Quarterly* 21 (1979), 31–40.

——, and SHEWRING, MARGARET (eds.), *Theatre of the English and Italian Renaissance* (Basingstoke, 1991).

NEELY, CAROL THOMAS, *Broken Nuptials in Shakespeare's Plays* (New Haven, Conn., 1985).

NEILL, KERBY, 'More Ado About Claudio: An Acquittal for the Slandered Groom', *SQ* 3 (1952), 91–107.

NELSON, ALAN H. ed., *Records of Early English Drama: Cambridge*, 2 vols. (Toronto, 1989).

NEUSS, PAULA, 'The Sixteenth-century English "Proverb" Play', *CD* 18 (1984), 1–18.

NEVO, RUTH, *Comic Transformations in Shakespeare* (London, 1980).

—— *Shakespeare's Other Language* (New York, 1987).

NEWMAN, KAREN, *Shakespeare's Rhetoric of Comic Character* (New York, 1985).

—— *Fashioning Femininity and English Renaissance Drama* (Chicago, 1991).

NORWOOD, GILBERT, *The Art of Terence* (Oxford, 1923).

—— *Plautus and Terence* (New York, 1932).

ORGEL STEPHEN, 'Shakespeare and the Kinds of Drama', *Critical Inquiry* 6 (1979), 107–23.

—— 'Nobody's Perfect: Or Why Did the English Stage Take Boys for Women', *South Atlantic Quarterly* 88 (1989), 7–29.

ORMEROD, DAVID, 'Faith and Fashion in "Much Ado About Nothing"', *ShS* 25 (1972), 93–105.

ORNSTEIN, ROBERT, *Shakespeare's Comedies: From Roman Farce to Romantic Mystery* (Newark, NJ, 1986).

ORR, DAVID, *Italian Renaissance Drama in England Before 1625* (Chapel Hill, NC, 1970).

OSBORNE, LAURIE, E., 'Dramatic Play in *Much Ado About Nothing*: Wedding the Italian *Novella* and English Comedy', *PQ* 69 (1990), 167–88.

OVERTON, BILL, *'The Merchant of Venice': Text and Performance* (Basingstoke, 1987).

PALMER, D. J., 'Twelfth Night and the Myth of Echo and Narcissus', ShS 32 (1979), 73–8.

PARKER, PATRICIA, 'The Merry Wives of Windsor and Shakespearean Translation', MLQ 52 (1991), 225–61.

——, and HARTMAN, GEOFFREY (eds.), Shakespeare and the Question of Theory, paper (New York, 1985).

——, and QUINT, DAVID (eds.), Literary Theory / Renaissance Texts (Baltimore, 1986).

PARKER, ROBERT W., 'Terentian Structure and Sidney's Original Arcadia', ELR 2 (1972), 61–78.

PARTEN, ANNE, 'Falstaff's Horns: Masculine Inadequacy and Feminine Mirth in The Merry Wives of Windsor', SP 82 (1985), 184–99.

PASTER, GAIL KERN, 'The City in Plautus and Middleton', RD 6 (1973), 29–44.

—— The Idea of the City in the Age of Shakespeare (Athens, Ga., 1985).

PEQUIGNEY, JOSEPH, 'The Two Antonios and Same-Sex Love in Twelfth Night and The Merchant of Venice', ELR 22 (1992), 201–21.

PERRY, BEN EDWIN, The Ancient Romances: A Literary-Historical Account of their Origins (Berkeley, 1967).

PFEIFFER, RUDOLPH, History of Classical Scholarship, 2 vols. (Oxford, 1968, 1976).

PHIALAS, PETER G., Shakespeare's Romantic Comedies (Chapel Hill, NC, 1966).

PHOTIADÈS, PÉNÉLOPE, 'Le type du Misanthrope dans la littérature grecque', Chronique d'Egypte 34 (1959), 305–26.

PITTALUGA, STEFANO, 'Pandolfo Collenuccio e la sua traduzione dell' "Amphitruo" di Plauto', Res Publica Litterarum: Studies in the Classical Tradition 6 (1983), 275–90.

PLETT, HEINRICH F. ed., Intertextuality (Berlin, 1991).

POTTER, LOIS, 'Twelfth Night': Text and Performance (Basingstoke, 1985).

PRAGER, CAROLYN, 'Heywood's Adaptation of Plautus' Rudens: The Problem of Slavery in The Captives', CD 9 (1975), 116–24.

PRAZ, MARIO, The Flaming Heart (Garden City, NY, 1958).

PRÉAUX, CLAIRE, 'Réflexions sur la Misanthropie au Théâtre', Chronique d'Egypte 34 (1959), 327–41.

PRICE, JOSEPH G., The Unfortunate Comedy: A Study of 'All's Well That Ends Well' and its Critics (Toronto, 1968).

PROUTY, CHARLES T., The Sources of 'Much Ado About Nothing' (New Haven, Conn., 1950).

PYLE, FITZROY, ' "Twelfth Night", "King Lear", and "Arcadia" ', MLR 43 (1948), 449–55.

RACKIN, PHYLLIS, 'Androgyny, Mimesis, and the Marriage of the Boy Heroine', PMLA 102 (1987), 29–41.

RADCLIFF-UMSTEAD, DOUGLAS, The Birth of Modern Comedy in Renaissance Italy (Chicago, 1969).

RADCLIFF-UMSTEAD, DOUGLAS, *Carnival Comedy and Sacred Play: The Renaissance Dramas of Giovan Maria Cecchi* (Columbia, Mo., 1986).

REDMOND, JAMES ed., *The Theatrical Space* (Cambridge, 1987).

—— *Women in Theatre* (Cambridge, 1989).

REED, JUN., ROBERT RENTOUL, *Bedlam on the Jacobean Stage* (Cambridge, Mass., 1952).

—— 'The Probable Origin of Ariel', *SQ* 11 (1960), 61–5.

REINHARDSTOETTNER, KARL VON, *Plautus: Spätere Bearbeitungen plautinischer Lustspiele* (Leipzig, 1886).

REYNOLDS, L. D. ed., *Texts and Transmission: A Survey of the Latin Classics* (Oxford, 1983).

——, and WILSON, N. G., *Scribes and Scholars,* 3rd edn. (Oxford, 1991).

RIBBECK, OTTO, *Alazon: Ein Beitrag zur Antiken Ethologie* (Leipzig, 1882).

RIEHLE, WOLFGANG, *Shakespeare, Plautus and the Humanist Tradition* (Cambridge, 1990).

RIEMER, A. P., *Antic Fables: Patterns of Evasion in Shakespeare's Comedies* (New York, 1980).

RIFFATERRE, MICHAEL, *Text Production*, tr. Terese Lyons (New York, 1983).

ROBBINS, EDWIN W., *Dramatic Characterization in Printed Commentaries on Terence 1473–1600* (Urbana, Ill., 1951).

ROBERTS, JEANNE ADDISON, *Shakespeare's English Comedy: 'The Merry Wives of Windsor' in Context* (Lincoln, Nebr., 1979).

—— 'Horses and Hermaphrodites: Metamorphoses in *The Taming of the Shrew*', *SQ* 34 (1983), 159–71.

ROBERTSON, JEAN ed., *The Countess of Pembroke's Arcadia* (Oxford, 1973).

ROOT, ROBERT KILBURN, *Classical Mythology in Shakespeare* (New York, 1903).

ROSE, MARY BETH, *The Expense of Spirit: Love and Sexuality in English Renaissance Drama* (Ithaca, NY, 1988).

—— ed., *Women in the Middle Ages and the Renaissance: Literary and Historical Perspectives* (Syracuse, NY, 1986).

ROWE, JUN., GEORGE E., *Thomas Middleton and the New Comedy Tradition* (Lincoln, Nebr., 1979).

RYDER, K. C., 'The *Senex Amator* in Plautus', *Greece and Rome* 31 (1984), 181–9.

SACCIO, PETER, 'Shrewd and Kindly Farce', *ShS* 37 (1984), 33–40.

ST CLARE BYRNE, M., 'The Shakespeare Season at The Old Vic, 1958–59 and Stratford-upon-Avon, 1959', *SQ* 10 (1959), 545–67.

SALINGAR, LEO, *Shakespeare and the Traditions of Comedy* (Cambridge, 1974).

—— *Dramatic Form in Shakespeare and the Jacobeans* (Cambridge, 1986).

SANDBACH, F. H., *The Comic Theatre of Greece and Rome* (London, 1977).

SANDERS, WALTER, 'Terence at Newberry, 1470–1700: A Rough Checklist', *RORD* 9 (1966), 62–76.

SANDYS, JOHN EDWIN, *A History of Classical Scholarship*, 3 vols., 3rd edn. (1921; repr. 1958).

SCHMELING, GARETH L., *Chariton* (New York, 1974).

—— *Xenophon of Ephesus* (Boston, 1980).

SCHMIDGALL, GARY, *Shakespeare and the Courtly Aesthetic* (Berkeley, 1981).

—— *Shakespeare and Opera* (New York, 1990).

SHOECK, R. J., *Intertextuality and Renaissance Texts* (Bamberg, 1984).

SCHWARTZ, MURRAY M., and KAHN, COPPÉLIA (eds.), *Representing Shakespeare: New Psychoanalytic Essays* (Baltimore, 1980).

SEGAL, ERICH, 'Scholarship on Plautus 1965–1976', *CW* 74 (1981), 353–433.

—— *Roman Laughter: The Comedy of Plautus*, (2nd edn., New York, 1987).

SHAPIRO, MICHAEL, ' "The Web of Our Life": Human Frailty and Mutual Redemption in *All's Well That Ends Well*', *JEGP* 71 (1972), 514–26.

SHERO, L. R., 'Alcmena and Amphitryon in Ancient and Modern Drama', *TAPA* 87 (1956), 192–238.

SIMMONS, J. L., 'A Source for Shakespeare's Malvolio: The Elizabethan Controversy with the Puritans', *HLQ* 36 (1973), 181–201.

SIMPSON, PERCY, *Studies in Elizabethan Drama* (Oxford, 1955).

SISKIN, CLIFFORD, 'Freedom and Loss in "The Tempest"', *ShS* 30 (1977), 147–55.

SKURA, MEREDITH ANNE, 'Discourse and the Individual: The Case of Colonialism in *The Tempest*', *SQ* 40 (1989), 42–69.

SLATER, ANN PASTERNAK, 'Variations within a Source: from Isaiah xxix to "The Tempest" ', *ShS* 25 (1972), 125–35.

SLATER, NIALL W., *Plautus in Performance: The Theatre of the Mind* (Princeton, 1985).

SMITH, BRUCE R., *Ancient Scripts and Modern Experience on the English Stage 1500–1700* (Princeton, 1988).

—— *Homosexual Desire in Shakespeare's England* (Chicago, 1991).

SMITH, JOHN HAZEL, *Shakespeare's 'Othello': A Bibliography* (New York, 1988).

SNYDER, SUSAN, *The Comic Matrix of Shakespeare's Tragedies* (Princeton, 1979).

SPENCER, CHRISTOPHER, *The Genesis of Shakespeare's Merchant of Venice* (Lewiston, NY, 1988).

SPEVACK, MARVIN, *A Complete and Systematic Concordance to the Works of William Shakespeare*, 9 vols. (Hildesheim, 1968–80).

STEADMAN, JOHN M., 'Falstaff as Actaeon: A Dramatic Emblem', *SQ* 14 (1963), 230–44.

STEWART, ZEPH, 'The *Amphitruo* of Plautus and Euripides' *Bacchae*', *TAPA* 89 (1958), 348–73.

STOCKHOLDER, KAY, *Dream Works: Lovers and Families in Shakespeare's Plays* (Toronto, 1987).

STOLL, ELMER EDGAR, 'Falstaff', *MP* 12 (1914), 197–240.

STONE, LAWRENCE, *The Family, Sex and Marriage in England 1500–1800* (New York, 1977).

—— *Road to Divorce, England 1530–1987* (Oxford, 1990).

STYAN, J. L., *Shakespeare in Performance: 'All's Well That Ends Well'* (Manchester, 1984).

SUMMERS, JOSEPH H., *Dreams of Love and Power* (Oxford, 1984).

TATUM, JAMES, *Apuleius and 'The Golden Ass'* (Ithaca, NY, 1979).

TÄUBLER, EUGEN, *Tyche: Historische Studien* (Leipzig, 1926).

TAYLOR, ANTHONY BRIAN, 'Shakespeare and Golding: Viola's Interview with Olivia and Echo and Narcissus', *ELN* 15 (1977), 103–06.

TAYLOR, GARY, and WARREN, MICHAEL (eds.), *The Division of the Kingdoms* (Oxford, 1983).

TERRY, ELLEN, *Four Lectures on Shakespeare*, ed. Christopher St John (1932; repr. New York, 1969).

THALER, ALWIN, 'Spenser and *Much Ado About Nothing*', *SP* 37 (1940), 225–35.

THOMPSON, ANN, *King Lear* (Atlanta Highlands, NJ, 1988).

THOMSON, J. A. K., *Shakespeare and the Classics* (1952; repr. London, 1966).

THOMSON, R. M., 'A Thirteenth-century Plautus Florilegium from Bury St Edmunds Abbey', *Antichthon* 8 (1974), 29–43.

TOBIAS, RICHARD C., and ZOLBROD, PAUL G. (eds.), *Shakespeare's Late Plays: Essays in Honor of Charles Crow* (Athens, OH, 1974).

TORRÃO, JOÃO MANUEL NUNES, 'Reflexos da *Rudens* de Plauto em *The Tempest* de Shakespeare', *Arquipélago* 4 (1982), 195–224.

TRAUB, VALERIE, *Desire and Anxiety: Circulations of Sexual Desire in Shakespearean Drama* (London, 1992).

TSCHERNJAJEW, PAUL, 'Shakespeare und Terenz', *Anglia* 55 (1931), 282–95.

TURNER, ROBERT Y., 'Dramatic Conventions in *All's Well That Ends Well*', *PMLA* 75 (1960), 497–502 [see also 79 (1964), 177–82].

VANDIVER, JUN., E. P., 'The Elizabethan Dramatic Parasite', *SP* 32 (1935), 411–27.

VAUGHAN, ALDEN, and VAUGHAN, VIRGINIA MASON, *Shakespeare's Caliban: A Cultural History* (Cambridge, 1991).

VELZ, JOHN W., *Shakespeare and the Classical Tradition: A Critical Guide to Commentary 1660–1960* (Minneapolis, 1968).

VICKERS, BRIAN, *The Artistry of Shakespeare's Prose* (London, 1968).

—— *Appropriating Shakespeare: Contemporary Critical Quarrels* (New Haven, Conn., 1993).

VON ROSADOR, K. TETZELI, 'Plotting the Early Comedies: *The Comedy of Errors, Love's Labour's Lost, The Two Gentlemen of Verona*', *ShS* 37 (1984), 13–22.

WARREN, ROGER, *Staging Shakespeare's Late Plays* (Oxford, 1990).

WAYNE, VALERIE, 'Refashioning the Shrew', *ShakS* 17 (1985), 159–87.

WEBBER, EDWIN J., 'The Literary Reputation of Terence and Plautus in Medieval and Pre-Renaissance Spain', *Hispanic Review* 24 (1956), 191–206.

WEBSTER, T. B. L., *Studies in Menander* (Manchester, 1950).

—— *Monuments Illustrating New Comedy*, 2nd edn., *University of London, Institute of Classical Studies, Bulletin Supplement*, 24 (1969).

—— *Studies in Later Greek Comedy*, 2nd edn. (1970; repr. Westport, Conn., 1981).

—— *An Introduction to Menander* (Manchester, 1974).

WEIMANN, ROBERT, *Shakespeare and the Popular Tradition in the Theatre*, ed. Robert Schwartz (Baltimore, 1978).

WEINBERG, BERNARD, *A History of Literary Criticism in the Italian Renaissance*, 2 vols. (Chicago, 1961).

WELLS, STANLEY ed., *'Twelfth Night': Critical Essays* (New York, 1986).

—— ed., *The Cambridge Companion to Shakespeare Studies* (Cambridge, 1986).

——, TAYLOR, GARY *et al.*, *William Shakespeare: A Textual Companion* (Oxford, 1987).

WENTERSDORF, KARL P., 'Hamlet's Encounter With the Pirates', *SQ* 34 (1983), 434–40.

WEST, DAVID, and WOODMAN, TONY (eds.), *Creative Imitation and Latin Literature* (Cambridge, 1979).

WEST, M. L., *Greek Metre* (Oxford, 1982).

WEST, MICHAEL, 'The Folk Background of Petruchio's Wooing Dance: Male Supremacy in *The Taming of the Shrew*', *ShakS* 7 (1974), 65–73.

WESTON, KARL E., 'The Illustrated Terence Manuscripts', *Harvard Studies in Classical Philology* 14 (1903), 37–54.

WHEELER, THOMAS, *'The Merchant of Venice': An Annotated Bibliography* (New York, 1985).

WIKANDER, MATTHEW H., 'As Secret as Maidenhead: The Profession of the Boy-Actress in *Twelfth Night*', *CD* 20 (1986), 349–63.

WILES, DAVID, *The Masks of Menander* (Cambridge, 1991).

WILLIAMS, GORDON, *Tradition and Originality in Roman Poetry* (1968; rev. Oxford, 1985).

WILLIAMS, GWYN, '"The Comedy of Errors" Rescued from Tragedy', *Review of English Literature* 5 (1964), 63–71.

WILLIS, DEBORAH, 'Shakespeare's *Tempest* and the Discourse of Colonialism', *SEL* 29 (1989), 277–89.

WINKLER, JOHN J., *Auctor and Actor: A Narratological Reading of Apuleius's 'Golden Ass'* (Berkeley, 1985).

WISLICENSUS, PAUL, 'Zwei neuentdeckte Shakespearequellen', *SJ* 14 (1879), 87–96.

WOOD, JAMES O., 'Shakespeare and the Belching Whale', *ELN* 11 (1973), 40–4.

WOODBRIDGE, LINDA, *Women and the English Renaissance: Literature and the Nature of Womankind, 1540–1620* (Urbana, Ill., 1984).

WORTON, MICHAEL, and STILL, JUDITH, *Intertextuality: Theories and Practice* (Manchester, 1990).

WRIGHT, JOHN, *Dancing in Chains: The Stylistic Unity of the Comoedia Palliata* (Rome, 1974).

WYRICK, DEBORAH BAKER, 'The Ass Motif in *The Comedy of Errors* and *A Midsummer Night's Dream*', *SQ* 33 (1982), 432–48.

YARDLEY, J. C., 'Propertius 4.5, Ovid *Amores* 1.6 and Roman Comedy', *Proceedings of the Cambridge Philological Society* 33 (1987), 179–89.

YOUNG, ALAN R., *The English Prodigal Son Plays* (Salzburg, 1979).

YOUNG, DAVID, *The Heart's Forest: A Study of Shakespeare's Pastoral Plays* (New Haven, Conn., 1972).

ZAGAGI, NETTA, *Tradition and Originality in Plautus* (Göttingen, 1980).

ZITNER, SHELDON, P., *Harvester New Critical Introductions to Shakespeare: 'All's Well That Ends Well'* (Hemel Hempstead, 1989).

Index